COMMON CORE ACHIEVE

Mastering Essential Test Readiness Skills

GED® Test Exercise Book

READING & WRITING

D1604785

Mc
Graw
Hill
Education

Bothell, WA • Chicago, IL • Columbus, OH • New York, NY

MHEonline.com

Copyright © 2015 McGraw-Hill Education

Send all inquiries to:
McGraw-Hill Education
8787 Orion Place
Columbus, OH 43240

ISBN: 978-0-02-135567-9
MHID: 0-02-135567-3

Printed in the United States of America.

2 3 4 5 6 7 8 9 RHR 17 16 15 14

Table of Contents

Congratulations! If you are using this book, it means that you are taking a key step toward achieving an important new goal for yourself. You are preparing to take a GED® Test, one of the most important steps in the pathway toward career, educational, and lifelong well-being and success.

Common Core Achieve: Mastering Essential Test Readiness Skills is designed to help you learn or strengthen the skills you will need when you take a GED® Test. The *Reading & Writing Exercise Book* provides you with additional practice using the key concepts and core skills required for success on test day and beyond.

How to Use This Book

This book is designed to follow the same lesson structure as the Core Student Module. Each lesson in the *Reading & Writing Exercise Book* is broken down into the same sections as the core module, with a page or more devoted to the key concepts covered in each section. Each lesson contains at least one Test-Taking Tip, which will help you prepare for a test by giving you hints such as how to approach certain question types, or strategies such as how to eliminate unnecessary information. At the back of this book, you will find the answer key for each lesson. The answer to each question is provided along with a rationale for why the answer is correct. If you get an answer incorrect, please return to the appropriate lesson and section in the online or the print Core Student Module to review the specific content.

About the GED® Reasoning through Language Arts Test

The GED® Reasoning through Language Arts test has two main sections. One section has objective questions (multiple choice, fill-in-the-blank, drag-and-drop, and drop-down), and the other section has a writing activity. These item types are described in detail below. Together, the two sections will assess your knowledge of reading and writing skills and concepts and your understanding and usage of standard written English. You will have 150 minutes to complete both sections of the GED® Reasoning through Language Arts Test. This time includes a 10-minute break. The software you use to take the test includes a timer that will allow you to keep track of the time left on the test.

Questions assess levels 1 through 3 of the Webb's Depth of Knowledge spectrum, asking you to answer questions that range from recall questions (DOK 1) to strategic thinking questions (DOK 3). Approximately 20% of the test items are at the DOK 1 level (recall). The remaining items are at the DOK 2 level (application of concepts) and DOK 3 level (strategic thinking).

The objective questions on the test have the following approximate breakdown:

- 35% focusing on analyzing and creating text features and techniques,

- 45% focusing on using evidence to understand, analyze, and create arguments, and

- 20% focusing on applying knowledge of English language conventions and usage

The objective portion of the test will have more than 50% multiple-choice items. There will be no more than 50 questions in this section. All the questions will be in response to a passage. These passages will be academic and workplace texts written at a range of difficulty levels. Each passage will range from 450–900 words. Seventy-five percent of the passages will be informational text. Twenty-five percent of the passages will be literary text.

The writing portion of the test will require you to use a keyboard to compose a response to a passage or passages. Do not worry, however, if you do not have strong typing or keyboarding skills. The test was designed to provide enough time for people who have minimal keyboarding skills. It would be helpful if you practice your keyboarding skills using a simple word processor prior to the test to ensure that you are as comfortable as possible when writing using a computer.

Item Types

The GED® Reasoning through Language Arts test consists of a variety of question types, including multiple choice, fill-in-the-blank, drop-down, drag-and-drop, and extended response. To prepare you for the GED® test, the *Reading & Writing Exercise Book* models these computer-based question types in a print format to help familiarize you with what you will experience on test day.

Multiple Choice Items

The multiple-choice question is the most common type of question you will encounter. Each multiple-choice question will contain four answer choices, of which there will be only one correct answer. When encountering a multiple-choice question, look for answers that cannot be correct based on the information given. You might also see extraneous information in the question that is used in the answer choices. Identify and eliminate this information so you can focus on the relevant information to answer the question.

> Which of the following best expresses the author's point of view?
>
> A. High standards leave some children behind.
>
> B. Parents and children have too many choices in education.
>
> C. The education system is not working and needs to be changed.
>
> D. Education in the United States allows everyone to be successful.

Drop-down Items

The drop-down items are activities that give a drop-down menu within the text with answer options. You select the correct option to complete a sentence. There can be multiple drop-down items in a text, each with a set of possible answers. When answering drop-down items, try to eliminate answer choices that are meant as a distraction, including choices with unnecessary information from the text or choices that reuse information from a previous drop-down item. Within this book, these items are simulated by showing an expanded drop down menu from which the correct answer can be selected.

>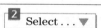
>
> A. large eyes, spotted skin, and incredible flexibility.
>
> B. makes the octopus different from many animals.
>
> C. not to mention its squishy, flexible body.
>
> D. and the fact that it is found in oceans around the world.

Fill-in-the-blank (FIB) Items

A fill-in-the-blank item requires you to complete a sentence by writing the word or phrase that completes the sentence. Fill-in-the-blank items may be used to test new vocabulary skills or to analyze a test passage. These items can be correctly completed by filling in one specific word or phrase. By asking you to provide the word rather than choose from a number of answer choices, fill-in-the-blank items test your understanding at a higher level. Make sure that you fill in the blank and check that the sentence makes sense, includes the correct part of speech, and follows proper grammar rules.

> The characteristics of "The Pit and the Pendulum" help me determine that its genre is _____.

Drag-and-drop Items

A drag-and-drop activity is an item type where you are required to drag text and drop it in a specific place. Examples of drag-and-drop items include categorizing, sequencing, or classifying ideas. For a drag-and-drop item, you will be given multiple items that need to be dragged, called draggables. Each draggable will need to be classified, categorized, or sequenced in the appropriate location, or target. Within this book, these items are simulated through writing the text from each draggable in the appropriate target area.

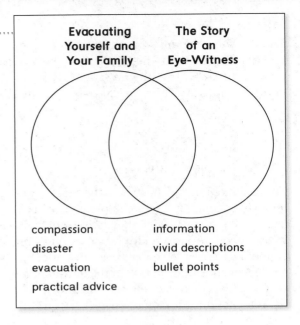

Evacuating Yourself and Your Family — **The Story of an Eye-Witness**

compassion

disaster

evacuation

practical advice

information

vivid descriptions

bullet points

Writing Practice

The Writing Practice in each lesson of the *Reading & Writing Exercise Book* is designed to help you prepare for extended response items on the GED® Test. A writing prompt guides you to produce responses that reflect the types of writing addressed in the extended response items. For an extended response item, you will be graded with a rubric focusing on three criteria: how well you support your position, how well you organize and develop your writing, and how well you write according to standard English conventions. The Writing Practice activities will help you practice and master these areas of writing competency.

Writing Practice

Sometimes when we tell stories about a past event, we may describe events out of order. When we do this, it is important to use transition words to indicate that we are breaking from chronological order.

Directions: Write a paragraph about an experience in which you taught someone how to do something. For example, it could be about teaching a younger sibling how to ride a bike or showing your grandfather how to write an e-mail. Include at least four steps. Include at least one detail that is out of sequence, and use transition words to indicate at which point in the process it occurred.

_____

_____

_____

_____

Strategies for Test Day

There are many things you should do to prepare for test day, including studying. Other ways to prepare you for the day of the test include preparing physically, arriving early, and recognizing certain strategies to help you succeed during the test. Some of these strategies are listed below.

- **Prepare physically.** Make sure you are rested physically and mentally on the day of the test. Eating a well-balanced meal will also help you concentrate while you are taking the test. Staying as stress-free as possible on the day of the test will make you more likely to stayed focused.

- **Arrive early.** Arrive at the testing center at least 20 minutes before the beginning of the test. Give yourself enough time to get seated and situated in the room. Keep in mind that some testing centers will not admit you if you are late.

- **Think positively.** Studies have shown that a positive attitude can help with success, although studying helps even more.

- **Relax during the test.** Stretching and deep breathing can help you relax and refocus. Try doing this a few times during the test, especially if you feel frustrated, anxious, or confused.

- **Read the test directions carefully.** Make sure that you understand what the directions are asking you to do, and complete the activity appropriately. If you have any questions about the test or how to input your answers, ask them before the beginning of the test.

- **Know the time limit for each test.** The GED® Reasoning through Language Arts test has a time limit of 150 minutes (including a 10-minute break). Try to work at a manageable pace. If you have extra time, go back to check your answers and finish any questions you might have skipped.

- **Have a strategy for answering questions.** For each question, read the question prompt, identifying the important information that you will need to answer the question. If necessary, reread the information and any answer choices that are provided.

- **Don't spend a lot of time on difficult questions.** If you are unable to answer a question or are not confident in your answer, you can click on *Flag for Review* in the test window to mark the question and move on to the next question. Answer easier questions first. At the end of the test, you will be able to answer and review flagged questions, if time permits.

- **Answer every question on the test.** If you do not know the answer, make your best guess. You will lose points leaving questions unanswered, but making a guess could possibly help you gain points.

Good luck with your studies, and remember that you are here because you have chosen to achieve important and exciting new goals for yourself. Every time you begin working within the program, keep in mind that the skills you develop in *Common Core Achieve: Mastering Essential Test Readiness Skills* are important for passing the GED® Test, but more importantly, they are keys to lifelong success.

This lesson will help you practice determining the main ideas and supporting details in two types of texts. Use it with core lesson 1.1 Determine the Main Idea to reinforce and apply your knowledge.

Key Concept

The main idea is the most important idea in a paragraph or passage. A main idea can be found in many different kinds of text

Core Skills

- Determine Main Ideas
- Identify Main Ideas in Various Texts

Main Idea in Informational Text

Informational texts explain, describe, instruct, or try to persuade. The main idea often states the purpose of the document. The supporting details of the text give facts, opinions, examples, and explanations that support the main idea.

Directions: Read the passage below. Then complete the activities.

New Purchasing System

To All Employees,

As you should be aware, the Purchasing Tracker (PT) system has been rolled out and is now required to be used for your purchasing activities. This new system will allow our company to easily organize and track all orders in one system and to cut back on the number of steps required to process an order. As with any new system, it will take some time to perfect the operation. However, to ensure that we realize the full benefit of PT, I need you to immediately start following the guidelines below:

Use of PT

Use of PT is mandatory for all new service orders. If you feel you have a special situation that cannot be accommodated in the system, let the PT team know immediately so a discussion can take place without delaying the project.

Purchase orders to supplier prior to project start

Corporate policy mandates that suppliers are not allowed to start work on a project without a fully approved PT purchase order. There should be no exceptions to this policy. A contract does not replace this requirement. If a contract is required for the project, the executed contract must be attached to the PT order. Suppliers can only start projects after they have received approved purchase orders (with attached contract, if applicable).

Use of rates in PT

If a service category in PT has associated rates, then the PT order must be built using the applicable rate-based line items. This means that the order should include a line specific to each rate-based item. Lump sums, combined totals, or use of "miscellaneous" items are not acceptable. Proper breakout of the order ensures that the company has full visibility of what we are purchasing and that our reporting is meaningful.

(continued)

Change orders

Orders should be created based on your original estimate, and if the project specs or scope changes, then the order should be updated via the Change Order process prior to the supplier submitting an invoice. Suppliers are not allowed to begin work on additional scope items until they have received the updated purchase order. Do not pad your requisitions in an attempt to avoid change orders. Additional funds on a purchase order open the door for the supplier to invoice for them.

1. Which text feature best helps you identify the main idea of each section?

   A. the passage title

   B. the headings

   C. the first sentence

   D. the last sentence

2. Which detail supports the main idea that suppliers must have a purchase order before starting work?

   A. "suppliers are not allowed to start work on a project without a fully approved PT purchase order"

   B. "let the PT team know immediately so a discussion can take place without delaying the project"

   C. "Lump sums, combined totals, or use of 'miscellaneous' items are not acceptable."

   D. "Additional funds on a purchase order open the door for the supplier to invoice for them."

3. What is the main idea of the "Use of rates in PT" section?

   A. PT must be used for all service requests.

   B. Contracts do not replace purchase orders.

   C. Rates must be listed for each rate-based item.

   D. Orders should be based on estimates.

4. In which section would you expect to find a detail about additional work on a project?

   A. Use of PT

   B. Purchase orders to supplier prior to project start

   C. Use of rates in PT

   D. Change orders

5. The _____ of the passage is that employees must follow the guidelines for using the PT system.

6. Why might the writer of this informational text state the topic sentence at the beginning of the passage?

   A. to make sure the reader knows what the passage is about

   B. to provide information in least-important to most-important order

   C. so that the reader does not have to read the entire passage to understand it

   D. because the reader would not understand the passage without the topic sentence

Main Idea in Literary Text

Fiction writers invent a self-contained world where imaginary events unfold. The writers also create characters who play roles in these events. Main ideas are presented in paragraphs and longer passages. As you read, look for the main idea and details. The main idea may be stated in a topic sentence, but it is more likely to be implied in a longer passage.

Directions: Read the passage below. Then choose the best answer to each question.

1 But all this—the mysterious, far-reaching hair-line trail, the absence of sun from the sky, the tremendous cold, and the strangeness and weirdness of it all—made no impression on the man. It was not because he was long used to it. He was a newcomer in the land, a *chechaquo*, and this was his first winter. The trouble with him was that he was without imagination. He was quick and alert in the things of life, but only in the things, and not in the significances.

2 Fifty degrees below zero meant eighty-odd degrees of frost. Such fact impressed him as being cold and uncomfortable, and that was all. It did not lead him to meditate upon his frailty as a creature of temperature, and upon man's frailty in general, able only to live within certain narrow limits of heat and cold; and from there on it did not lead him to the conjectural field of immortality and man's place in the universe. Fifty degrees below zero stood for a bite of frost that hurt and that must be guarded against by the use of mittens, ear-flaps, warm moccasins, and thick socks. Fifty degrees below zero was to him just precisely fifty degrees below zero. That there should be anything more to it than that was a thought that never entered his head….

3 At the man's heels trotted a dog, a big native husky, the proper wolf-dog, gray-coated and without any visible or temperamental difference from its brother, the wild wolf.

4 The animal was depressed by the tremendous cold. It knew that it was no time for travelling. Its instinct told it a truer tale than was told to the man by the man's judgment. In reality, it was not merely colder than fifty below zero; it was colder than sixty below, than seventy below. It was seventy-five below zero. Since the freezing-point is thirty-two above zero, it meant that one hundred and seven degrees of frost obtained.

5 The dog did not know anything about thermometers. Possibly in its brain there was no sharp consciousness of a condition of very cold such as was in the man's brain. But the brute had its instinct. It experienced a vague but menacing apprehension that subdued it and made it slink along at the man's heels, and that made it question eagerly every unwonted movement of the man as if expecting him to go into camp or to seek shelter somewhere and build a fire. The dog had learned fire, and it wanted fire, or else to burrow under the snow and cuddle its warmth away from the air.

—Excerpted from "To Build a Fire" by Jack London, 1908

1. What is the main idea of this excerpt?

   A. The dog has survival instincts that the man lacks.

   B. The man has more knowledge than the dog.

   C. The man and dog are dependent on each other.

   D. The man and dog are experiencing the same things.

2. Which detail shows that the man is not prepared for the environment?

   A. "he was long used to it"

   B. "he was quick and alert in the things of life"

   C. "he was without imagination"

   D. "such a fact impressed him as being cold"

3. What is the main idea of paragraph 4?

   A. The dog is like a wild wolf.

   B. The dog can tolerate the cold.

   C. The dog trusts the man's judgment.

   D. The dog knows how cold it really is.

4. Which phrase would best express the main idea of the passage?

   A. instinct or knowledge

   B. experience or inexperience

   C. mortality or immortality

   D. happiness or sadness

5. Which of the following definitions best fits the meaning of the word **tremendous** as it is used in paragraphs 1 and 4?

   A. large

   B. extreme

   C. excellent

   D. vast

6. Which of the following statements is true about the main idea of the passage?

   A. The writer does not include a main idea.

   B. The writer wants the reader to provide the main idea.

   C. The main idea is obvious and, therefore, does not need to be stated.

   D. The reader can infer the main idea through details.

 Test-Taking Tip

The more you practice reading different types of texts of different lengths, the better prepared you will be to read and understand passages presented in reading tests. A good way to practice is to read as much as you can about subjects that interest you. Not only will you become a better reader when taking a test, you will also increase your enjoyment of reading.

Language Practice

Commas are used in a number of situations, such as to separate items in a series, to separate introductory information, to separate independent ideas, and to separate text that provides additional details.

Directions: Read the passage below. Then choose the option that correctly punctuates each sentence.

Reality television is not a new phenomenon.  **1** Select . . . ▼ such as *Candid Camera* and *What's My Line* were hits in television's earliest days. PBS broke new ground in 1973 with An American Family by following the Loud family as they went about **2** Select . . . ▼ Louds decided on camera to divorce, millions of viewers were shocked.

By the 2000s, reality television shows were common on nearly every network. The shows were clearly **3** Select . . . ▼ were also cheaper to make than scripted shows. A typical reality show uses a smaller crew, hires fewer performers, needs fewer sets, and requires very few writers. These less-expensive shows give networks a **4** Select . . . ▼ shows mean big money.

1 Select . . . ▼

A. In fact reality shows

B. in fact, reality shows

C. In fact reality shows,

D. In fact reality, shows

2 Select . . . ▼

A. their everyday life and when the

B. their everyday life, and, when the

C. their everyday life, and when the

D. their everyday life. And, when the

3 Select . . . ▼

A. entertaining to viewers but they

B. entertaining to viewers, but they

C. entertaining to viewers but, they

D. entertaining to viewers, but, they

4 Select . . . ▼

A. larger profit margin so hit reality

B. larger profit margin. So, hit reality

C. larger profit margin so, hit reality

D. larger profit margin, so hit reality

 Test-Taking Tip

Some tests may have several drop-down items on a page. When there is a lot of text on the page or when the drop-down list is small, it can be easy to miss items. Carefully review the page to make sure you have selected answers for all the drop-down items before moving on.

Writing Practice

Some people have nicknames that describe their appearance or abilities. For instance, Hall of Fame basketball player Hakeem "The Dream" Olajuwon earned his nickname through his amazing talents on the court. He was considered a "dream" athlete because he was such a talented player in all aspects of the game.

Directions: Write a brief paragraph in which you explain how someone received a nickname. You may write about yourself, a friend, a relative, or a famous person. Think about the main idea. You may state the main idea in a topic sentence or imply the main idea through the details. Make sure the key details all support the main idea sentence.

_____

_____

_____

_____

_____

_____

_____

_____

_____

_____

_____

_____

_____

_____

_____

_____

_____

_____

This lesson will help you practice identifying supporting details in two informational texts. Use it with core lesson 1.2 Identify Supporting Details to reinforce and apply your knowledge.

Key Concept

Supporting details are concrete ideas that develop the main idea in a passage. There are many types of supporting details.

Core Skills

- Identify Supporting Details
- Cite Details

Identifying Supporting Details

The main idea of a passage is its most important idea. Supporting details are ideas in sentences and paragraphs that support this main idea. The supporting details in a text may include facts, examples, reasons, and descriptions.

Directions: Read the passage below. Then complete the activities.

Civilizations Begin to Interact

The Fertile Crescent

1   The Middle East and the coastal regions of the Mediterranean Sea, as well as the Nile Delta, were the locations for the beginning of many early civilizations, including Egyptian, Babylonian, Sumerian, Phoenician, Persian, and Greek. The close proximity of these civilizations allowed for trade and also created competition for land and resources. The interaction among various cultures created changes in and exchanges of traditions and technology.

2   The classical civilizations that had the largest impact on the world's cultural development are the Greek and Roman Empires. Greek civilization continued the Egyptian priorities of art, literature, music, theater, architecture, and the sciences. The first major citizen participation in government occurred in ancient Athens, a powerful Greek city-state. All male citizens participated in the assembly, which determined laws and policies.

3   During the golden age of ancient Greece (500 BCE to 300 BCE, before the common era), many great philosophers and educators such as Socrates, Plato, and Aristotle shared their wisdom with the world. For the first time, the improvement of the mind and the body was viewed as an important priority for society. The challenge of improved physical fitness was the reason why the Olympic Games began in ancient Greece.

4   Eventually the Romans conquered the Greeks, copying their architecture, art forms, and poetry, and even some of their mythological gods. The Greeks and the Romans had maintained early people's practice of using myth to explain natural phenomena such as seasonal changes, flooding and severe weather, and success in agriculture. To make the myths easier to understand and appreciate, the Greeks and Romans had gods with human attributes. Greek and Roman mythology has continued to exist even after our understanding of the universe had outgrown the need for storylike explanations. Many of the planets, including Jupiter, Neptune, Mars, Venus, and Mercury, were named for Roman gods.

(continued)

5 The Romans were interested in military strength and acquiring land for the empire. Thus, athletic competition and training for combat as a form of entertainment developed in Rome. The Roman government differed from the Athenian model. One, two, or sometimes three consuls were chosen by the Roman senate, a group of the wealthiest landholders, or patricians. The vast majority of the citizens were plebeians—the small farmers, tradesmen, artisans, and merchants.

6 Wealth and connections among family members thus determined position in the social classes within Roman culture. This status determined whether a member of the society was considered to be worthy of having a vote. The Roman system of government was called a republic. The lower class of slaves and the common class of farmers and tradesmen were limited in their rights of marriage partners and land ownership.

7 One lasting contribution of the Romans was the calendar introduced by Julius Caesar in 46 BCE Caesar made the months of unequal days and added leap years to make the reckoning more equal to an actual year. This Julian calendar, with some modifications, is still in use today.

1. Information about mythology and the calendar are _____ details that develop the main idea.

2. Which detail supports the main idea that Greek and Roman empires contributed to the culture of the surrounding area?

   A. "For the first time, the improvement of the mind and the body was viewed as an important priority for society."

   B. "The vast majority of the citizens were plebeians—the small farmers, tradesmen, artisans, and merchants."

   C. "The challenge of improved physical fitness was the reason why the Olympic Games began in ancient Greece."

   D. "The interaction among various cultures created changes in and exchanges of traditions and technology."

3. Which detail could be added to paragraph 4 to support the main idea of the paragraph?

   A. When the Romans conquered the Greeks, much of Greek culture was destroyed.

   B. The Romans' astronomical discoveries included the discovery of several planets and constellations.

   C. Although Roman gods shared similar stories, they had different names and personalities.

   D. The Romans made many contributions to culture, including a series of roadways and aqueducts.

4. You would expect to find a supporting detail about the Greek government in paragraph

_____.

5. Which detail could you cite to support an idea about the structure of Roman society?

   A. "To make the myths easier to understand and appreciate, the Greeks and Romans had gods with human attributes."

   B. "One, two, or sometimes three consuls were chosen by the Roman senate, a group of the wealthiest landholders, or patricians."

   C. "Thus, athletic competition and training for combat as a form of entertainment developed in Rome."

   D. "One lasting contribution of the Romans was the calendar introduced by Julius Caesar in 46 BCE."

Using Details to Make Generalizations

Writers use many types of detail to help the reader understand a passage. By thinking carefully about these details, the reader can make generalizations, or broad statements about the text.

Directions: Read the passage below. Then choose the best answer to each question.

Marshes

1 Marshes are defined as wetlands frequently or continually inundated with water, characterized by emergent soft-stemmed vegetation adapted to saturated soil conditions. There are many different kinds of marshes, ranging from the prairie potholes to the Everglades, coastal to inland, freshwater to saltwater. All types receive most of their water from surface water, and many marshes are also fed by groundwater. Nutrients are plentiful and the pH is usually neutral leading to an abundance of plant and animal life. . . . [W]e have divided marshes into two primary categories: non-tidal and tidal.

2 Marshes recharge groundwater supplies and moderate streamflow by providing water to streams. This is an especially important function during periods of drought. The presence of marshes in a watershed helps to reduce damage caused by floods by slowing and storing flood water. As water moves slowly through a marsh, sediment and other pollutants settle to the substrate, or floor of the marsh. Marsh vegetation and microorganisms also use excess nutrients for growth that can otherwise pollute surface water. . . . This wetland type is very important to preserving the quality of surface waters. In fact, marshes are so good at cleaning polluted waters that people are now building replicas of this wetland type to treat wastewater from farms, parking lots, and small sewage plants.

3 Non-tidal marshes are the most prevalent and widely distributed wetlands in North America. They are mostly freshwater marshes, although some are brackish or alkaline. They frequently occur along streams in poorly drained depressions, and in the shallow water along the boundaries of lakes, ponds, and rivers. Water levels in these wetlands generally vary from a few inches to two or three feet. . . . [S]ome marshes, like prairie potholes, may periodically dry out completely.

4 It is easy to recognize a non-tidal marsh by its characteristic soils, vegetation, and wildlife. Highly organic, mineral rich soils of sand, silt, and clay underlie these wetlands. . . . [L]ily pads, cattails . . . , reeds, and bulrushes provide excellent habitat for waterfowl and other small mammals. . . . Prairie potholes, playa lakes, vernal pools, and wet meadows are all examples of non-tidal marshes.

5 Due to their high levels of nutrients, freshwater marshes are one of the most productive ecosystems on earth. They can sustain a vast array of plant communities that in turn support a wide variety of wildlife within this vital wetland ecosystem. As a result, marshes sustain a diversity of life that is way out of proportion with its size. In addition . . . , non-tidal marshes serve to mitigate flood damage and filter excess nutrients from surface runoff.

6 Unfortunately, like many other wetland ecosystems, freshwater marshes have suffered major acreage losses to human development. Some have been degraded by excessive deposits of nutrients and sediment from construction and farming. Severe flooding and nutrient deposition to downstream waters have often followed marsh destruction and degradation. Such environmental problems prove the vital roles these wetlands play. This realization has spurred enhanced protection and restoration of marsh ecosystems. . . .

(continued)

7 Tidal marshes can be found along protected coastlines in middle and high latitudes worldwide. They are most prevalent in the United States on the eastern coast from Maine to Florida and continuing on to Louisiana and Texas along the Gulf of Mexico. Some are freshwater marshes, others are brackish (somewhat salty), and still others are saline (salty). . . . [T]hey are all influenced by the motion of ocean tides. Tidal marshes are normally categorized into two distinct zones, the lower or intertidal marsh and the upper or high marsh.

8 In saline tidal marshes, the lower marsh is normally covered and exposed daily by the tide. It is predominantly covered by the tall form of Smooth Cordgrass. . . . The saline marsh is covered by water only sporadically, and is characterized by Short Smooth Cordgrass, Spike Grass, and Saltmeadow Rush. . . . Saline marshes support a highly specialized set of life adapted for saline conditions. . . .

9 Tidal marshes serve many important functions. They buffer stormy seas, slow shoreline erosion, and are able to absorb excess nutrients before they reach the oceans and estuaries. High concentrations of nutrients can cause oxygen levels low enough to harm wildlife. . . . Tidal marshes also provide vital food and habitat for clams, crabs, and juvenile fish, as well as offering shelter and nesting sites for several species of migratory waterfowl.

10 Pressure to fill in these wetlands for coastal development has lead to significant and continuing losses of tidal marshes, especially along the Atlantic coast. Pollution . . . also remains a serious threat to these ecosystems. Fortunately, most states have enacted special laws to protect tidal marshes, but much diligence is needed to assure that these protective measures are actively enforced.

—From "Marshes" by the U.S. Environmental Protection Agency

1. What generalization could be drawn from the details in the first paragraph?

    A. Marshes are inhospitable to many animal and plant species.

    B. Marshes are very fragile and highly susceptible to droughts and flooding.

    C. Marshes, because of their plentiful water, provide an excellent location for the development of new housing.

    D. Marshes can be found in many geographic locations across the United States.

2. Which of the following details supports the generalization that marshes are important to water quality?

    A. "We have divided marshes into two primary categories: non-tidal and tidal."

    B. "As water moves slowly through a marsh, sediment and other pollutants settle to the substrate, or floor of the marsh."

    C. "Tidal marshes can be found along protected coastlines in middle and high latitudes worldwide."

    D. "Pressure to fill in these wetlands for coastal development has led to significant and continuing losses of tidal marshes, especially along the Atlantic coast."

3. Which detail provides an example to support the generalization that marshes have diversity in their ecosystems?

    A. "Lily pads, cattails . . . , reeds, and bulrushes provide excellent habitat for waterfowl and other small mammals."

    B. "They frequently occur along streams in poorly drained depressions, and in the shallow water along the boundaries of lakes, ponds, and rivers."

    C. "Water levels in these wetlands generally vary from a few inches to two or three feet . . ."

    D. "Unfortunately, like many other wetland ecosystems, freshwater marshes have suffered major acreage losses to human development."

4. Which of the following definitions best fits the meaning of the word **absorb** as it is used in paragraph 9?

    A. to capture someone's attention

    B. to occupy completely

    C. to take in or soak up

    D. to spread across a large area

Language Practice

A complete sentence must have a subject and predicate. It must be able to stand alone. When you write, check your text for sentence fragments. Change fragments into complete sentences.

Directions: The passage below is incomplete. Choose the option that correctly completes each sentence.

As a scuba diver, I enjoy looking at the amazing underwater animals. One of my favorites **1** Select . . . ▼ What makes it so special? A gigantic head attached to eight wiggly arms **2** Select . . . ▼ However, what fascinates me most is its behavior. Using specialized pigment cells, **3** Select . . . ▼ I, as well as its predators, have often swum by the octopus without noticing it. When it is discovered, **4** Select . . . ▼ This startles the predator, allowing the octopus a chance to escape.

 **1** Select . . . ▼

    A. among the thousands of creatures I have seen.

    B. although it is hard to choose.

    C. is the distinctive octopus.

    D. the incredibly flexible octopus.

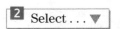 **2** Select . . . ▼

    A. large eyes, spotted skin, and incredible flexibility.

    B. makes the octopus different from many animals.

    C. not to mention its squishy, flexible body.

    D. and the fact that it is found in oceans around the world.

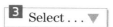 Select . . . ▼

   A. changing the color of its skin to match its environment.

   B. located in the muscles of its skin.

   C. creating a variety of colors and patterns.

   D. it can blend in with almost any environment.

 Select . . . ▼

   A. the octopus can release a puff of black ink.

   B. by a predator or even a diver like myself.

   C. great, thick clouds of black ink.

   D. which does not occur frequently.

 Test-Taking Tip

When taking a paper test, you can highlight important details. This is often not possible on a computer-based exam. Therefore, when reading a passage, you might want to use a dry-erase board to take notes on important details. Later you can use your notes to determine a main idea or to make generalizations.

Writing Practice

There are many kinds of natural disasters, including hurricanes, tornados, forest fires, and earthquakes. Reporters who cover these events write to inform people about what happened. They must be able to give facts, descriptions, explanations, and reasons to help their readers understand the main idea.

Directions: Write a brief paragraph about a real or imagined natural disaster. Include a generalization that accurately describes the type of disaster. Use at least three types of supporting details in your paragraph to help the reader experience and understand what happened.

_____

_____

_____

_____

_____

_____

_____

_____

_____

_____

This lesson will help you practice identifying directly stated main ideas and determining implied main ideas from supporting details. Use it with core lesson 1.3 Identify Direct and Implied Main Ideas to reinforce and apply your knowledge.

Key Concept	Core Skills
The main idea may be stated directly in a topic sentence or sentences, or it may be implied. An implied main idea must be inferred from supporting details.	• Determine Implied Main Ideas • Use Details to Deduce Central and Supporting Ideas

Direct and Implied Main Ideas

In some texts, the main idea is directly stated. In others, the main idea is implied, or expressed indirectly, through the details in the text. To figure out the implied main idea, you need to think about what the details are about and how they are related to each other.

Directions: Read the passage below. Then complete the activities.

Early Domestic and Foreign Policy

The years between 1791 and 1803 saw the United States expand geographically. Between 1791 and 1796, Vermont, Kentucky, and Tennessee were admitted to the Union under the administration of George Washington, the first US president. In 1803, under President Thomas Jefferson, Ohio was admitted to the Union, and the largest acquisition of land for the United States occurred with the Louisiana Purchase. By paying France $15 million for the territory, Jefferson doubled the size of the country. He subsequently appointed Lewis and Clark to explore the acquired territory.

The Monroe Doctrine

A strong sense of nationalism developed after the War of 1812. For the first time the United States could afford to look inward and pay less attention to European affairs. As a result, US westward expansion continued, with victories over several Native American tribes.

In 1823 President James Monroe proclaimed to the world that European powers would no longer be allowed to colonize the Americas. He indicated that the United States would remain neutral in European conflicts as long as the European powers left the emerging republics in North and South America alone. Known as the Monroe Doctrine, this foreign policy statement marked the appearance of the United States on the world political stage.

Jacksonian Democracy and the Mexican War

After Monroe left office, sectionalism became a problem for the United States. Sectionalism refers to the political, cultural, and economic differences among regions of the country—in this case the agricultural South and West and the industrial Northeast. The conflicting demands that each section put upon the government caused great political turmoil.

(continued)

The first US president elected to office as a result of these factional differences was Andrew Jackson in 1828. A Southerner and hero in the War of 1812, Jackson was considered to be a populist, a man who represented the interests of the common people. He believed that *all* people, not just the propertied few, should have a voice in deciding how the government should be run.

As the champion of the common people, Jackson opposed the establishment of a national bank because he believed that it would only benefit the wealthy and because he feared the Eastern merchants and industrialists would control it. Under Jacksonian democracy, farmers and craftspeople gained a louder voice in government than they had had under previous administrations. Despite pressure to annex Texas during his second term, Jackson refused, fearing a war with Mexico.

President James Polk, Jackson's successor, had no such fear. Congress, agreeing to the demands of the Texans, annexed the Texas Republic in 1845. Thus, the expansionist fervor in the United States was renewed. Manifest Destiny—the drive to extend the US borders to the Pacific Ocean—became a rallying cry. When President Polk was unable to purchase the territory that included New Mexico and California, the United States declared war on Mexico in 1846 as a result of a territorial dispute between the two countries.

The Treaty of Guadalupe Hidalgo that ended the war in 1848 resulted in the United States gain of the land that would later become California, Utah, Nevada, and parts of Colorado, New Mexico, Arizona, and Wyoming. Thus, the United States had set its continental boundaries.

1. The overall main idea of this passage is expressed _____.

2. Which sentence best expresses the main idea of the entire passage?

   A. The Louisiana Purchase doubled the size of the country.

   B. US domestic and foreign policy changed throughout the years.

   C. Exploration of new lands was a main priority to early Americans.

   D. Relationships between the United States and Mexico were strained.

3. Which sentence best expresses the main idea of the first paragraph?

   A. "The years between 1791 and 1803 saw the United States expand geographically."

   B. "In 1803, under President Thomas Jefferson, Ohio was admitted to the Union, and the largest acquisition of land for the United States occurred with the Louisiana Purchase."

   C. "By paying France $15 million for the territory, Jefferson doubled the size of the country."

   D. "He subsequently appointed Lewis and Clark to explore the acquired territory."

4. Which part of the passage best implies a main idea that the United States expanded through territorial wars with other countries?

   A. "Early Domestic and Foreign Policy"

   B. "The Monroe Doctrine"

   C. paragraph 6

   D. paragraph 7

Implied Main Ideas and Supporting Details

The main idea of a text may be directly stated, but it is often implied. To identify an implied main idea, look for sentences that contain key phrases and details. Think about how these details are related.

Directions: Read the passage below. Then complete the activities.

The Golden Windows

1 All day long the little boy worked hard, in field and barn and shed, for his people were poor farmers, and could not pay a workman; but at sunset there came an hour that was all his own, for his father had given it to him. Then the boy would go up to the top of a hill and look across at another hill that rose some miles away. On this far hill stood a house with windows of clear gold and diamonds. They shone and blazed so that it made the boy wink to look at them: but after a while the people in the house put up shutters, as it seemed, and then it looked like any common farmhouse.

2 The boy supposed they did this because it was supper-time; and then he would go into the house and have his supper of bread and milk, and [go] to bed.

3 One day the boy's father called him and said: "You have been a good boy, and have earned a holiday. Take this day for your own; but remember that God gave it, and try to learn some good thing."

4 The boy thanked his father and kissed his mother; then he put a piece of bread in his pocket, and started off to find the house with the golden windows.

5 It was pleasant walking[, for h]is bare feet made marks in the white dust, and when he looked back, the footprints seemed to be following him, and making company for him. His shadow, too, kept beside him, and would dance or run with him as he pleased; so it was very cheerful. . . .

6 After a long time he came to a high green hill; and when he had climbed the hill, there was the house on the top; but it seemed that the shutters were up, for he could not see the golden windows. He came up to the house, and then he could well have wept, for the windows were of clear glass, like any others, and there was no gold anywhere about them.

7 A woman came to the door, and looked kindly at the boy, and asked him what he wanted.

8 "I saw the golden windows from our hilltop," he said, "and I came to see them, but now they are only glass." . . .

9 "We are poor farming people," she said, "and are not likely to have gold about our windows; but glass is better to see through."

10 She bade the boy sit down on the broad stone step at the door, and brought him a cup of milk and a cake, and bade him rest; then she called her daughter, a child of his own age, and nodded kindly at the two, and went back to her work.

(continued)

11 The little girl was barefooted like himself, and wore a brown cotton gown, but her hair was golden like the windows he had seen, and her eyes were blue like the sky at noon. She led the boy about the farm, and showed him her black calf with the white star on its forehead, and he told her about his own at home, which was red like a chestnut, with four white feet. Then when they had eaten an apple together, and so had become friends, the boy asked her about the golden windows. The little girl nodded, and said she knew all about them, only he had mistaken the house. . . .

12 "Come with me, and I will show you the house with the golden windows, and then you will see for yourself."

13 They went to a knoll that rose behind the farmhouse, and as they went the little girl told him that the golden windows could only be seen at a certain hour, about sunset. . . .

14 When they reached the top of the knoll, the girl turned and pointed; and there on a hill far away stood a house with windows of clear gold and diamond, just as he had seen them. And when they looked again, the boy saw that it was his own home.

15 Then he told the little girl that he must go; and he gave her his best pebble, the white one with the red band, that he had carried for a year in his pocket; and she gave him three horse-chestnuts, one red like satin, one spotted, and one white like milk. He kissed her, and promised to come again, but he did not tell her what he had learned; and so he went back down the hill, and the little girl stood in the sunset light and watched him.

16 The way home was long, and it was dark before the boy reached his father's house; but the lamplight and firelight shone through the windows, making them almost as bright as he had seen them from the hilltop; and when he opened the door, his mother came to kiss him, and his little sister ran to throw her arms about his neck, and his father looked up and smiled from his seat by the fire. . . .

17 "[H]ave you learned anything?" asked his father.

18 "Yes!" said the boy. "I have learned that our house has windows of gold and diamond."

— From *The Pig Brother and Other Fables and Stories* by Laura E. Richards

1. To identify the _____ of "The Golden Windows," look for details in the boy's dialogue and actions at the top of both hills that tell what the passage is about.

2. Which of the following sentences best describes how the main idea is presented in this passage?

A. The main idea is stated as a topic sentence.

B. The writer wants the reader to provide the main idea.

C. The main idea is stated at the end of the story.

D. The reader can infer the main idea through the details.

3. Which statement best describes the main idea of this passage?

   A. Things are not always as they seem.

   B. Hard work always pays off in the end.

   C. Sometimes friends are the best kind of family.

   D. Sometimes home is not the easiest place to stay.

4. Identify the excerpt from the passage that best supports the main idea.

   A. "The way home was long, and it was dark before the boy reached his father's house; but the lamplight and firelight shone through the windows, making them almost as bright as he had seen them from the hilltop . . ."

   B. "The little girl nodded, and said she knew all about them, only he had mistaken the house . . ."

   C. "She bade the boy sit down on the broad stone step at the door, and brought him a cup of milk and a cake, and bade him rest; then she called her daughter, a child of his own age, and nodded kindly at the two, and went back to her work."

   D. "The boy thanked his father and kissed his mother; then he put a piece of bread in his pocket, and started off to find the house with the golden windows."

5. Which of the following definitions best fits the meaning of the word **holiday** as it is used in this passage?

   A. celebration

   B. religious feast day

   C. time of relaxation

   D. date on a calendar

 Test-Taking Tip

Note how much time you are given to complete a test. Keep an eye on the time as you are taking the test. Stop periodically to make sure that you are on target to finish. Plan ahead so you have time at the end of the exam to review your answers. Make sure that you have answered all the questions and have not made any errors.

Writing Practice

You walk into a dark room. What is the first thing you do? Do you turn on a light? We use lights to help us work, play, drive, and stay safe. A standard light bulb is relatively simple—it's just a filament and a glass covering—yet it's hard to imagine our lives without this amazing invention.

Directions: Write a brief paragraph in which you tell about a real or imagined invention. Before beginning to write, determine your main idea. You may directly state the main idea in a topic sentence or imply the main idea through the details. Make sure the key details are related and support the main idea.

_____

_____

_____

_____

_____

_____

_____

_____

_____

_____

_____

_____

_____

_____

_____

_____

_____

_____

This lesson will help you practice summarizing details in two passages. Use it with core lesson 1.4 Summarize Details to reinforce and apply your knowledge.

Key Concept	**Core Skills**
Explaining the most important ideas in a passage in a concise way is called summarizing. A summary includes the main idea and the key supporting details.	• Summarize Key Information • Summarize a Text

Summarizing Key Information

To write a concise and effective summary, you must first identify the most important points. Begin by identifying the main idea. Then identify the most important supporting details. When these details are identified, paraphrase by restating the main idea and important supporting details in your own words.

Directions: Read the passage below. Then complete the activities.

Excerpt from *Up From Slavery: An Autobiography*

The first pair of shoes that I recall wearing were wooden ones. They had rough leather on the top, but the bottoms, which were about an inch thick, were of wood. When I walked they made a fearful noise, and besides this they were very inconvenient, since there was no yielding to the natural pressure of the foot. In wearing them one presented [an] exceedingly awkward appearance. The most trying ordeal that I was forced to endure as a slave boy, however, was the wearing of a flax shirt. In the portion of Virginia where I lived it was common to use flax as part of the clothing for the slaves. That part of the flax from which our clothing was made was largely the refuse, which of course was the cheapest and roughest part. I can scarcely imagine any torture, except, perhaps, the pulling of a tooth, that is equal to that caused by putting on a new flax shirt for the first time. It is almost equal to the feeling that one would experience if he had a dozen or more chestnut burrs, or a hundred small pin-points, in contact with his flesh. Even to this day I can recall accurately the tortures that I underwent when putting on one of these garments. The fact that my flesh was soft and tender added to the pain. But I had no choice. I had to wear the flax shirt or none; and had it been left to me to choose, I should have chosen to wear no covering. In connection with the flax shirt, my brother John, who is several years older than I am, performed one of the most generous acts that I ever heard of one slave relative doing for another. On several occasions when I was being forced to wear a new flax shirt, he generously agreed to put it on in my stead and wear it for several days, till it was "broken in." Until I had grown to be quite a youth this single garment was all that I wore.

—From *Up From Slavery: An Autobiography* by Booker T. Washington

1. One major _____ of the passage is the pain and discomfort of clothing made for slaves.

2. Which of the following best paraphrases the main idea of the passage?

   A. New clothing was a luxury and reward for slaves.

   B. The comfort of slaves was not a factor in clothing choice.

   C. Clothing for slaves was simple, practical, and durable.

   D. The life of a slave was determined by which clothes he was given.

3. Which supporting detail about the wooden shoes should be included in a summary of the passage?

   A. They made a fearful noise when the narrator walked.

   B. The leather from which the top was made was very rough.

   C. Someone wearing the shoes looked awkward and strange.

   D. The wood sole did not give when the foot pressed against it.

4. Choose the detail that you should paraphrase and include in a summary of the passage.

   A. "When I walked, they made a fearful noise . . ."

   B. "In the portion of Virginia where I lived it was common to use flax . . ."

   C. "That part of the flax from which our clothing was made was largely the refuse . . ."

   D. "I can scarcely imagine any torture . . . equal to . . . putting on a new flax shirt . . ."

5. Which of the following definitions best fits the meaning of the word **refuse** as it is used in this passage?

   A. waste

   B. decline

   C. recycle

   D. fabric

 Test-Taking Tip

Passage-based questions take more time than questions without a passage. One helpful strategy for planning your time is to take the total time allotted and divide it by the number of passages. This will let you know how much time to spend per section.

Summarizing a Text

To create an effective summary, identify the main idea and most important supporting details. Paraphrase these in concise statements to tell what the passage is about. One way to summarize is to group related details to make one statement.

Directions: Read the passage below. Then complete the activities.

Travel Alert

US DEPARTMENT OF STATE

Bureau of Consular Affairs

Hurricane Season

May 30, 2013

1 The Department of State alerts US citizens to the upcoming Hurricane Season in the Atlantic, the Caribbean, and the Gulf of Mexico. Hurricane season in the Atlantic begins June 1 and ends November 30.

2 The National Oceanic and Atmospheric Administration's (NOAA) Climate Prediction Center . . . expects to see an active or extremely active season in the Atlantic Basin this year[. There's] a 70 percent chance of 13 to 20 named storms, of which seven to eleven are predicted to strengthen to a hurricane. . . . Of those, three to six are expected to become major hurricanes . . . NOAA recommends that those in hurricane-prone regions begin preparations for the upcoming season now.

3 During and after some previous storms, US citizens traveling abroad encountered dangerous and often uncomfortable conditions[. These conditions] lasted for several days while awaiting transportation back to the United States. In the past, many US citizens were forced to delay travel . . . due to infrastructure damage to airports and limited flight availability. Roads were also washed out or obstructed by debris. [This damage adversely affected] access to airports and land routes out of affected areas. Reports of looting and sporadic violence in the aftermath of natural disasters have occurred. Security personnel may not always be readily available to assist. In the event of a hurricane, travelers should be aware that they may not be able to depart the area for 24–48 hours or longer.

(continued)

4 If you travel to these areas during hurricane season, we recommend you obtain travel insurance to cover unexpected expenses during an emergency. [You might be in a situation that] requires an evacuation from an overseas location. [If this occurs,] the US Department of State will work with commercial airlines to ensure that US citizens are repatriated as safely and efficiently as possible. Commercial airlines are the Department's primary source of transportation in an evacuation[. O]ther means of transport are utilized only as a last resort. The US Department of State will not provide no-cost transportation, but [it] does have the authority to provide repatriation loans to those in financial need.

5 If you live in or are traveling to storm-prone regions, prepare for hurricanes and tropical storms by organizing a kit in a waterproof container that includes a supply of bottled water, non-perishable food items, a battery-powered or hand-crank radio, any medications taken regularly, and vital documents . . . Emergency shelters often provide only very basic resources and may have limited medical and food supplies. NOAA and the Federal Emergency Management Agency (FEMA) have additional tips on their websites.

—From "Travel Alert" by the US Department of State

1. Hurricane season in the Atlantic runs through the summer and part of the fall. The area affected includes the Atlantic, the Caribbean, and the Gulf of Mexico. US citizens should read the following advice from the Department of State.

   The statement above is a _____ of paragraph 1.

2. Which of the following best paraphrases the main idea of the passage?

   A. People should use caution when they are traveling to other countries.

   B. The upcoming hurricane season will be active and destructive.

   C. As hurricane season approaches, people should make preparations.

   D. NOAA and FEMA are good sources of hurricane information.

3. Which supporting detail is most important to include in the summary?

   A. "There's a 70 percent chance of 13 to 20 storms . . ."

   B. "Of those, three to six are expected to become major hurricanes . . ."

   C. "These conditions lasted for several days while awaiting transportation back to the United States."

   D. "[W]e recommend you obtain travel insurance to cover unexpected expenses during an emergency."

4. Choose the sentence that best paraphrases and summarizes the details in paragraph 3.

    A. Risks to travelers include delays, unsafe travel conditions, and risks to personal safety.

    B. US citizens often experience hardships such as looting and violence when they travel to other countries.

    C. Drivers should be cautious during hurricane season as roadways might be washed away or have obstacles.

    D. Security personnel might be too busy with other issues to help US citizens traveling in hurricane-prone areas.

5. Which text features identify important information that should be included in a summary of this passage?

    A. boldfaced headings

    B. italicized text

    C. section headings

    D. paragraph breaks

6. Choose and write the best paraphrases of the main idea and supporting details that could be used to write a summary of the travel alert in the concept web.

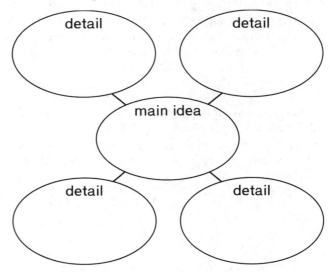

During hurricane season, travelers should be prepared for emergencies.

The NOAA does not recommend travel to other countries during hurricane season.

Purchasing traveler's insurance can help travelers with the unexpected expense of emergency evacuation.

Hurricane season affects certain regions from June through November.

Travelers should consider bringing a well-stocked emergency kit.

There is a 70 percent chance of 13 to 20 named storms this season.

Travelers should be prepared for unsafe and uncomfortable conditions after a hurricane.

Roads may be washed out or obstructed by debris.

 Test-Taking Tip

When reading test passages, it is tempting to read the questions and then skim the passage to find the answers. Unfortunately, when you do not read the entire passage, you can miss important themes or details. The gaps can cause confusion, especially with questions that ask you to perform higher-level thinking such as summarizing or synthesizing information. Take the time to read the passage thoroughly, and then skim the passage to find the details needed to answer the questions.

Writing Practice

When you tell a friend about a favorite book or movie, you are providing a summary. You might explain the characters, the problem faced, how the problem was solved, and the major events. Paraphrasing and including only the important details make a precise and effective summary.

Directions: Write a summary of a movie you have seen or a book you have read. As you write, summarize the main idea. Then paraphrase the key details in concise statements.

_____

_____

_____

_____

_____

_____

_____

_____

_____

_____

_____

_____

_____

_____

_____

_____

_____

_____

_____

_____

This lesson will help you practice identifying a theme in two different passages. Use it with core lesson 1.5 Identify a Theme to reinforce and apply your knowledge.

Key Concept

The theme is the underlying meaning of a story. An author reveals the theme in a work of fiction through characters, setting, language, and other literary elements.

Core Skills

- Synthesize Details That Relate to the Theme
- Understand the Relationships among Ideas

Using Fictional Elements to Determine Theme

The theme is the central message of a text, and it may express a belief or an opinion about life. The theme, however, is not always stated; it may be implied. The author may reveal the theme through narrators' or characters' comments or actions.

Directions: Read the passage below. Then complete the activities.

Legend of Tu-Tok-A-Nu'-La (El Capitan)

1   Here were once two little boys living in the valley who went down to the river to swim. After paddling and splashing about to their hearts' content, they went on shore and crept up on a huge boulder which stood beside the water. They lay down in the warm sunshine to dry themselves, but fell asleep. They slept so soundly that they knew nothing, though the great boulder grew day by day, and rose night by night, until it lifted them up beyond the sight of their tribe, who looked for them everywhere.

2   The rock grew until the boys were lifted high into the heaven, even far up above the blue sky, until they scraped their faces against the moon. And still, year after year, among the clouds they slept.

3   Then there was held a great council of all the animals to bring the boys down from the top of the great rock. Every animal leaped as high as he could up the face of the rocky wall. Mouse could only jump as high as one's hand; Rat, twice as high. Then Raccoon tried; he could jump a little farther. One after another of the animals tried, and Grizzly Bear made a great leap far up the wall, but fell back. Last of all Lion tried, and he jumped farther than any other animal, but fell down upon his back. Then came tiny Measuring-Worm, and began to creep up the rock. Soon he reached as high as Raccoon had jumped, then as high as Bear, then as high as Lion's leap, and by and by he was out of sight, climbing up the face of the rock. For one whole snow, Measuring-Worm climbed the rock, and at last he reached the top. Then he wakened the boys, and came down the same way he went up, and brought them down safely to the ground. Therefore the rock is called Tutokanula, the measuring worm. But white men call it El Capitan.

—From *Myths and Legends of California and the Old Southwest*, edited by Katherine Berry Judson

1. The actions of the Measuring-Worm express the story's _____, or central message.

2. Which sentence below *best* states the theme of the passage?

   A. When you work together, you can solve a problem.

   B. Never judge someone by the way he or she looks.

   C. By making a continued effort, you will finish the job.

   D. The strongest person will survive in the end.

3. Which detail from the passage helps you understand the theme?

   A. "For one whole snow, Measuring-Worm climbed the rock, and at last he reached the top."

   B. "Every animal leaped as high as he could up the face of the rocky wall."

   C. "Then there was held a great council of all the animals to bring the boys down from the top of the great rock."

   D. "And still, year after year, among the clouds they slept."

4. Which of the following definitions best fits the meaning of the word **creep** as it is used in paragraph 3?

   A. a hateful, mean, or unpleasant person

   B. a feeling of things crawling on your body

   C. spreading out or growing on a surface

   D. moving slowly, low to the ground

Synthesizing Multiple Main Ideas to Determine Theme

Sometimes you have to synthesize information from fictional elements such as setting, plot, characterization, point of view, language, and conflict to determine the theme. As you read, also think about the main idea of each paragraph and synthesize these to state the theme.

Directions: Read the passage below. Then complete the activities.

The Ingenious Patriot

1 Having obtained an audience of the King an Ingenious Patriot pulled a paper from his pocket, saying:

2 "May it please your Majesty, I have here a formula for constructing armour-plating which no gun can pierce. If these plates are adopted in the Royal Navy our warships will be invulnerable, and therefore invincible. Here, also, are reports of your Majesty's Ministers, attesting the value of the invention. I will part with my right in it for a million tumtums."

3 After examining the papers, the King put them away and promised him an order on the Lord High Treasurer of the Extortion Department for a million tumtums.

4 "And here," said the Ingenious Patriot, pulling another paper from another pocket, "are the working plans of a gun that I have invented, which will pierce that armour. Your Majesty's Royal Brother, the Emperor of Bang, is anxious to purchase it, but loyalty to your Majesty's throne and person constrains me to offer it first to your Majesty. The price is one million tumtums."

(continued)

5 Having received the promise of another check, he thrust his hand into still another pocket, remarking: "The price of the irresistible gun would have been much greater, your Majesty, but for the fact that its missiles can be so effectively averted by my peculiar method of treating the armour plates with a new—"

6 "The King signed to the Great Head Factotum to approach.

7 "Search this man," he said, "and report how many pockets he has."

8 "Forty-three, Sire," said the Great Head Factotum, completing the scrutiny.

9 "May it please your Majesty," cried the Ingenious Patriot, in terror, "one of them contains tobacco."

10 "Hold him up by the ankles and shake him," said the King; "then give him a check for forty-two million tumtums and put him to death. Let a decree issue declaring ingenuity a capital offence."

—From *Fantastic Fables* by Ambrose Bierce

1. How can determining the point of view help you understand the theme?

   A. Looking from the king's perspective, you understand how difficult it is to protect one's kingdom.

   B. Looking from the patriot's perspective, you learn the dangers of greed with those in authority.

   C. Looking from the perspective of the Great Head Factotum, you learn a lesson about money.

   D. Looking from the narrator's perspective, you understand what the king and the patriot learn about loyalty.

2. How is the author's characterization of the main character as a patriot helpful in understanding the theme?

   A. The character presents himself as a trusted and wise adviser to the king.

   B. The character calls himself loyal, but his actions show otherwise.

   C. The character acts with cunning, and enriches himself by doing so.

   D. The character is penalized for his ingenuity and sales tactics.

3. Which sentence below is the best statement of the theme of the passage?

   A. Rulers are not always fair.

   B. Weapons are dangerous.

   C. You can't always trust what a person says.

   D. You should always listen to wise advice.

4. The theme can be determined by _____ information from the characterization of the king and the patriot, the language used in the dialog, and the outcome of the interaction between the characters.

 Test-Taking Tip

Some test answers can be found directly in a passage. For others, such as identifying theme and implied main ideas, you might need to synthesize information from several places. When you synthesize, make a list of important ideas. Mark out any that are not relevant. Then look for ways that the ideas are connected.

Writing Practice

There are many different types of short stories. Satires, such as "The Ingenious Patriot," reveal problems in society in a humorous way. Fables, such as "Legend of Tu-Tok-A-Nu'-La (El Capitan)," are another type of short story. Fables sometimes explain how something was created and often have a moral. Topics for short stories range from solving a mystery to going on a magical adventure to explaining how bluebonnets came to Texas.

Directions: Write a short story. You may invent your own or retell in your own words a story you have read. Your short story should have a beginning, middle, and end. It should have a theme that is stated or implied, with details to support the theme.

_____

_____

_____

_____

_____

_____

_____

_____

_____

_____

_____

_____

_____

_____

_____

_____

_____

This lesson will help you practice determining the sequence of events in two types of texts. Use it with core lesson 2.1 Sequence Events to reinforce and apply your knowledge.

Key Concept

The sequence of events is the order in which the events in a text occur.

Core Skills

• Sequence Information
• Use Text Features

Sequence of Time

To fully comprehend narrative passages and procedural texts, readers need to understand the order of events or steps. When reading a passage, use transitions and text features to help determine the sequence of events.

Directions: Read the passage below. Then complete the activities.

Athletic Shoes

1   Picking a pair of athletic shoes used to be easy. When only a few brands and styles of shoes existed, you could just choose the most comfortable pair. But today, athletic shoes are a multibillion-dollar business. With thousands of different styles, colors, and features, picking a pair of athletic shoes can be complicated. Nevertheless, there are ways to find the ideal pair of shoes.

2   First, you should choose different shoes for working out than for everyday use. For everyday shoes, comfort and appearance are the most important selection criteria. For exercising, finding the right shoe involves several factors. Consider the type of activities you will engage in. If you mainly participate in a specific sport or activity, such as running, walking, or playing tennis, you will want to get shoes designed specifically for that activity. Running shoes, for example, contain extra padding to make running easier on your feet. Tennis shoes contain extra padding to cushion the toes. Walking shoes are specially designed to help you walk quickly and effortlessly. If you participate in many sports, a pair of cross-training shoes is a good idea. These shoes have enough padding for runners, but they also meet the needs of other athletes.

3   After you have decided which kind of shoe you would like, begin to look at individual pairs of shoes. When you try on shoes, make sure you are wearing the same kind of socks that you will be wearing when you work out. Also make sure you do more than just look at the shoes in a mirror; take a short walk around the shoe department to determine how they feel. Make sure they fit snugly but are not too tight. The tip of the shoe should be roomy enough for you to wiggle your toes. If your feet are jammed in, you run the risk of injuring yourself.

4   Finally, look for style and special features. For example, if you run early in the morning or late at night, you should select shoes with reflective material so drivers can see you in the dark. If you are interested in measuring the distance that you run or walk, consider shoes with a built-in pedometer. If you have trouble with your feet, shoes filled with air or gel provide extra cushioning that could help.

5   After you buy your shoes, make sure you break them in before your first workout. As you continue to wear them, watch for signs of wear and tear. Worn-out shoes can be just as harmful to your feet as improper footwear.

1. According to the passage, what was easy to do *before* so many brands and styles of athletic shoes existed?

   A. use one pair of shoes to cross train

   B. walk around the store with the shoes on

   C. purchase the top-selling brand

   D. choose the most comfortable pair

2. Which transition word in the text tells you that style and special features should be the last things to consider before purchasing shoes?

   A. next

   B. after

   C. finally

   D. then

3. Which of the following phrases could logically replace the underlined text and convey the intended meaning?

   When you try on shoes, make sure you are wearing the same kind of socks that you will be wearing when you work out.

   A. While you are trying on shoes

   B. After you have tried on shoes

   C. Until you try on shoes

   D. Subsequent to trying on shoes

4. Which of the following definitions best fits the meaning of the word **improper** as it is used in paragraph 5?

   A. not in good taste

   B. not well suited to one's needs

   C. not current or trendy

   D. not following cultural expectations

5. Write the steps of buying and using athletic shoes in the correct sequence according to the passage, starting with the first step at the top.

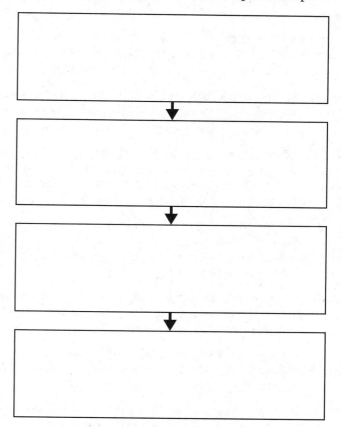

try on different shoes

decide what kind of shoes you will need

break in your shoes

consider additional features you might want

Sequence in a Process

When texts do not use clear transition words in describing a procedure or process, you can usually assume that the steps are being presented in chronological order. In some cases, text features such as headings can also help you see how a text is organized and understand the order of events or actions.

Directions: Read the passage below. Then complete the activities.

Natural Gas Basics

How Was Natural Gas Formed?

The main ingredient in natural gas is methane, a gas (or compound) composed of one carbon atom and four hydrogen atoms. Millions of years ago, the remains of plants and animals (diatoms) decayed and built up in thick layers. This decayed matter from plants and animals is called organic material—it was once alive. . . . Pressure and heat changed some of this organic material into coal, some into oil (petroleum), and some into natural gas—tiny bubbles of odorless gas.

In some places, gas escapes from small gaps in the rocks into the air; then, if there is enough activation energy from lightning or a fire, it burns. When people first saw the flames, they experimented with them and learned they could use them for heat and light.

How Do We Get Natural Gas?

The search for natural gas begins with geologists, who study the structure and processes of the Earth. They locate the types of rock that are likely to contain gas and oil deposits.

Today, geologists' tools include seismic surveys that are used to find the right places to drill wells. Seismic surveys use echoes from a vibration source at the Earth's surface (usually a vibrating pad under a truck built for this purpose) to collect information about the rocks beneath. Sometimes it is necessary to use small amounts of dynamite to provide the vibration that is needed.

Scientists and engineers explore a chosen area by studying rock samples from the earth and taking measurements. If the site seems promising, drilling begins. Some of these areas are on land, but many are offshore, deep in the ocean. Once the gas is found, it flows up through the well to the surface of the ground and into large pipelines.

Some of the gases that are produced along with methane, such as butane and propane (also known as "by-products"), are separated and cleaned at a gas processing plant. The by-products, once removed, are used in a number of ways. For example, propane can be used for cooking on gas grills.

Dry natural gas is also known as consumer-grade natural gas. In addition to natural gas production, the U.S. gas supply is augmented by imports, withdrawals from storage, and by supplemental gaseous fuels.

Most of the natural gas consumed in the United States is produced in the United States. Some is imported from Canada and shipped to the United States in pipelines. A small amount of natural gas is shipped to the United States as liquefied natural gas (LNG).

We can also use machines called "digesters" that turn today's organic material (plants, animal wastes, etc.) into natural gas. This process replaces waiting for millions of years for the gas to form naturally.

—From "Natural Gas Basics" by the U.S. Energy Information Administration

1. In the section "How Was Natural Gas Formed?", the sequence of events describes a _____.

2. Which of the following best describes how this text is arranged?

   A. two processes described in chronological order and placed in sections that are also in chronological order

   B. two processes described in reverse chronological order and placed in sections that are in chronological order

   C. two processes described in chronological order and placed in sections that appear in order of importance

   D. two processes with interrupting flashbacks, placed in sections that are in chronological order

3. Which text feature indicates to the reader that the process of natural gas being formed comes *before* the process of obtaining it?

   A. the order of visual graphics

   B. the order of the title

   C. the order of bolded headings

   D. the order of underlined phrases

4. According to the section "How Do We Get Natural Gas?" which transition word would accurately complete the following sentence: Scientists study samples and take measurements _____ taking a seismic survey.

   A. before

   B. after

   C. while

   D. until

Test-Taking Tip

The text features that you use to determine the sequence of events can also help you find the correct answer in a test question more quickly. When you first read a passage, make a mental note of any section headings that are used to organize the passage. Later, when you read the questions, notice whether the question tells you where in the passage to look for the answer. If it does, go straight to that section and make sure your answer corresponds to the information found in that section.

Writing Practice

Sometimes when we tell stories about a past event, we may describe events out of order. When we do this, it is important to use transition words to indicate that we are breaking from chronological order.

Directions: Write a paragraph about an experience in which you taught someone how to do something. For example, it could be about teaching a younger sibling how to ride a bike or showing your grandfather how to write an e-mail. Include at least four steps. Include at least one detail that is out of sequence, and use transition words to indicate at which point in the process it occurred.

_____

_____

_____

_____

This lesson will help you practice inferring relationships within two literary texts. Use it with core lesson 2.2 Infer Relationships between Events, People, and Ideas to reinforce and apply your knowledge.

Key Concept

Making an inference is determining the most likely explanation for the given information.

Core Skills

- Make Inferences
- Cite Evidence

Inferring a Writer's Meaning

To make inferences about a text, use a combination of explicit details and implied information as clues. Then combine this information with your personal knowledge to draw conclusions about the relationships among characters, events, setting, and ideas in a text.

Directions: Read the passage below. Then complete the activities.

Dick Baker's Cat

1 One of my comrades . . . was one of the gentlest spirits that ever bore its patient cross in a weary exile: grave and simple Dick Baker, pocket-miner of Dead-Horse Gulch. He was forty-six, grey as a rat, earnest, thoughtful, slenderly educated, slouchily dressed and clay-soiled, but his heart was finer metal than any gold his shovel ever brought to light—than any, indeed, that ever was mined or minted.

2 Whenever he was out of luck and a little downhearted, he would fall to mourning over the loss of a wonderful cat he used to own . . . [H]e always spoke of the strange sagacity of that cat with the air of a man who believed in his secret heart that there was something human about it—maybe even supernatural.

3 I heard him talking about this animal once. He said:

4 "Gentlemen, I used to have a cat here, by the name of Tom Quartz . . . I had him here eight year—and he was the remarkablest cat I ever see. He was a large grey one of the Tom specie, an' he had more hard, natchral sense than any man in this camp . . . He never ketched a rat in his life—'peared to be above it. He never cared for nothing but mining. He knowed more about mining . . . than any man I ever, ever see. You couldn't tell *him* noth'n' 'bout placer-diggin's . . . [A]s for pocket-mining, why he was just born for it. He would dig out after me an' Jim when we went over the hills prospect'n', and he would trot along behind us for as much as five mile . . . [I]f the ground suited him, he would lay low 'n' keep dark till the first pan was washed . . . [T]hen he would sidle up 'n' take a look, an' if there was about six or seven grains of gold *he* was satisfied . . . [T]hen he would lay down on our coats and snore like a steamboat till we'd struck the pocket, an' then get up 'n' superintend. He was nearly lightnin' on superintending.

(continued)

5 "Well, by an' by, up comes this yer quartz excitement. Everybody was into it—everybody was pick'n' 'n' blast'n' instead of shovelin' dirt on the hillside—everybody was putt'n' down a shaft instead of scrapin' the surface. Noth'n' would do Jim, but *we* must tackle the ledges, too, 'n' so we did. We commenced putt'n' down a shaft . . . Tom Quartz he begin to wonder what in the Dickens it was all about. *He* hadn't ever seen any mining like that before, 'n' he was all upset, as you may say—he couldn't come to a right understanding of it no way . . . But that cat, you know, was *always* agin new-fangled arrangements . . . *You* know how it is with old habits. But by an' by Tom Quartz begin to git sort of reconciled a little, though he never *could* altogether understand that eternal sinkin' of a shaft an' never pannin' out anything. At last he got to comin' down in the shaft, hisself, to try to cipher it out. An' when he'd git the blues . . . knowin' as he did, that the bills was runnin' up all the time an' we warn't makin' a cent—he would curl up on a gunny-sack in the corner an' go to sleep. Well, one day when the shaft was down about eight foot, the rock got so hard that we had to put in a blast—the first blast'n' we'd ever done since Tom Quartz was born. An' then we lit the fuse 'n' clumb out 'n' got off 'bout fifty yards—'n' forgot 'n' left Tom Quartz sound asleep on the gunny-sack. In 'bout a minute we seen a puff of smoke bust up out of the hole . . . [E]verything let go with an awful crash . . . [A]bout four million ton of rocks 'n' dirt 'n' smoke 'n' splinters shot up 'bout a mile an' a half into the air . . .

6 [B]y George, right in the dead centre of it was old Tom Quartz a-goin' end over end, an' a-snortin' an' a-sneez'n, an' a-clawin' an' a-reach'n' for things like all possessed. . . . An' that was the last we see of *him* for about two minutes 'n' a half . . . [T]hen all of a sudden it begin to rain rocks and rubbage an' directly he come down ker-whoop about ten foot off f'm where we stood. Well, I reckon he was p'raps the orneriest-lookin' beast you ever see. One ear was sot back on his neck, 'n' his tail was stove up, 'n' his eye-winkers was singed off . . . [H]e was all blacked up with powder an' smoke, an' all sloppy with mud 'n' slush f'm one end to the other. . . . He took a sort of a disgusted look at hisself, 'n' then he looked at us . . . [T]hen he turned on his heel 'n' marched off home without ever saying another word.

7 "That was jest his style. . . . [A]fter that you never see a cat so prejudiced agin quartz-mining as what he was. . . .

8 I said, "Well, Mr. Baker, his prejudice against quartz-mining *was* remarkable, considering how he came by it. Couldn't you ever cure him of it?"

9 "*Cure him!* No! When Tom Quartz was sot once, he was *always* sot."

—From "Dick Baker's Cat" by Mark Twain

1. Based on the description in Paragraph 1, the reader can infer that the narrator's opinion of the character Dick Baker is that he is

A. clever but ultimately cruel.

B. simple and uneducated but kind.

C. good at mining but bad with money.

D. well educated and a sharp dresser.

2. In the second paragraph, the narrator makes it explicit that Dick Baker speaks highly of his cat. However, the narrator _____ that he, himself, has doubts about the cat's near-human intelligence.

3. In paragraph 4, beginning with the phrase "[I]f the ground suited him . . ." through the end of the paragraph, the cat's behavior would be best described as

A. so unbelievable that it would seem supernatural to any observer.

B. impressive for a cat, but regarded by its owner as unremarkable.

C. normal for most cats, but interpreted by the owner as being human-like.

D. typical of a trained circus animal but not of a pet cat.

4. In paragraph 5, Dick Baker describes the miners' enthusiasm for quartz. Based on his word choice and description, you can infer that the cat

A. hopes to find a large supply of quartz.

B. does not think quartz is salable.

C. prefers digging deep to searching the topsoil.

D. thinks underground mining is not worthwhile.

5. Based on the description in paragraphs 5 and 6 of what happened to Tom Quartz, what can you infer about the Dick Baker's feelings about the event?

A. It was devastating.

B. It was amusing.

C. It was pleasing.

D. It was frightening.

Citing Evidence

When making inferences about a text, a reader must look for evidence in the text. Evidence can include opinions, examples that support a point, and factual information.

Directions: Read the passage below. Then complete the activities.

The House in the Mist

1 It was a night to drive any man indoors. Not only was the darkness impenetrable, but the raw mist enveloping hill and valley made the open road anything but desirable to a belated wayfarer like myself.

2 Being young, untrammelled, and naturally indifferent to danger, I was not averse to adventure; and having my fortune to make, was always on the lookout for El Dorado, which to ardent souls lies ever beyond the next turning. Consequently, when I saw a light shimmering through the mist at my right, I resolved to make for it and the shelter it so opportunely offered.

3 But I did not realise then, as I do now, that shelter does not necessarily imply refuge, or I might not have undertaken this adventure with so light a heart. Yet who knows? The impulses of an unfettered spirit lean toward daring, and youth, as I have said, seeks the strange, the unknown, and sometimes the terrible.

(continued)

4   My path towards this light was by no means an easy one. After confused wanderings through tangled hedges, and a struggle with obstacles of whose nature I received the most curious impression in the surrounding murk . . . I arrived in front of a long, low building, which, to my astonishment, I found standing with doors and windows open to the pervading mist, save for one square casement, through which the light shone from a row of candles placed on a long mahogany table.

5   The quiet and seeming emptiness of this odd and picturesque building made me pause. I am not much affected by visible danger, but this silent room, with its air of sinister expectancy, struck me most unpleasantly . . . I was about to reconsider my first impulse and withdraw again to the road, when a second look thrown back upon the comfortable interior I was leaving convinced me of my folly, and sent me straight toward the door which stood so invitingly open.

6   But half-way up the path my progress was again stayed by the sight of a man issuing from the house I had so rashly looked upon as devoid of all human presence. He seemed in haste, and at the moment my eye first fell on him was engaged in replacing his watch in his pocket.

7   But he did not shut the door behind him, which I thought odd, especially as his final glance had been a backward one, and seemed to take in all the appointments of the place he was so hurriedly leaving.

8   As we met he raised his hat. This likewise struck me as peculiar, for the deference he displayed was more marked than that usually bestowed on strangers . . . [H]is lack of surprise at an encounter more or less startling in such a mist, was calculated to puzzle an ordinary man like myself. Indeed, he was so little impressed by my presence there that he was for passing me without a word or any other hint of good-fellowship . . . But this did not suit me. I was hungry, cold, and eager for creature comforts . . . [T]he house before me gave forth, not only heat, but a savoury odour which in itself was an invitation hard to ignore. I therefore accosted the man.

9   "Will bed and supper be provided for me here?" I asked. "I am tired out with a long tramp over the hills, and hungry enough to pay anything in reason———"

10 I stopped, for the man had disappeared. He had not paused at my appeal, and the mist had swallowed him. But at the break in my sentence his voice came back in good-natured tones, and I heard:

11 "Supper will be ready at nine, and there are beds for all. Enter, sir; you are the first to arrive, but the others cannot be far behind."

12 A queer greeting certainly. But when I strove to question him as to its meaning, his voice returned to me from such a distance that I doubted if my words had reached him any more than his answer had reached me.

13 "Well," thought I, "it isn't as if a lodging had been denied me. He invited me to enter, and enter I will."

(continued)

14 The house, to which I now naturally directed a glance of much more careful scrutiny than before, was no ordinary farm-building, but a rambling old mansion . . . Though furnished, warmed, and lighted with candles, . . . it had about it an air of disuse which made me feel myself an intruder, in spite of the welcome I had received. But I was not in a position to stand upon ceremony . . . [E]re long I found myself inside the great room and before the blazing logs whose glow had lighted up the doorway and added its own attraction to the other allurements of the inviting place.

15 Though the open door made a draught which was anything but pleasant, I did not feel like closing it, and was astonished to observe the effect of the mist through the square thus left open to the night. It was not an agreeable one, and, instinctively turning my back upon that quarter of the room, I let my eyes roam over the wainscoted walls and the odd pieces of furniture which gave such an air of old-fashioned richness to the place. . . . But the solitude of the place . . . struck cold to my heart, and I missed the cheer rightfully belonging to such attractive surroundings.

—From *Room Number 3 and Other Detective Stories* by Anna Katharine Green

1. In paragraph 1, the phrases "darkness [was] impenetrable" and "raw mist [was] enveloping hill and valley" are

   A. opinions expressed by the narrator about weather conditions.

   B. inferences made by the reader about the story's setting.

   C. facts about weather conditions where the author lived.

   D. examples to illustrate the idea that it was not a good night to be outdoors.

2. The narrator's descriptions of what he sees and his opinions about what he sees are two types of
   _____.

3. Which of the following definitions best fits the meaning of the word **unfettered** as it is used in paragraph 3?

   A. unrestrained

   B. unnatural

   C. unguarded

   D. unforgiving

4. Which of the following statements from paragraph 14 could you cite to support the inference that the narrator feels uneasy in this setting?

   A. "The house . . . was no ordinary farm-building, but a rambling old mansion . . ."

   B. "Though furnished, warmed, and lighted with candles, . . . it had about it an air of disuse . . ."

   C. . . . which made me feel myself an intruder, in spite of the welcome I had received . . ."

   D. "I found myself . . . before the blazing logs whose glow had . . . added its own attraction . . ."

Test-Taking Tip

Use your prior knowledge when making inferences about a passage on a test. Before reading the passage, read the title, look at any illustrations or graphics that accompany it, and skim the text for any words that are highlighted or repeated throughout. Based on these, use what you already know about the words and ideas mentioned to predict what topics will be discussed in the passage. While you read, combine details in the text with what you already know to make inferences and to better understand what you are reading.

Writing Practice

When writing, authors do not explain every opinion they have. Many details are implicit; readers must make inferences to understand the entire meaning of the text.

Directions: Think of a person whom you find inspiring. Make a list of two facts about that person and two opinions you hold about him or her, as well as one additional detail (fact or opinion). Analyze your details to see how they are related to one another. Then write a paragraph that explicitly states two facts and two opinions, and implies one additional detail. Make sure that the relationships among the details on your list are implied by the text and can be inferred by your reader.

_____

_____

_____

_____

_____

_____

_____

_____

_____

_____

_____

_____

_____

_____

_____

_____

This lesson will help you practice analyzing relationships between text elements in two literary passages. Use it with core lesson 2.3 Analyze Relationships between Ideas to reinforce and apply your knowledge.

Key Concept

Relationships exist between different text elements—between characters, between characters and setting, between plot and setting, or between ideas.

Core Skills

- Identify Literary Elements
- Analyze the Relationship between Plot and Setting

Identifying Literary Elements

Literary texts, especially stories, contain certain key elements that help build the narrative, or the story that is being told. The key elements include plot, setting, theme, and character. Writers use characterization to describe their characters through details such as dialogue, actions, and descriptions.

Directions: Read the passage below. Then complete the activities.

1 Once upon a time—of all the good days in the year, on Christmas Eve—old Scrooge sat busy in his counting-house. It was cold, bleak, biting weather: foggy withal: and he could hear the people in the court outside, go wheezing up and down, beating their hands upon their breasts, and stamping their feet upon the pavement stones to warm them. The city clocks had only just gone three, but it was quite dark already—it had not been light all day—and candles were flaring in the windows of the neighbouring offices, like ruddy smears upon the palpable brown air. The fog came pouring in at every chink and keyhole, and was so dense without, that although the court was of the narrowest, the houses opposite were mere phantoms. To see the dingy cloud come drooping down, obscuring everything, one might have thought that Nature lived hard by, and was brewing on a large scale.

2 The door of Scrooge's counting-house was open that he might keep his eye upon his clerk, who in a dismal little cell beyond, a sort of tank, was copying letters. Scrooge had a very small fire, but the clerk's fire was so very much smaller that it looked like one coal. But he couldn't replenish it, for Scrooge kept the coal-box in his own room; and so surely as the clerk came in with the shovel, the master predicted that it would be necessary for them to part. Wherefore the clerk put on his white comforter, and tried to warm himself at the candle; in which effort, not being a man of a strong imagination, he failed.

3 "A merry Christmas, uncle! God save you!" cried a cheerful voice. It was the voice of Scrooge's nephew, who came upon him so quickly that this was the first intimation he had of his approach.

4 "Bah!" said Scrooge, "Humbug!"

5 He had so heated himself with rapid walking in the fog and frost, this nephew of Scrooge's, that he was all in a glow; his face was ruddy and handsome; his eyes sparkled, and his breath smoked again.

6 "Christmas a humbug, uncle!" said Scrooge's nephew. "You don't mean that, I am sure?"

7 "I do," said Scrooge. "Merry Christmas! What right have you to be merry? What reason have you to be merry? You're poor enough."

(continued)

8 "Come, then," returned the nephew gaily. "What right have you to be dismal? What reason have you to be morose? You're rich enough."

9 Scrooge having no better answer ready on the spur of the moment, said, "Bah!" again; and followed it up with "Humbug."

—From *A Christmas Carol: A Ghost Story of Christmas* by Charles Dickens

---

1. Scrooge, his clerk, and his nephew are the three _____ in this passage.

2. The phrases "cold, bleak, biting weather: foggy withal" and "it had not been light all day" are details about the story's

A. characters.

B. narrative.

C. setting.

D. theme.

3. Write the details from the passage under the appropriate literary element category.

Setting	Character

3 PM on Christmas Eve

Scrooge's control over the coal-box

description of the fog

Scrooge's counting-house

nephew's response to Scrooge

Scrooge's reaction to his nephew

4. Which detail from the passage describes the story's main character, Scrooge?

A. He had a cheerful voice.

B. He did not have much money.

C. He was in a bad mood.

D. He felt very cold.

Analyzing Relationships in Text

When you read a text, the various relationships between the setting, characters, and events in the plot can help you understand or infer the story's theme.

Directions: Read the passage below. Then complete the activities.

Room Number 3

1 "What door is that? You've opened all the others; why do you pass that one by?"

2 "Oh, that! That's only Number 3. A mere closet, gentlemen," responded the landlord in a pleasant voice. "To be sure, we sometimes use it as a sleeping-room when we are hard pushed. Jake, the clerk you saw below, used it last night. But it's not on our regular list. Do you want a peep at it?"

3 "Most assuredly. As you know, it's our duty to see every room in this house, whether it is on your regular list or not."

4 "All right. I haven't the key of this one with me. But—yes, I have. There, gentlemen!" he cried, unlocking the door and holding it open for them to look inside. "You see it no more answers the young lady's description than the others do. And I haven't another to show you. You have seen all those in front, and this is the last one in the rear. You'll have to believe our story. The old lady never put foot in this tavern."

5 The two men he addressed peered into the shadowy recesses before them, and one of them, a tall and uncommonly good-looking young man of stalwart build and unusually earnest manner, stepped softly inside. He was a gentleman farmer living near, recently appointed deputy sheriff on account of a recent outbreak of horse-stealing in the neighbourhood.

6 "I observe," he remarked, after a hurried glance about him, "that the paper on these walls is not at all like that she describes. She was very particular about the paper; said that it was of a muddy pink colour and had big scrolls on it which seemed to move and crawl about in whirls as you looked at it. This paper is blue and striped. Otherwise——"

7 "Let's go below," suggested his companion, who, from the deference with which his most casual word was received, was evidently a man of some authority. "It's cold here, and there are several new questions I should like to put to the young lady. Mr. Quimby,"—this to the landlord, "I've no doubt you are right, but we'll give this poor girl another chance. I believe in giving every one the utmost chance possible."

8 "My reputation is in your hands, Coroner Golden," was the quiet reply. Then, as they both turned, "my reputation against the word of an obviously demented girl."

(continued)

9 The words made their own echo. As the third man moved to follow the other two into the hall, he seemed to catch this echo, for he involuntarily cast another look behind him as if expectant of some contradiction reaching him from the bare and melancholy walls he was leaving. But no such contradiction came. Instead, he appeared to read confirmation there of the landlord's plain and unembittered statement. The dull blue paper with its old-fashioned and uninteresting stripes seemed to have disfigured the walls for years. It was not only grimy with age, but showed here and there huge discoloured spots, especially around the stovepipe-hole high up on the left-hand side. Certainly he was a dreamer to doubt such plain evidences as these. Yet——

10 Here his eye encountered Quimby's, and pulling himself up short, he hastily fell into the wake of his comrade now hastening down the narrow passage to the wider hall in front. Had it occurred to him to turn again before rounding the corner—but no, I doubt if he would have learned anything even then. The closing of a door by a careful hand—the slipping up behind him of an eager and noiseless step—what is there in these to re-awaken curiosity and fix suspicion? Nothing, when the man concerned is Jacob Quimby; nothing. Better that he failed to look back; it left his judgment freer for the question confronting him in the room below.

11 Three Forks Tavern has been long forgotten, but at the time of which I write it was a well-known but little-frequented house, situated just back of the highway on the verge of the forest lying between the two towns of Chester and Danton in southern Ohio. It was of ancient build, and had all the picturesquesness of age and the English traditions of its original builder. Though so near two thriving towns, it retained its own quality of apparent remoteness from city life and city ways. This in a measure was made possible by the nearness of the woods which almost enveloped it; but the character of the man who ran it had still more to do with it, his sympathies being entirely with the old, and not at all with the new. . . . This, while it appealed to a certain class of summer boarders, did not so much meet the wants of the casual traveller, so that while the house might from some reason or other be overfilled one night, it was just as likely to be almost empty the next. . . . The building itself was of wooden construction, high in front and low in the rear, with gables toward the highway, projecting here and there above a strip of rude old-fashioned carving. These gables were new, that is, they were only a century old; the portion now called the extension, in the passages of which we first found the men we have introduced to you, was the original house.

—From *Room Number 3 and Other Detective Stories* by Anna Katharine Greene

1. Which statement best describes the relationship between the setting and plot of this passage?

   A. A man makes observations about a room possibly involved in a crime.

   B. A conversation between three men reveals information about a crime.

   C. Three men walk down a hallway of an old tavern.

   D. A man questions the sanity of a young woman involved in a crime.

2. Which statement describes the relationship between the characters and events in this passage?

   A. A coroner and a deputy sheriff discover that a tavern owner is the prime suspect in a crime.

   B. A demented young woman tells a deputy sheriff that a tavern owner committed a crime.

   C. A coroner convinces a suspicious deputy sheriff to investigate a local tavern owner.

   D. A tavern owner cooperates with the investigation of a coroner and a deputy sheriff.

3. Which of the following phrases best describes the relationship between Three Forks Tavern and its owner, as it is explained in Paragraph 11?

    A. The tavern has an impact on the owner's mood.

    B. The owner wants to keep the tavern from changing.

    C. The tavern is important in changing the owner's life.

    D. The owner is indifferent to the tavern.

4. A key detail that ties the story's plot to its setting is the color of the _____.

5. Which of the following definitions best fits the meaning of the word **retained** as it is used in paragraph 11?

    A. employed

    B. restrained

    C. preserved

    D. remembered

6. The deputy sheriff's thoughts about Jacob Quimby in Paragraph 10 could be evidence to support which of the following themes?

    A. the importance of intuition and careful observations in judgments

    B. the importance of considering other people's point of view

    C. the importance of considering everyone to be a suspect at first

    D. the importance of being truthful and transparent about one's objectives

---

✔ **Test-Taking Tip**

Understanding what a question is asking is an important part of taking a test. When you come across a long or complex question, especially one referring to a passage, read it carefully. Then try breaking the question into parts. For example: Does part of the question tell you where to look for the answer? What is the question asking you about the passage you read? What is the question asking or telling you about the answer options?

Writing Practice

All narratives have a setting, and the setting often plays an important role in the events that occur in a narrative. For example, the place where a wedding is held might make the event romantic, memorable, or even comical. A journey might be exciting because of the surprises that come from experiencing a new place. The events that unfold might be affected as much by the environment as by the characters involved.

Directions: Write a paragraph describing an important event in your life that happened in a memorable place. Be sure to describe the place as well as the event. Make clear why the place was important for this particular event.

_____

_____

_____

_____

_____

_____

_____

_____

_____

_____

_____

_____

_____

_____

_____

_____

_____

_____

_____

This lesson will help you practice determining implicit relationships between ideas in two types of texts. Use it with core lesson 2.4 Determine Implicit Relationships between Ideas between Implicit Ideas to reinforce and apply your knowledge.

Key Concept	Core Skills
Like ideas, relationships between ideas in a text may be implied. When this occurs, readers must find clues in the text to help them understand how the ideas connect.	• Determine Implied Relationships between Ideas • Predict Outcomes

Interpreting Implied Relationships between Ideas

Authors sometimes present explicit ideas with implicit relationships among them. Readers often need to make inferences about these relationships for a full understanding of a text. Readers can use language structure, punctuation, the proximity of words and ideas to support their inferences.

Directions: Read the passage below. Then complete the activities.

Warm and Cold Air Masses

1 Humidity and temperature affect how an air mass or body of air interacts in the atmosphere. Air masses are created when a body of air takes on the characteristics from the land or water over which it forms. The central region of Canada usually creates cold and dry air masses. Air masses that form over the Gulf of Mexico are warm and have high humidity. The Pacific Northwest creates air masses that are cool but also humid. The air masses that begin over the southwestern region of the United States are often dry but warm. Meteorologists track these air masses to help them make weather forecasts. The air masses that move across the United States from west to east help meteorologists predict the weather.

2 Cold air masses tend to be unstable and turbulent and move faster than warm air masses. When a cold air mass comes into contact with a warm air mass, it forces the warmer air upward. This forces any moisture in that air to condense quickly. The clouds that are formed by quick vertical air movements are cumulus clouds—puffy, cottonlike clouds. If the air is holding a great deal of moisture, the instant vertical draft creates a cumulonimbus or thunderhead. These are the storm clouds that drop a heavy load of precipitation quickly. Very often the quick rush of moist air will create a separation of electric charges within the cloud. This is how lightning is created. The release of the charged particles through the air superheats the individual air particles. They expand so fast that small sonic booms, or thunder, are heard.

3 Warm air masses are usually stable, and the wind that accompanies them is steady. Clouds that are formed by warm air masses are stratus clouds—low-lying, level clouds that in warm weather bring precipitation in the form of drizzle. As the warm air continues over the cooler air mass, the cloud formation becomes higher and thinner. The highest wispy clouds are cirrus clouds and do not contain enough moisture to bring precipitation.

(continued)

Air Masses Cause Fronts

4 A front occurs when two air masses collide and a boundary between the two masses forms. The weather for the land below is affected. Fronts may be either weak or strong. Strong fronts generally bring precipitation. When cold air acts like a plow and pushes warm air back, a cold front forms. If the cold air retreats, and the warm air pushes it away, a warm front occurs. Sometimes, the boundary between the two air masses does not move, and the front becomes stationary. Stationary fronts bring conditions similar to those brought by warm fronts. The precipitation that results, however, is usually milder and lasts longer.

5 More commonly, these collisions of fronts take place at the change of seasons. In the central part of the United States, spring means collisions of the newly arriving warm, moist air from the Gulf of Mexico with the retreating dry and cold air from central Canada. This annual springtime tradition generates the conditions that cause tornadoes. Tornadoes are the result of a very isolated strong updraft of warm, moist air. The rotation of the planet puts the circulation pattern of a counterclockwise spin into the updraft. (This is known as the Coriolis Effect and is demonstrated by all wind and water currents in both hemispheres. It is the reason the trade vessels in the Atlantic Ocean coming from Europe to North America must travel south to the equator instead of straight across the Atlantic.) Tornadoes can have wind speeds of up to 300 miles per hour, and they travel across the ground at around 30 miles per hour. Most tornadoes are produced in a region known as Tornado Alley: an area starting in the northern sections of Texas, through Oklahoma, Kansas, Missouri, and parts of Iowa and Illinois.

6 Hurricanes are also seasonal storms. As the energy from the Sun leaves the northern hemisphere in the late summer, the oceans near the Equator develop air mass and water-current low-pressure systems. Hurricane season is August through October, when the conditions are right for the start of these large circulation patterns that are fueled by the warm ocean waters near the equator.

---

1. The word patterns at the beginning of paragraphs 2 and 3 make it clear that the author is

   A. comparing similar characteristics of warm and cold air masses.

   B. contrasting different characteristics of warm and cold air masses.

   C. explaining how warm air masses slowly become cold air masses.

   D. explaining how cold air masses slowly become warm air masses.

2. In paragraph 1, what information is implied by explicit details about air masses?

   A. Air masses over the Gulf of Mexico are warm.

   B. The weather in Canada is cold and dry.

   C. Air masses in the Southwest are dry.

   D. Humidity affects how air masses interact.

3. In paragraph 3, language patterns and the _____ of ideas help readers infer that the authors is comparing the different movements of cold air masses and the resulting fronts.

4. Based on the details describing cold and warm air masses in Paragraphs 2 and 3, a reader could infer that

   A. rain only occurs when cold air masses come in contact with warm air masses.

   B. puffy, cottonlike clouds form when warm air masses and cold air masses meet.

   C. cold air masses cause heavier rain than warm air masses.

   D. the winds in warm air masses are gustier than in cold air masses.

Citing Evidence of Implied Relationships

When inferring the relationship between ideas, a reader must support inferences with evidence supporting the implied relationship. Based on this evidence, the reader can predict outcomes within the text or predict how this evidence might apply to other texts or to situations outside of one particular text.

Directions: Read the passage below. Then complete the activities.

Supreme Court Decision on Repealing the Defense of Marriage Act (DOMA)

1   DOMA's principal effect is to identify a subset of state-sanctioned marriages and make them unequal. The principal purpose is to impose inequality, not for other reasons like governmental efficiency. Responsibilities, as well as rights, enhance the dignity and integrity of the person. And DOMA contrives to deprive some couples married under the laws of their State, but not other couples, of both rights and responsibilities. By creating two contradictory marriage regimes within the same State, DOMA forces same-sex couples to live as married for the purpose of state law but unmarried for the purpose of federal law, thus diminishing the stability and predictability of basic personal relations the State has found it proper to acknowledge and protect. By this dynamic DOMA undermines both the public and private significance of state-sanctioned same-sex marriages; for it tells those couples, and all the world, that their otherwise valid marriages are unworthy of federal recognition. This places same-sex couples in an unstable position of being in a second-tier marriage. The differentiation demeans the couple, whose moral and sexual choices the Constitution protects . . . and whose relationship the State has sought to dignify. And it humiliates tens of thousands of children now being raised by same-sex couples. The law in question makes it even more difficult for the children to understand the integrity and closeness of their own family and its concord with other families in their community and in their daily lives.

2   Under DOMA, same-sex married couples have their lives burdened, by reason of government decree, in visible and public ways. By its great reach, DOMA touches many aspects of married and family life, from the mundane to the profound. It prevents same-sex married couples from obtaining government health care benefits they would otherwise receive. . . . It deprives them of the Bankruptcy Code's special protections for domestic-support obligations. . . . It forces them to follow a complicated procedure to file their state and federal taxes jointly. . . . It prohibits them from being buried together in veterans' cemeteries. . . .

3   DOMA also brings financial harm to children of same-sex couples. It raises the cost of health care for families by taxing health benefits provided by employers to their workers' same-sex spouses. . . . And it denies or reduces benefits allowed to families upon the loss of a spouse and parent, benefits that are an integral part of family security. . . .

(continued)

4 DOMA divests married same-sex couples of the duties and responsibilities that are an essential part of married life and that they in most cases would be honored to accept were DOMA not in force. For instance, because it is expected that spouses will support each other as they pursue educational opportunities, federal law takes into consideration a spouse's income in calculating a student's federal financial aid eligibility. . . . Same-sex married couples are exempt from this requirement. The same is true with respect to federal ethics rules. Federal executive and agency officials are prohibited from "participat[ing] personally and substantially" in matters as to which they or their spouses have a financial interest. . . . A similar statute prohibits Senators, Senate employees, and their spouses from accepting high-value gifts from certain sources . . . , and another mandates detailed financial disclosures by numerous high-ranking officials and their spouses. . . . Under DOMA, however, these Government-integrity rules do not apply to same-sex spouses. . . .

5 The class to which DOMA directs its restrictions and restraints are those persons who are joined in same-sex marriages made lawful by the State. DOMA singles out a class of persons deemed by a State entitled to recognition and protection to enhance their own liberty. It imposes a disability on the class by refusing to acknowledge a status the State finds to be dignified and proper. DOMA instructs all federal officials, and indeed all persons with whom same-sex couples interact, including their own children, that their marriage is less worthy than the marriages of others. The federal statute is invalid, for no legitimate purpose overcomes the purpose and effect to disparage and to injure those whom the State, by its marriage laws, sought to protect in personhood and dignity. By seeking to displace this protection and treating those persons as living in marriages less respected than others, the federal statute is in violation of the Fifth Amendment. This opinion and its holding are confined to those lawful marriages.

6 The judgment of the Court of Appeals for the Second Circuit is affirmed.

7 It is so ordered.

> —from U.S. Supreme Court decision on UNITED STATES v. WINDSOR,
> delivered by Justice Anthony Kennedy

1. The statement in paragraph 4 that "Under DOMA . . . Government-integrity rules do not apply to same-sex spouses . . ." is evidence to support which of the following predicted outcomes?

   A. The Court of Appeals will uphold DOMA.

   B. The Court of Appeals will overturn DOMA.

   C. The Court of Appeals will uphold Government-integrity rules.

   D. The Court of Appeals will overturn Government-integrity rules.

2. In paragraph 5, which of these details helps the reader to infer that the Court of Appeals based their final decision on existing legislation?

   A. "DOMA singles out a class of persons deemed by a State entitled to recognition and protection . . ."

   B. "[DOMA] is invalid, [and in displacing State] protection, [is] in violation of the Fifth Amendment."

   C. "[DOMA] imposes a disability . . . by refusing to acknowledge a status the State finds to be dignified and proper . . ."

   D. "[The Court's] opinion and its holding are confined to those lawful marriages [protected by the State]."

3. Based on the proximity of these two statements, what conclusion can the reader infer? "Responsibilities, as well as rights, enhance the dignity and integrity of the person. And DOMA contrives to deprive some couples married under the laws of their State, but not other couples, of both rights and responsibilities."

   A. Therefore, DOMA diminishes the dignity and integrity of all couples.

   B. Therefore, DOMA diminishes the dignity and integrity of some couples.

   C. Therefore, DOMA diminishes the rights and responsibilities of all couples.

   D. Therefore, DOMA diminishes the rights and responsibilities of some couples.

4. Based on the Court of Appeals' decision about DOMA, what type of statutes might you predict would also be overturned by the same court?

   A. those that deny underage couples with parental consent the right to marry

   B. those that deny citizens the types of responsibilities that enhance integrity

   C. those that impact the financial disclosures of high-ranking federal officials and their spouses

   D. those that enable the federal government to deny rights already recognized by the state

5. Which of the following definitions best fits the meaning of the word **concord** as it is used in paragraph 1?

   A. sympathy

   B. serenity

   C. unity

   D. tranquility

 Test-Taking Tip

When you answer questions about a reading passage, go back to the passage to find the answer. Before looking for the answer in the passage, read the question carefully to see whether some of the context in the question or in the answer options can help you find the answer when you reread.

Writing Practice

When writing a text, an author can use structure and patterns to reveal his or her ideas without directly stating them. For example, an author can describe one item with very favorable language but then describe the negative attributes of a similar item. It will then be inferred by the reader that the author prefers the item that he or she described with more positive words.

Directions: Write a paragraph comparing and contrasting two different cities you have visited or lived in. Structure your sentences so it is clear that you are comparing and contrasting these cities without saying so explicitly. Include at least two similarities and two differences. Include at least one statement that implies but does not state that one city is better than the other city.

_____

_____

_____

_____

_____

_____

_____

_____

_____

_____

_____

_____

_____

_____

_____

_____

_____

_____

This lesson will help you practice analyzing details to understand two types of complex texts. Use it with core lesson 2.5 Analyze the Role of Details in Complex Texts to reinforce and apply your knowledge.

Key Concept

The details in complex informational and literary texts provide clues to the main ideas, significance of events, and relationships implied by the author.

Core Skills

- Comprehend Complex Texts
- Use Details to Analyze Complex Texts

Examining Complex Literary Texts

Complex literary texts often contain challenging words, abstract ideas, or implicit purposes. In addition, the subject might be unfamiliar, the text might have more than one theme, and the text structure might be unusual. To understand complex literary texts, you should scan the text to pick up clues from the title and key details, combine these clues with your knowledge, and draw from your life experiences.

Directions: Read the passage below. Then complete the activities.

The Black Cat

1 For the most wild, yet most homely narrative which I am about to pen, I neither expect nor solicit belief. Mad indeed would I be to expect it in a case where my very senses reject their own evidence. Yet mad am I not—and very surely do I not dream. But tomorrow I die, and today I would unburthen my soul. My immediate purpose is to place before the world plainly, succinctly, and without comment, a series of mere household events. In their consequences these events have terrified—have tortured—have destroyed me. Yet I will not attempt to expound them. To me they presented little but horror—to many they will seem less terrible than *baroques*. Hereafter, perhaps, some intellect may be found which will reduce my phantasm to the commonplace—some intellect more calm, more logical, and far less excitable than my own, which will perceive, in the circumstances I detail with awe, nothing more than an ordinary succession of very natural causes and effects.

2 From my infancy I was noted for the docility and humanity of my disposition. My tenderness of heart was even so conspicuous as to make me the jest of my companions. I was especially fond of animals, and was indulged by my parents with a great variety of pets. With these I spent most of my time, and never was so happy as when feeding and caressing them. This peculiarity of character grew with my growth, and in my manhood I derived from it one of my principal sources of pleasure. To those who have cherished an affection for a faithful and sagacious dog, I need hardly be at the trouble of explaining the nature or the intensity of the gratification thus derivable. There is something in the unselfish and self-sacrificing love of a brute which goes directly to the heart of him who has had frequent occasion to test the paltry friendship and gossamer fidelity of mere *Man*.

3 I married early, and was happy to find in my wife a disposition not uncongenial with my own. Observing my partiality for domestic pets, she lost no opportunity of procuring those of the most agreeable kind. We had birds, gold-fish, a fine dog, rabbits, a small monkey, and *a cat*.

(continued)

4 This latter was a remarkably large and beautiful animal, entirely black, and sagacious to an astonishing degree. In speaking of his intelligence, my wife, who at heart was not a little tinctured with superstition, made frequent allusion to the ancient popular notion which regarded all black cats as witches in disguise. Not that she was ever *serious* upon this point, and I mention the matter at all for no better reason than that it happens just now to be remembered.

—From "The Black Cat" by Edgar Allan Poe

1. By scanning the title and the first sentence of each paragraph, the reader can tell that the narrator is discussing

   A. cats and superstitions.

   B. his life and his cat.

   C. his childhood and relatives.

   D. marriage and fiction writing.

2. Choose the phrase that best completes the following summary of paragraph 1: The narrator says that perhaps readers will _____ the events he is about to describe.

   A. be persuaded to agree with

   B. be terrified yet entertained by

   C. determine a logical explanation for

   D. understand why he has written about

3. Which statement best summarizes the main idea of paragraph 3?

   A. The narrator's wife had pets of all different kinds.

   B. The narrator married someone who was agreeable.

   C. The narrator married someone who shared his love of animals.

   D. The narrator's wife allowed him to get fish, birds, a dog, and a cat.

4. Which of the following definitions best fits the meaning of the word **brute** as it is used in paragraph 2?

   A. monster

   B. savage

   C. thug

   D. animal

Understanding Complex Informational Texts

Complex informational texts can be challenging when the reader is not familiar with technical vocabulary and concepts. It is helpful to scan for recurring words, make predictions and connections based on prior knowledge, and visualize as you read. Paraphrase difficult words, concepts, and complex sentences using your own words; summarize the main points implied by the details; and try to identify the author's main ideas. As you read, think about how the details relate to the main ideas.

Directions: Read the passage below. Then complete the activities.

Remarks by the President on College Affordability

1 A higher education is the single best investment you can make in your future. And I'm proud of all the students who are making that investment. . . . And that's not just me saying it. Look, right now, the unemployment rate for Americans with at least a college degree is about one-third lower than the national average. The incomes of folks who have at least a college degree are more than twice those of Americans without a high school diploma. So more than ever before, some form of higher education is the surest path into the middle class.

(continued)

2 But what I want to talk about today is what's become a barrier and a burden for too many American families—and that is the soaring cost of higher education. . . .

3 This is something that everybody knows you need—a college education. On the other hand, college has never been more expensive. Over the past three decades, the average tuition at a public four-year college has gone up by more than 250 percent—250 percent. Now, a typical family's income has only gone up 16 percent. So think about that—tuition has gone up 250 percent; income gone up 16 percent. That's a big gap. . . .

4 The average student who borrows for college now graduates owing more than $26,000. Some owe a lot more than that. And I've heard from a lot of these young people who are frustrated that they've done everything they're supposed to do—got good grades in high school, applied to college, did well in school—but now they come out, they've got this crushing debt that's crippling their sense of self-reliance and their dreams. It becomes hard to start a family and buy a home if you're servicing $1,000 worth of debt every month. It becomes harder to start a business if you are servicing $1,000 worth of debt every month, right? . . .

5 So at a time when a higher education has never been more important or more expensive, too many students are facing a choice that they should never have to make: Either they say no to college and pay the price for not getting a degree—and that's a price that lasts a lifetime—or you do what it takes to go to college, but then you run the risk that you won't be able to pay it off because you've got so much debt. . . .

6 So the bottom line is this—we've got a crisis in terms of college affordability and student debt. And over the past four years, what we've tried to do is to take some steps to make college more affordable. So we enacted historic reforms to the student loan system, so taxpayer dollars stop padding the pockets of big banks and instead help more kids afford college. . . .

7 Because what was happening was the old system, the student loan programs were going through banks; they didn't have any risk because the federal government guaranteed the loans, but they were still taking billions of dollars out of the program. We said, well, let's just give the loans directly to the students and we can put more money to helping students.

8 Then we set up a consumer watchdog. And that consumer watchdog is already helping students and families navigate the financial options that are out there to pay for college without getting ripped off by shady lenders. . . .

9 Then, we took action to cap loan repayments at 10 percent of monthly income for many borrowers who are trying to responsibly manage their federal student loan debt. . . . So overall, we've made college more affordable for millions of students and families through tax credits and grants and student loans that go farther than they did before. And then, just a few weeks ago, Democrats and Republicans worked together to keep student loan rates from doubling. . . .

(continued)

10 So that's all a good start, but it's not enough. The problem is, is that even if the federal government keeps on putting more and more money in the system, if the cost is going up by 250 percent, tax revenues aren't going up 250 percent—and so [at] some point, the government will run out of money, which means more and more costs are being loaded on to students and their families.

11 The system's current trajectory is not sustainable. And what that means is state legislatures are going to have to step up. They can't just keep cutting support for public colleges and universities. . . . That's just the truth. Colleges are not going to be able to just keep on increasing tuition year after year, and then passing it on to students and families and taxpayers. . . . Our economy can't afford the trillion dollars in outstanding student loan debt, much of which may not get repaid because students don't have the capacity to pay it. We can't price the middle class and everybody working to get into the middle class out of a college education. We're going to have to do things differently. We can't go about business as usual.

—from "Remarks by the President on College Affordability" (speech) by Barack Obama

---

1. Scan the title and the first two paragraphs to determine which of the following is the main theme of this speech.

A. The incomes of college graduates needs to increase.

B. The importance of higher education is overestimated.

C. The unemployment rate for college graduates is too high.

D. The cost of higher education is too high.

2. What detail offers the strongest support for the idea that college tuition is no longer affordable to the average American?

A. Some college graduates owe more than $26,000 in loan debt.

B. It's hard to start a family if you have to pay $1000 in debt each month.

C. Average tuition increased 250 percent, and average income increased 16 percent.

D. Federal tax revenues have not increased by 250 percent, but college costs have.

3. By imagining a college graduate sending a check for $1000 to a bank each month, you are _____ the details of the text.

4. The technical information in paragraphs 7, 8, and 9 can be best summarized in which of the following statements?

A. The government took lending away from the banks to offer more money to students.

B. The government offered tax credits and grants to make college more affordable.

C. The government took several steps to help and protect students who take out loans.

D. The government's political parties worked together to keep loan rates from doubling.

5. Based on the first sentences of paragraph 10 and paragraph 11, what is the author's conclusion?

A. Some changes were made to the old system, but more must be made.

B. The old system was not sustainable, so changes were made.

C. The changes made will redirect the trajectory of the current system.

D. If the current system does not change, the government will run out of money.

Language Practice

In writing, it is important to use the correct pronoun to match the antecedent to which it refers.

Directions: Read the following passage. Then choose the option with the correct pronoun to match the antecedent.

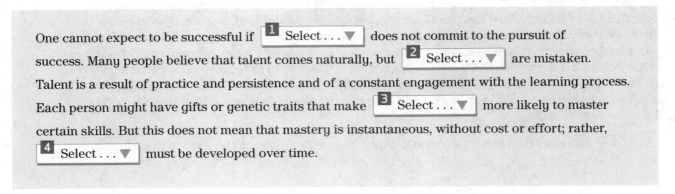

One cannot expect to be successful if **1** Select . . . ▼ does not commit to the pursuit of success. Many people believe that talent comes naturally, but **2** Select . . . ▼ are mistaken. Talent is a result of practice and persistence and of a constant engagement with the learning process. Each person might have gifts or genetic traits that make **3** Select . . . ▼ more likely to master certain skills. But this does not mean that mastery is instantaneous, without cost or effort; rather, **4** Select . . . ▼ must be developed over time.

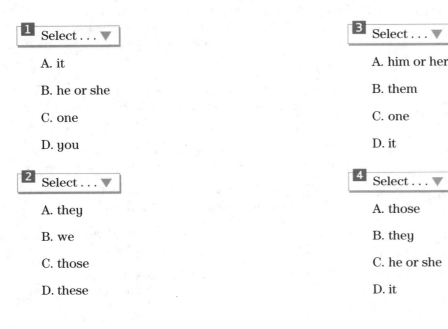

1 Select . . . ▼

A. it

B. he or she

C. one

D. you

2 Select . . . ▼

A. they

B. we

C. those

D. these

3 Select . . . ▼

A. him or her

B. them

C. one

D. it

4 Select . . . ▼

A. those

B. they

C. he or she

D. it

Test-Taking Tip

The extended response portion of the test is used to assess numerous abilities. These include your organizational skills and stylistic choices, the effectiveness of your arguments, your use of evidence, and your grasp of standard English conventions. In other words, your score will take into account what you write and how you write it. Therefore, it's important to become comfortable with content and presentation.

Writing Practice

Not all English speakers use exactly the same vocabulary. We all learn new words through our daily experiences, our jobs, and our interests. Anyone who plays a sport, has a hobby, or works in a particular industry learns the specialized terms and procedures that go along with that activity. Sometimes without realizing it, in different areas of our lives, we communicate in ways that not all of our family and friends can understand.

Directions: Write a paragraph explaining a particular rule or procedure that pertains to your job, a sport you watch or play, or a hobby or special interest you have. Be sure to use clear writing, but include the words and ideas that are specific to that activity without defining them to your reader.

_____

_____

_____

_____

_____

_____

_____

_____

_____

_____

_____

_____

_____

_____

_____

_____

_____

This lesson will help you practice determining connotative and figurative meanings in two types of texts. Use it with core lesson 3.1 Determine Connotative and Figurative Meanings to reinforce and apply your knowledge.

Key Concept

The connotative meaning of a word or phrase is the meaning suggested by the word. Figurative language includes words or phrases that imply more than their literal meaning.

Core Skills

- Analyze and Evaluate Word Choice
- Interpret Words and Phrases

Identifying Connotative and Figurative Meanings

Authors use connotative and figurative language to set the tone and mood of a text. The tone conveys the author's attitude about a subject; the mood is how the writing makes the reader feel. As you read, analyze the author's use of specific words and phrases to identify the text's mood and tone.

Directions: Read the passage below. Then complete the activities.

The Pony Express

1 From 1860 to 1861, the young riders of the Pony Express galloped their way across the western United States into American history. When the Pony Express first began its operation, there was no quick way for people on the East Coast of the United States to communicate with people on the West Coast. Mail was delivered by steamship or stagecoach. The founders of the Pony Express came up with a better—and faster—method.

2 They created a mail service between St. Joseph, Missouri, and Sacramento, California, that consisted of riders, horses, and way stations. Most of the riders were young teenagers, often orphans. They were lightweight, hard-working, and brave enough to take on incredible risks. Each rider would mount a fresh horse and ride at breakneck speed to the next station, about ten to fifteen miles away. There the rider would mount another fresh horse and ride on from station to station until he had covered about 75 miles. Then a new rider would take over the mailbag and complete the next section of the Pony Express route.

3 At its busiest point of operation, the Pony Express had more than 80 riders, between 400 and 500 horses, and more than 100 stations. The riders were often heroic for their dedication to getting the mail through. They rode during the day and during the night. They crossed mountains and deserts and rough trails in all kinds of weather. They carried firearms to protect themselves from the many dangers they encountered while crossing the Wild West.

4 The Pony Express had a short but glorious history. It ended after 19 months of operation when the Pacific Telegraph line was completed in October, 1861. Then the Pony Express and its riders ended their exciting chapter in American history.

1. Which sentence from the passage is an example of figurative language?

   A. "The riders were often heroic for their dedication to getting the mail through."

   B. "... the young riders of the Pony Express galloped their way across the western United States into American history."

   C. "Then a new rider would take over the mailbag and complete the next section of the Pony Express route."

   D. "Most of the riders were young teenagers, often orphans."

2. What is the mood of the article?

   A. concerned

   B. suspenseful

   C. longing

   D. exciting

3. What is the tone in the article?

   A. suspicious

   B. complimentary

   C. sympathetic

   D. indifferent

4. The sentence "Then the Pony Express and its riders ended their exciting chapter in American history" is an example of a _____.

5. What is the connotative meaning of the word **breakneck** in the second paragraph?

   A. dangerous

   B. cautious

   C. torturous

   D. relaxed

6. Which of the following definitions best fits the meaning of the word **glorious** as it is used in final paragraph?

   A. famous

   B. interesting

   C. troubled

   D. wonderful

Understanding Connotative and Figurative Meanings in Literary Text

Connotative and figurative language add depth to literary texts. An author's descriptions and word choices indicate the author's tone, the mood that the text conveys, and how the reader should feel toward the characters and about the events in the story. As you read, reflect on the author's reason for using certain words and phrases.

Directions: Read the passage below. Then complete the activities.

Rip Van Winkle

1   Rip Van Winkle was one of those happy mortals of foolish, pleasant dispositions who take the world easy, eat white bread or brown (which ever can be got with least thought or trouble), and would rather starve on a penny than work for a pound. He would have whistled life away in perfect contentment but for his wife's continual harping about his idleness, his carelessness, and the ruin he was bringing on his family. Morning, noon, and night, her tongue was incessantly going. Every thing he said or did was sure to produce a torrent of criticism. Rip had but one way of replying to all lectures of the kind. He shrugged his shoulders, shook his head, cast up his eyes, but said nothing. This, however, always provoked a fresh volley from his wife. He was then forced to retreat to the outside of the house—the only side which, in truth, belongs to a henpecked husband.

2   Rip's sole domestic adherent was his dog Wolf, who was as much henpecked as his master. Dame Van Winkle regarded them as companions in idleness, looking upon Wolf with an evil eye as the cause of his master's so often going astray. True, he was as courageous an animal as ever scoured the woods—but what courage can withstand the terrors of a woman's tongue? The moment Wolf entered the house, his crest fell, his tail drooped to the ground, or curled between his legs. He sneaked about with a gallows air, casting many a sidelong glance at Dame Van Winkle. At the least flourish of a broomstick or ladle, he flew to the door with a pre-emptive yelp.

3   Times grew worse and worse with Rip Van Winkle as years of matrimony rolled on. A tart temper never mellows with age, and a sharp tongue is the only edge tool that grows keener by constant use. For a long while he used to console himself by frequenting a kind of club of the sages, philosophers, and other idle men of the village. Sessions were held on a bench before a small inn designated by a ruddy portrait of his majesty George the Third. Here they used to sit in the shade of a long lazy summer's day, talk listlessly over village gossip, or tell endless sleepy stories about nothing. But it would have been worth any statesman's money to have heard the profound discussions that sometimes took place when by chance an old newspaper fell into their hands from some passing traveller. How solemnly they would listen to the contents, as drawled out by Derrick Van Bummel, the schoolmaster. A dapper learned little man, he was not to be daunted by the most gigantic word in the dictionary. Then how sagely they would deliberate upon public events some months after they had taken place.

4   The opinions of this band were completely controlled by Nicholas Vedder, a patriarch of the village and landlord of the inn. At the inn's door he took his seat from morning till night, just moving sufficiently to avoid the sun and keep in the shade of a large tree. The neighbours could tell the hour by his movements as accurately as by a sun dial. It is true, he was rarely heard to speak, but smoked his pipe incessantly. His adherents, however, (for every great man has his adherents) perfectly understood him and knew how to gather his opinions. When any thing that was read or related displeased him, he was observed to smoke his pipe vehemently and send forth short, frequent, and angry puffs. When pleased, he would inhale the smoke slowly and tranquilly, emitting it in light and placid clouds. Sometimes he would even deign to take the pipe from his mouth to let the fragrant vapour curl about his nose, gravely nodding his head in token of approval.

(continued)

5 From even this strong hold the unlucky Rip was at length thwarted by his unruly wife, who would suddenly break in upon the tranquility of the meeting and call the members all to task. That honourable personage, Nicholas Vedder himself, was hardly safe from the daring tongue of this terrible shrew who charged him outright with encouraging her husband in habits of idleness.

6 Poor Rip was at last reduced almost to despair. His only alternative to escape from the labour of the farm and the clamour of his wife was to take gun in hand and stroll away into the woods. Here he would sometimes seat himself at the foot of a tree and share the contents of his wallet with Wolf, with whom he sympathized as a fellow sufferer in persecution. "Poor Wolf," he would say, "thy mistress leads thee a dog's life of it; but never mind, my lad, while I live thou shalt never want a friend to stand by thee!" Wolf would wag his tail, look wistfully in his master's face, and if dogs can feel pity, I truly believe he reciprocated the sentiment with all his heart.

—From "Rip Van Winkle," by Washington Irving, 1819

1. How does the author want readers to feel toward Rip Van Winkle?

A. irritated

B. understanding

C. loyal

D. sympathetic

2. The _____ in the third paragraph is one of amusement.

3. Review paragraphs 2 and 4. Which pair of words could replace "adherent" and "adherents" to give the connotation of someone who supports or believes in another?

A. student/students

B. friend/friends

C. enemy/enemies

D. pet/pets

4. How does the mood change between paragraphs 4 and 5?

A. It changes from calm to frenzied.

B. It changes from unpleasant to pleasant.

C. It changes from riotous to peaceful.

D. It changes from humorous to serious.

5. Write three words that describe Dame Van Winkle in the character web.

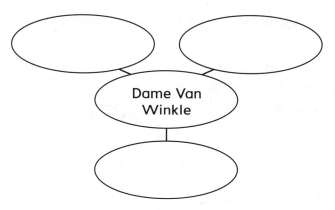

brash   passive

dominant   unpleasant

meek

6. Reread the first paragraph. Based on the paragraph's context, what is the connotative meaning of the word **henpecked**?

A. enjoying lovely solitude

B. suffering constant nagging

C. feeling spiritually fulfilled

D. taking pleasure in silence

Test-Taking Tip

If you can't identify all the correct answers in a drag-and-drop activity, begin with the one or two that you know. Eliminate the choices that you know are incorrect, and then select the best option from the remaining choices. Blank answer spaces will count against your overall score.

Language Practice

Homophones are words that sound the same but are spelled differently and have different meanings. Using the correct homophones is an important part of crafting a text that is clear and easy to understand.

Directions: Circle the correct homophone to complete each sentence.

1. Juan | Select . . . ▼ | that something was wrong as soon as he stepped into the house.
   - knew
   - new

2. Courtney and Malik couldn't wait to move out of | Select . . . ▼ | old apartment.
   - they're
   - there
   - their

3. One shoe alone does not make a | Select . . . ▼ |.
   - pear
   - pair
   - pare

4. We're leaving now, | Select . . . ▼ | you're ready or not.
   - weather
   - whether

 Test-Taking Tip

It is easy to stray off course while completing a timed extended response. Before you begin to write, closely reread the directions. Then write a brief outline of the points you want to address. The outline serves as a roadmap that will keep you on track and help you use the time to thoroughly answer the question.

Writing Practice

Connotative and figurative language brings depth to your writing. These types of descriptive language add interest while guiding the reader to react to the text in a specific way. For example, "Jaime was silent" simply tells that Jaime didn't make any noise. "Jaime was as quiet as a mouse" is more descriptive. It still relates that Jaime was quiet, but it also makes Jaime seem small and meek.

Directions: Write a paragraph describing an emotional moment in your life. It can be a memory filled with happiness, sadness, anger, or humor. Use connotative and figurative language to give the reader a vivid description of the situation and the emotions you felt at the time.

_____

_____

_____

_____

_____

_____

_____

_____

_____

_____

_____

_____

_____

_____

_____

_____

_____

_____

_____

This lesson will help you practice analyzing tone in two types of texts. Use it with core lesson 3.2 Analyze Tone to reinforce and apply your knowledge.

Key Concept

Tone is the expression of a writer's attitude through stylistic choices.

Core Skills

- Analyze Word Choice
- Interpret Words and Phrases to Draw Conclusions

Identifying Author's Tone in an Informational Text

The tone an author conveys is much like the tone of your voice when you speak. In writing, authors convey tone through word choices and sentence structure. The tone of an informational text should be appropriate to the author's purpose for writing and for the text's topic and genre.

Directions: Read the passage below. Then complete the activities.

Manager

Value Inn Hotel

122 Massachusetts Avenue

Washington, DC 20027

Dear Manager,

1 I am writing about a number of problems I had when I stayed at your hotel in May of this year. The headaches began at the front desk, where I had to wait in line for 10 minutes. When I finally reached the desk, the employee was unable to find my reservation even after I spelled my name several times and gave her my reservation number. She then said there were no more non-smoking rooms, even though I had reserved one weeks ago. She also informed me that only rooms on the twenty-second floor were available despite the fact that I had reserved a lower floor room.

2 Naturally, I had trouble with my room key and had to return to the desk, where more customers were in line. The clerk who checked me in wasn't there, and the new clerk huffily told me to wait in line with the others. I had to wait 15 more minutes to get a key to my room. When I finally entered my room, it was nothing short of a disaster. I returned to the front desk for a third time. Imagine my surprise when the clerk offered me a non-smoking room on a lower floor!

3 Despite the better room, my troubles were far from over. Your website clearly said that Internet access was free, yet I had to pay $9.95 in order to access it. When I made my reservation, I was told that the pool was open. Once at the hotel, however, I learned that the pool was not scheduled to open until the following weekend, which was Memorial Day. As the cherry on top, the air conditioner in my room broke that night. I called the front desk, but the engineer was not at all successful in his attempts to repair it. Since there were no other rooms available (not even those on the twenty-second floor, apparently), I had to sleep in a stuffy, uncomfortable room.

4 I complained to a desk clerk about all these problems, but she said that there was nothing she could do to solve them. Because of the problems I experienced, I would like the cost of my stay refunded to me.

Sincerely,

Charles Walters

1. How does the topic of this letter affect its tone?

   A. The topic, a compliment about a hotel stay, sets a tone of congratulations.

   B. The topic, a complaint about a hotel stay, sets a tone of anger or frustration.

   C. The topic, a compliment about a hotel stay, sets a tone of neutrality.

   D. The topic, a complaint about a hotel stay, sets a tone of disappointment or sadness.

2. Which sentence from paragraph 2 best expresses the tone in the letter?

   A. "Naturally, I had trouble with my room key and had to return to the desk."

   B. "I had to wait 15 more minutes to get a key to my room."

   C. "I returned to the front desk for a third time."

   D. "Imagine my surprise when the clerk offered me a non-smoking room on a lower floor!"

3. In paragraph 1, the word _____ is a metaphor that conveys the tone by showing the author's frustration with the staff.

4. What tone does the word "Sincerely" convey as used at the end of the letter?

   A. dismissive

   B. flattering

   C. respectful

   D. furious

5. In paragraph 3, replacing "As the cherry on top," with "Thankfully," would change the _____ of the sentence to gratitude.

✓ Test-Taking Tip

Fill-in-the-blank items are sentences that have a blank space or line in the place of a word or phrase. You are expected to give the word or phrase that completes the sentence. Fill-in-the-blank items often test your knowledge of vocabulary words, key terms, or important facts. Read the fill-in-the-blank item, looking for clues in the surrounding words to help you identify a specific term or fact.

Analyzing Tone in a Literary Text

Tone plays an important role in literary writing. It can help build suspense in a mystery story, or create a sense of urgency in an adventure story. When writers carefully craft the details of a story, the words and phrases they choose help express the tone.

Directions: Read the passage below. Then complete the activities.

The Thief

1   "And now, if you have all seen the coin and sufficiently admired it, you may pass it back. I make a point of never leaving it off the shelf for more than fifteen minutes."

2   The half dozen or more guests seated about the board of the genial speaker, glanced casually at each other as though expecting to see the object mentioned immediately produced.

3   But no coin appeared.

4   "I have other amusements waiting," suggested their host, with a smile in which even his wife could detect no signs of impatience. "Now let Robert put it back into the cabinet."

5   Robert was the butler.

6   Blank looks, negative gestures, but still no coin.

7   "Perhaps it is in somebody's lap," timidly ventured one of the younger women. "It doesn't seem to be on the table."

8   Immediately all the ladies began lifting their napkins and shaking out the gloves which lay under them, in an effort to relieve their own embarrassment and that of the gentlemen who had not even so simple a resource as this at their command.

9   "It can't be lost," protested Mr. Sedgwick, with an air of perfect confidence. "I saw it but a minute ago in somebody's hand. Darrow, you had it; what did you do with it?"

10   "Passed it along."

11   "Well, well, it must be under somebody's plate or doily." And he began to move about his own and such dishes as were within reach of his hand.

12   Each guest imitated him, lifting glasses and turning over spoons till Mr. Sedgwick himself bade them desist. "It's slipped to the floor," he nonchalantly concluded. "A toast to the ladies, and we will give Robert the chance of looking for it."

13   As they drank this toast, his apparently careless, but quietly astute, glance took in each countenance about him. The coin was very valuable and its loss would be keenly felt by him. Had it slipped from the table some one's eye would have perceived it, some hand would have followed it. Only a minute or two before, the attention of the whole party had been concentrated upon it. Darrow had held it up for all to see, while he discoursed upon its history. He would take Darrow aside at the first opportunity and ask him—But—it! how could he do that? These were his intimate friends. He knew them well, more than well, with one exception, and he—Well, he was the handsomest of the lot and the most debonair and agreeable. A little more gay than usual to-night, possibly a trifle too gay, considering that a man of Mr. Blake's social weight and business standing sat at the board; but not to be suspected, no, not to be suspected, even if he was the next man after Darrow and had betrayed something like confusion when the eyes of the whole table turned his way at the former's simple statement of "I passed it on. . . ."

(continued)

14 "And now, some music!" he cheerfully cried, as with lingering glances and some further pokings about of the table furniture, the various guests left their places and followed him into the adjoining room.

15 But the ladies were too nervous and the gentlemen not sufficiently sure of their voices to undertake the entertainment of the rest at a moment of such acknowledged suspense; and notwithstanding the exertions of their host and his quiet but much discomfited wife, it soon became apparent that but one thought engrossed them all, and that any attempt at conversation must prove futile so long as the curtains between the two rooms remained open and they could see Robert on his hands and knees searching the floor and shoving aside the rugs.

16 Darrow, who was Mr. Sedgwick's brother-in-law and almost as much at home in the house as Sedgwick himself, made a move to draw these curtains, but something in his relative's face stopped him and he desisted with some laughing remark which did not attract enough attention, even, to elicit any response. . . .

17 "Robert will find it if it is there." Then, distressed at this involuntary disclosure of his thought, added in his whole-hearted way: "It's such a little thing, and the room is so big and a round object rolls unexpectedly far, you know. Well, have you got it?" he eagerly demanded, as the butler finally showed himself in the door.

18 "No, sir; and it's not in the dining-room. I have cleared the table and thoroughly searched the floor."

19 Mr. Sedgwick knew that he had. He had no doubts about Robert. Robert had been in his employ for years and had often handled his coins and, at his order, sometimes shown them.

20 "Very well," said he, "we'll not bother about it any more to-night; you may draw the curtains."

21 But here the clear, almost strident voice of the youngest man of the party interposed.

22 "Wait a minute," said he. "This especial coin is . . . unique in this country, and not only worth a great deal of money, but cannot be duplicated at any cost. . . . Gentlemen—I leave the ladies entirely out of this—I do not propose that he shall have further opportunity to associate me with this very natural doubt. I demand the privilege of emptying my pockets here and now, before any of us have left his presence. I am a connoisseur in coins myself and consequently find it imperative to take the initiative in this matter."

—*Room Number 3 and Other Detective Stories* by Anna Katherine Greene, 1913

1. What tone can a reader expect from a story of this genre?

   A. a tone of disbelief

   B. a tone of wonder

   C. a tone of suspense

   D. a tone of neutrality

2. Which of the following definitions best fits the meaning of the word **futile** as it is used in paragraph 15?

   A. annoying

   B. pointless

   C. careless

   D. useful

3. The effect of short phrases and short sentences in paragraphs 3 through 6 conveys a tone of

   A. lightheartedness and fun.

   B. confusion.

   C. suspicion.

   D. anticipation.

4. What is the tone in the story?

   A. intense

   B. terrifying

   C. friendly

   D. frantic

5. How does paragraph 13 affect the tone of the passage?

   A. The paragraph supplies a demonstration of the building tension by revealing Mr. Sedgwick's suspicions.

   B. Paragraph 13 gives details about Robert's search for the coin, which slows the pace and relieve the tension.

   C. In paragraph 13, the author misleads readers by naming Darrow as the culprit, changing the tone to confusion.

   D. The descriptions in the paragraph focus on Mr. Blake, which creates a humorous tone.

6. Reread the last paragraph of the passage. Which words listed below could replace "demand" while maintaining the tone of the paragraph? Write your answers in the concept web.

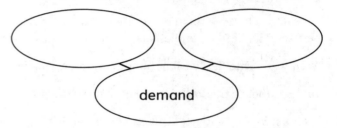

ask	call upon
crave	insist on
plead	urgently request

 Test-Taking Tip

Some test items ask about specific words or phrases, paragraphs, or sections of a passage. Before answering a question about a text detail, reread the related sentence or paragraph whether or not the item directs you to reread it. As you reread, focus on what the question is about. For example, if the item is about the meaning of a word, think about how the word is used as you reread.

Writing Practice

Connotative words, figurative language, and sentence structure are the building blocks that an author uses to express tone in a story. Think about the words you would use to tell a ghost story versus the words you would use to talk about an exciting baseball play. As a writer, expressing your tone can deepen the reader's understanding of and interest in the story.

Directions: Write a paragraph in which you describe the adult responsibilities you now have that you did not have when you were a child. For example, you are responsible for waking yourself up and getting to work on time. Before you write, decide on your purpose for writing. Choose words, descriptions, and sentence structures that will convey your desired tone.

_____

_____

_____

_____

_____

_____

_____

_____

_____

_____

_____

_____

_____

_____

_____

_____

_____

_____

_____

This lesson will help you practice analyzing word choice in two speeches. Use it with core lesson 3.3 Analyze Word Choice to reinforce and apply your knowledge.

Key Concept	Core Skills
To communicate accurately, authors make careful decisions about the words they use.	• Analyze Word Choice • Evaluate Word Choice

Choosing the Right Word

An author's word choices determine the tone, mood, and impact of a text. Readers or listeners can gain a deeper understanding about what an author wants them to feel, think, and understand by analyzing his or her word choices and writing style.

Directions: Read the passage below. Then complete the activities.

President Updates America on Operations Liberty Shield and Iraqi Freedom

1 Right now men and women from every part of America, supported by a strong coalition, are fighting to disarm a dangerous regime and to liberate an oppressed people.

2 It has been 11 days since the major ground war began. In this short time, our troops have performed brilliantly, with skill and with bravery. . . . In 11 days, coalition forces have taken control of most of western and southern Iraq. In 11 days, we've seized key bridges, opened a northern front, achieved—nearly achieved complete air superiority, and are delivering tons of humanitarian aid. By quick and decisive action, our troops are preventing Saddam Hussein from destroying the Iraqi people's oil fields. Our forces moved into Iraqi missile launch areas that threatened neighboring countries. Many dangers lie ahead, but day by day, we are moving closer to Baghdad. Day by day, we are moving closer to victory. . . .

3 Our victory will mean the end of a tyrant who rules by fear and torture. Our victory will remove a sponsor of terror, armed with weapons of terror. Our victory will uphold the just demands of the United Nations and the civilized world. And when victory comes, it will be shared by the long-suffering people of Iraq, who deserve freedom and dignity. . . .

4 The dictator's regime has ruled by fear and continues to use fear as a tool of domination to the end. Many Iraqis have been ordered to fight or die by Saddam's death squads. Others are pressed into service by threats against their children. Iraqi civilians attempting to flee to liberated areas have been shot and shelled from behind by Saddam's thugs. Schools and hospitals have been used to store military equipment. . . . Iraqis who show friendship toward coalition troops are murdered in cold blood by the regime's enforcers.

5 The people of Iraq have lived in this nightmare world for more than two decades. It is understandable that fear and distrust run deep. Yet, here in the city where America itself gained freedom, I give this pledge to the citizens of Iraq: We're coming with a mighty force to end the reign of your oppressors. We are coming to bring you food and medicine and a better life. And we are coming, and we will not stop, we will not relent until your country is free. . . .

(continued)

6   We know that our enemies are desperate; we know that they're dangerous. The dying regime in Iraq may try to bring terror to our shores. Other parts of the global terror network may view this as a moment to strike, thinking that we're distracted. They're wrong.

7   . . . The United States and allied troops are shattering the al Qaeda network. We're hunting them down, one at a time. We're finding them, we're interrogating them, and we're bringing them to justice. . . .

8   We will end the Iraqi regime, an ally of terrorist groups and a producer of weapons of mass destruction. . . . Shortly before we begin the liberation of Iraq, we launched Operation Liberty Shield, to implement additional measures to defend the American homeland against terrorist attacks.

9   This nationwide effort is focused on five specific areas. First, we are taking even greater security measures at our borders and ports. We have relocated hundreds of security personnel on our borders. We've added additional reconnaissance aircraft patrols at our borders. . . . Friends and immigrants will always be welcome in this land. Yet we will use all our power to keep out the terrorists and the criminals so they can't hurt our citizens. . . .

10 Second, we are strengthening protections throughout our national transportation system. We're enforcing temporary flight restrictions over some of our major cities. We've stepped up surveillance of hazardous material shipments within our country and taken measures to keep them away from places where large numbers of people gather. . . . We will do all in our power to make sure our skies and rails and roads are safe from terror.

11 Third, we've increased surveillance of suspected terrorists. Certain individual[s] with ties to Iraqi intelligence services have been ordered out of this country. We're interviewing Iraqi-born individuals on a voluntary basis for two reasons: to gain information on possible terrorist plans, and to make sure they've not experienced discrimination or hate crimes. . . . Iraqi Americans will be protected, and enemy agents will be stopped. . . .

12 Fourth, under Operation Liberty Shield, we are guarding our nation's most important infrastructure with greater vigilance. Under the direction of our governors, thousands of National Guardsmen and state police officers are protecting chemical facilities and nuclear power sites, key electrical grids and other potential targets. . . .

13 And, finally, we're strengthening the preparedness of our public health system. The Departments of Agriculture and Health and Human Services have increased field inspections of livestock and crops. Public health officials have increased medical surveillance in major cities. . . .

14 After our nation was attacked on September the 11th, 2001, America made a decision: We will not wait for our enemies to strike before we act against them. We're not going to permit terrorists and terror states to plot and plan and grow in strength while we do nothing.

15 The actions we're taking in Operation Liberty Shield are making this nation more secure. And the actions we're taking abroad against a terror network and against the regime in Iraq are removing a grave danger to all free nations. In every case, by acting today, we are saving countless lives in the future.

—From "President Updates America on Operations Liberty Shield and Iraqi Freedom"
by George W. Bush

1. How does the author's word choice in paragraphs 1–7 support his purpose to persuade readers of the necessity of Operation Liberty Shield?

   A. He uses words such as "regime" and "network" to describe the initiative.

   B. He uses words such as "brilliantly" and "skill" to describe the troops on the ground.

   C. He uses words such as "nightmare" and "murdered" to describe the atrocities happening.

   D. He uses words such as "distracted" and "interrogating" to describe the work of the troops.

2. In paragraph 4, why does the author use the word *thugs* to describe the people working with Saddam Hussein?

   A. to show that Hussein depends on soldiers who served in prison

   B. to highlight that Hussein has been resistant to attempts at diplomacy

   C. to communicate the idea that Hussein's soliders are criminals

   D. to emphasize that Hussein has been working with fighters from many nations

3. In paragraph 4, how does President Bush show his feelings about Saddam Hussein?

   A. He refers to Hussein's people as "Iraqis."

   B. He refers to Hussein's rule as a "dictator's regime."

   C. He refers to the demands of the United Nations as "just."

   D. He refers to members of Hussein's military as "troops."

4. Reread paragraphs 8–15. Add the words that contribute to the speech's focus on safety to the appropriate box in the graphic organizer.

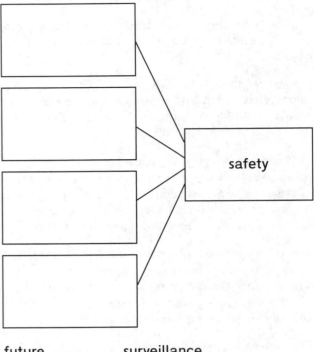

   future   surveillance

   vigilance   information

   secure   protection

5. Why is the word *attacked* used in paragraph 14?

   A. to show that the United States was not responsible for the events of September 11

   B. to remind listeners of the violent nature of the events that occurred on September 11

   C. to provide a neutral explanation of what happened on September 11

   D. to persuade listeners that the events of September 11 could not be prevented

Analyzing and Evaluating Word Choice in Various Texts

Word choice is particularly important when a text is written for the purpose of persuasion. The author's word choices, including connotative language and figurative language, inform the reader about how the writer wants him or her to feel about the topic.

Directions: Read the passage below. Then complete the activities.

1   Friends and Fellow Citizens: I stand before you tonight under indictment for the alleged crime of having voted at the last presidential election, without having a lawful right to vote. It shall be my work this evening to prove to you that in thus voting, I not only committed no crime, but, instead, simply exercised my citizen's rights, guaranteed to me and all United States citizens by the National Constitution, beyond the power of any State to deny.

2   Our democratic-republican government is based on the idea of the natural right of every individual member thereof to a voice and a vote in making and executing the laws. We assert the province of government to be to secure the people in the enjoyment of their unalienable rights. We throw to the winds the old dogma that governments can give rights. Before governments were organized, no one denies that each individual possessed the right to protect his own life. liberty and property. And when 100 or 1,000,000 people enter into a free government, they do not barter away their natural rights; they simply pledge themselves to protect each other in the enjoyment of them, through prescribed judicial and legislative tribunals. They agree to abandon the methods of brute force in the adjustment of their differences, and adopt those of civilization. . . .

3   The preamble of the Federal Constitution says: "We, the people of the United States, in order to form a more perfect union, establish justice, insure domestic tranquility, provide for the common defense, promote the general welfare, and secure the blessings of liberty to ourselves and our posterity, do ordain and establish this Constitution for the United States of America."

4   It was we, the people; not we, the white male citizens; nor yet we, the male citizens; but we, the whole people, who formed the Union. And we formed it, not to give the blessings of liberty, but to secure them; not to the half of ourselves and the half of our posterity, but to the whole people— women as well as men. And it is a downright mockery to talk to women of their enjoyment of the blessings of liberty while they are denied the use of the only means of securing them provided by this democratic-republican government—the ballot.

—From "Is It a Crime for a Citizen of the United States to Vote?" by Susan B. Anthony

1. Susan B. Anthony gave this speech and chose her words to _____ people that women have the right to vote.

2. The speaker chose her words to influence which audience?

   A. male landowners

   B. women

   C. politicians

   D. average citizens

3. Which of the following definitions best fits the meaning of the word **exercised** as it is used in paragraph 1?

   A. eliminated

   B. used

   C. ignored

   D. maintained

4. The phrase *throw to the winds* in paragraph 2 is an example of _____ language.

5. What idea is conveyed by the word *mockery* in paragraph 4?

   A. It is meaningless to talk of rights when women are not able to vote.

   B. It is silly to talk of rights when women are not able to vote.

   C. It is difficult to talk of rights when women are not able to vote.

   D. It is encouraging to talk of rights when women are not able to vote.

6. How does Anthony want her audience to feel as a result of her word choices?

   A. hopeful

   B. angry

   C. depressed

   D. excited

 Test-Taking Tip

Context clues can help you figure out the meaning of a word used in a test question. If you come across a test question that has an unfamiliar word, search the rest of the question for clues to its meaning. You can also refer to the test's introduction and directions for context clues.

Writing Practice

Powerful writing comes from the heart. Authors convey their feelings about a particular subject through the use of carefully chosen words meant to evoke feelings or emotions in the reader. As a writer, it is important to bring your passion to life with connotative and figurative language, as well as vivid descriptions to give the reader a clear picture of your feelings.

Directions: Write a paragraph describing your viewpoint on a current social or political topic, such as forced school closings or mandatory health insurance. Choose words that will convey your point of view and persuade the reader to agree with you.

_____

_____

_____

_____

_____

_____

_____

_____

_____

_____

_____

_____

_____

_____

_____

_____

_____

_____

_____

_____

This lesson will help you practice analyzing the development of ideas within fiction and nonfiction texts. Use it with core lesson 4.1 Analyze the Development of Ideas to reinforce and apply that knowledge.

Key Concept	Core Skills
Every piece of writing has a structure. Writers develop their ideas in texts through organization.	• Recognize Organization • Analyze Text Structure

Identifying Text Structure

A common type of text structure is sequence. Stories and other narratives relate events in the order in which they happened. Often, such texts include words such as *first, second, next,* and *last.* Another way writers organize their writing is by comparing or contrasting two or more things or ideas with words such as *although, both,* and *in contrast.* A third way to organize a text is through cause and effect. Words and phrases such as *so, therefore, since,* and *as a result* identify cause-and-effect structure.

Directions: Read the passage below. Then complete the activities.

The Maiden Voyage of the *Titanic*

1 Ever was [an] ill-starred voyage more [promising] than when the *Titanic* . . . steamed majestically out of the port of Southampton. [The ship left] at noon on Wednesday, April 10th, bound for New York.

2 Elaborate preparations had been made for the maiden voyage. Crowds of eager watchers gathered to witness the departure[.] Everyone was more interested because of the notable people who were to travel aboard her. Friends and relatives of many of the passengers were at the dock to bid Godspeed to their departing loved ones. The passengers themselves were unusually gay and happy.

3 Majestic and beautiful the ship rested on the water, marvel of shipbuilding, worthy of any sea. As this new queen of the ocean moved slowly from her dock, no one questioned her construction[.] She [had] an elaborate system of water-tight compartments, calculated to make her unsinkable[.] She had been pronounced the safest as well as the most [luxurious] Atlantic liner afloat.

4 There was silence just before the boat pulled out. . . . [Then] the heavy whistles sounded[.] The splendid *Titanic*, her flags flying and her band playing, churned the water and plowed heavily away.

5 [Before departure] the people on board wav[ed] handkerchiefs and shout[ed] good-byes[.] [Their voices] could be heard only as a buzzing murmur on shore[.] [Next, the *Titanic*] rode away on the ocean, proudly [and] majestically. . . .

6 And so it was only her due that the *Titanic* steamed out of the harbor bound on her maiden voyage[.] A thousand "God-speeds" were [called] after her, while [she dwarfed] every other vessel that she passed. . . .

(continued)

The Ship's Captain

7 In command of the *Titanic* was Captain E. J. Smith. . . . The next six officers, in the order of their rank, were Murdock, Lightollder,{sic} Pitman, Boxhall, Lowe and Moody. Dan Phillips was chief wireless operator, with Harold Bride as assistant.

8 From the forward bridge, fully ninety feet above the sea, peered out the [kind] face of the ship's master[.] [He was] cool of aspect, deliberate of action, [and] impressive in [his confidence.]

9 From far below the bridge sounded the strains of the ship's orchestra, playing a favorite air from "The Chocolate Soldier." All went as merry as a wedding bell. Indeed, among that gay ship's company were two score or more at least for whom the wedding bells had sounded. . . . Some were on their honeymoon tours[.] [Others] were returning to their motherland after having passed the weeks of the honeymoon. . . .

10 [Who] would have [predicted] that within the span of six days that ship . . . would lie at the bottom of the Atlantic[?]

    —From *Sinking of the Titanic and Great Sea Disasters* edited by Logan Marshall, 1912

---

1. What is the structure of this passage?

  A. compare and contrast

  B. problem and solution

  C. sequence of events

  D. cause and effect

2. This quotation from paragraph 6 is structured to serve what purpose: "A thousand 'God-speeds' were [called] after her, while [she dwarfed] every other vessel that she passed. . . ."?

  A. to describe the cause of the *Titanic's* sinking

  B. to describe the effect of the *Titanic's* sinking

  C. to compare the *Titanic* with other ships

  D. to contrast the *Titanic* with other ships

3. Which word in paragraph 5 is specific to the sequence text structure?

  A. could

  B. next

  C. on

  D. and

4. One _____ of the large crowds at the departure of the *Titanic* was that many friends and family of the ship's passengers wanted to say good-bye.

Variations in Organization

Often, a text's organization includes more than one structure or variations on a particular structure. Chronological order, also known as time order, expresses a clear sequence, relating what happened first, second, third, and so on. When writers interrupt the sequence to introduce events that took place before the story began, this is called a flashback. Slow pacing, another way that writers express time, moves gradually through events, using details and description. Fast pacing moves through events quickly to arrive at an important moment.

Directions: Read the passage below. Then complete the activities.

1   Holmes had been seated for some hours in silence with his long, thin back curved over a chemical vessel in which he was brewing a particularly malodorous product. His head was sunk upon his breast, and he looked from my point of view like a strange, lank bird, with dull gray plumage and a black top-knot.

2   "So, Watson," said he, suddenly, "you do not propose to invest in South African securities?"

3   I gave a start of astonishment. Accustomed as I was to Holmes's curious facilities, this sudden intrusion into my most intimate thoughts was utterly inexplicable.

4   "How on earth do you know that?" I asked.

5   He wheeled around upon his stool, with a steaming test-tube in his hand, and a gleam of amusement in his deep-set eyes.

6   "Now, Watson, confess yourself utterly taken aback," said he.

7   "I am."

8   "I ought to make you sign a paper to that effect."

9   "Why?"

10   "Because in five minutes you will say that it is all so absurdly simple."

11   "I am sure I will say nothing of the kind."

12   "You see, my dear Watson"—he propped his test-tube in the rack, and began to lecture with the air of a professor addressing his class—"it is not really difficult to construct a series of inferences, each dependent upon its predecessor and each simple in itself. If, after doing so, one simply knocks out all the central inferences and presents one's audience with the starting-point and the conclusion, one may produce a startling, though possibly a meretricious, effect. Now, it was not really difficult, by an inspection of the groove between your left forefinger and thumb, to feel sure that you did not propose to invest your small capital in the gold fields."

(continued)

13 "I see no connection."

14 "Very likely not; but I can quickly show you a close connection. Here are the missing links of the very simple chain: 1. You had chalk between your left finger and thumb when you returned from the club last night. 2. You put chalk there when you play billiards, to steady the cue. 3. You never play billiards except with Thurston. 4. You told me, four weeks ago, that Thurston had an option on some South African property which would expire in a month, and which he desired you to share with him. 5. Your check book is locked in my drawer, and you have not asked for the key. 6. You do not propose to invest your money in this manner."

15 "How absurdly simple!" I cried.

16 "Quite so!" said he, a little nettled. "Every problem becomes very childish once it is explained to you. Here is an unexplained one. See what you can make of that, friend Watson." He tossed a sheet of paper upon the table, and turned once more to his chemical analysis.

17 I looked with amazement at the absurd hieroglyphics upon the paper.

18 "Why, Holmes, it is a child's drawing," I cried.

19 "Oh, that's your idea!"

20 "What else should it be?"

21 "That is what Mr. Hilton Cubitt, of Riding Thorpe Manor, Norfolk, is very anxious to know. This little conundrum came by the first post, and he was to follow by the next train. There's a ring at the bell, Watson, I should not be very much surprised if this were he."

A heavy step was heard upon the stairs, and an instant later there entered a tall, ruddy, clean-shaven gentleman, whose clear eyes and florid cheeks told of a life led far from the fogs of Baker Street. He seemed to bring a whiff of his strong, fresh, bracing, east-coast air with him as he entered. Having shaken hands with each of us, he was about to sit down, when his eye rested upon the paper with the curious markings, which I had just examined and left upon the table.

22 "Well, Mr. Holmes, what do you make of these?" he cried. "They told me that you were fond of queer mysteries, and I don't think you can find a queerer one than that. I sent the paper on ahead, so that you might have time to study it before I came."

23 "It is certainly rather a curious production," said Holmes. "At first sight it would appear to be some childish prank. It consists of a number of absurd little figures dancing across the paper upon which they are drawn. Why should you attribute any importance to so grotesque an object?"

24 "I never should, Mr. Holmes. But my wife does. It is frightening her to death. She says nothing, but I can see terror in her eyes. That's why I want to sift the matter to the bottom."

25 Holmes held up the paper so that the sunlight shone full upon it. It was a page torn from a notebook. The markings were done in pencil . . . .

26 Holmes examined it for some time, and then, folding it carefully up, he placed it in his pocketbook.

27 "This promises to be a most interesting and unusual case," said he. "You gave me a few particulars in your letter, Mr. Hilton Cubitt, but I should be very much obliged if you would kindly go over it all again for the benefit of my friend, Dr. Watson."

—From "The Mystery of the Dancing Men" by Sir Arthur Conan Doyle

1. Which text structure is used in paragraph 21?

   A. chronological order

   B. compare and contrast

   C. problem and solution

   D. cause and effect

2. Which of the following definitions best fits the meaning of the word **inferences** as it is used in paragraph 12?

   A. statements

   B. conclusions

   C. evidence

   D. reasoning

3. How is this passage structured?

   A. It relates a story in the sequence that the events happened.

   B. It compares Watson's and Holmes's methods of solving mysteries.

   C. It contrasts Watson's and Holmes's methods of solving mysteries.

   D. It shows the causes that led to Holmes taking Cubitt's case.

4. Review the following events from the story. Then write the events into the chart in the order in which they occur in the passage, with the first event at the top and the last event at the bottom.

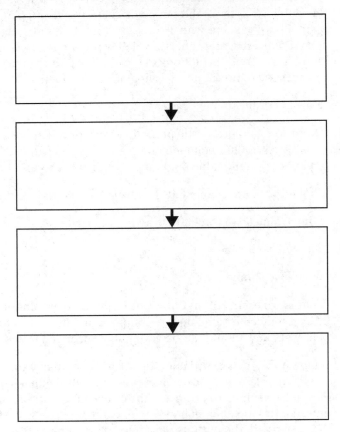

Holmes tells Watson the six missing links of the simple chain.

Holmes brews a product with his back curved over a chemical vessel.

Mr. Hilton Cubitt rings the doorbell.

Holmes holds up a piece of notebook paper into the sunshine.

Test-Taking Tip

The more you practice identifying the purposes of passages, the quicker that process will become for you. You will be able to notice words that are specific to the text structure, such as *first* and *as a result*, and you will know that you are reading a sequence passage or a cause-and-effect passage. If you start to pay attention to words such as these when you are reading a passage on a test, this will help you understand the passage and questions.

Writing Practice

Every piece of writing has an important structure that helps develop ideas. Certain pieces of writing, such as texts using sequence structure, use transition words that are specific to their structure, such as *first, second, next*, and *last*. Other pieces of writing, such as texts describing cause and effect, use different transition words that are specific to their structure, such as *so, therefore, since*, and *as a result*. Using these words helps the writer move between ideas. It helps develop ideas so the reader can understand them.

Directions: Using the compare-and-contrast text structure, write a brief paragraph in which you compare and contrast two of your favorite family traditions. You may choose traditions that exist in your immediate family, in your extended family, or traditions that you would like to start. While writing this piece, make sure you use words that are specific to the compare-and-contrast text structure.

_____

_____

_____

_____

_____

_____

_____

_____

_____

_____

_____

_____

_____

This lesson will help you practice analyzing text structure and how it impacts key ideas. Use it with core lesson 4.2 Analyze How Structure Impacts Key Ideas to reinforce and apply your knowledge.

Key Concept	Core Skills
Authors structure what they write to communicate and reinforce key ideas.	• Analyze the Relationship between Paragraphs • Understand Organization

Distinguishing between Text Structures

Writers often use one of five main types of text structures. These five text structures are sequence, compare and contrast, cause and effect, description, and problem and solution.

A text that has a sequence text structure places events in time order or points in order of importance. In texts that use compare-and-contrast structure, a writer compares, contrasts, or compares and contrasts ideas. Cause-and-effect texts describe how events cause other events. An event can have multiple causes or multiple effects. Texts that have the description text structure use the five senses to paint a vivid picture. Finally, problem-and-solution texts offer one or more solutions to a problem.

Directions: Read the passage below. Then complete the activities.

Graduated Driver Licensing: A Proven Road to Improved Teen Safety

1 The National Safety Council is a leader in promoting Graduated Driver Licensing (GDL).

2 GDL is a novice driver licensing system that is proven effective at reducing teen drivers' high crash risk by 20–40%. States with stronger, comprehensive GDL systems see a higher reduction in teen crashes. GDL reduces teen driver exposure to high crash risk situations, such as nighttime driving and teen passengers.

3 GDL systems have three stages of licensure:

   1 A learner's permit that allows driving only while supervised by a fully licensed driver.

   2 An intermediate (sometimes called provisional) license that allows unsupervised driving under certain restrictions including nighttime and passenger limits.

   3 A full license.

4 All new drivers can make wrong decisions behind the wheel. However teens are the most at jeopardy. They bring to the road a unique mix of inexperience, distraction, peer pressure and a tendency to underestimate risk. . . .

5 Most Americans typically learn to drive during the teen years, when the brain is not fully mature yet. Recent research is beginning to give us insight into why many teens have difficulty regulating risk-taking behavior:

   • The area of the brain that weighs consequences, suppresses impulses and organizes thoughts does not fully mature until about age 25.

(continued)

- Hormones are more active in teens, which influence the brain's neurochemicals that regulate excitability and mood. The result can be thrill-seeking behavior and experiences that create intense feelings.

6 Learning to regulate driving behavior comes with time and practice. Defensive Driving Course-Alive at 25® offers a balanced approach to help teens not only regulate their own driving behavior, but also help them deal with the actual issues that can influence their driving behavior.

7 Driver education programs play a role in preparing teens to drive, but should not be viewed as the end of the learning-to-drive process. In order to develop safe driving skills, inexperienced drivers need opportunities to improve through gradual exposure to increasingly-challenging driving tasks. Teens become safer drivers with more driving experience.

8 In some states, the completion of driver education qualifies a teen for full driving privileges. The National Safety Council believes this is not a wise approach. Research shows that significant hours of behind-the-wheel experience are necessary to reduce crash risk. Parent involvement and Graduated Driver Licensing play important roles in developing skills.

9 DriveitHOME is a new program offering specially-created resources to help parents keep their teens safer on the roads, especially after a teen gets a driver's license. Designed by parents for parents, the unique program includes an interactive website featuring engaging videos, practice tips and other critical resources. Parents can sign up to receive weekly practice tips and suggestions via email, and are encouraged to share their own teaching techniques and experiences.

—From "Graduated Drivers" by National Safety Council

1. Which text structure best describes the way the ideas in paragraph 3 are organized?

   A. compare and contrast

   B. cause and effect

   C. order of importance

   D. sequence

2. Which quotation from the passage offers one solution to the problem of teen drivers' high crash risk?

   A. "All new drivers can make wrong decisions behind the wheel."

   B. "However teens are the most at jeopardy."

   C. "They bring to the road a unique mix of inexperience, distraction, peer pressure and a tendency to underestimate risk. . . ."

   D. "Teens become safer drivers with more driving experience."

3. Paragraph _____ presents causes for why teens have a hard time managing risky behavior behind the wheel.

4. Fill in the concept web with the descriptions of the effects of GDL.

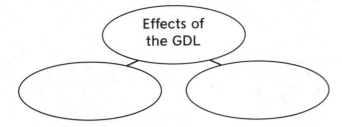

"States with stronger, comprehensive GDL systems see a higher reduction in teen crashes."

"GDL reduces teen driver exposure to high crash risk situations, such as nighttime driving and teen passengers."

"In some states, the completion of driver education qualifies a teen for full driving privileges...."

"Designed by parents for parents, the unique program includes an interactive website featuring engaging videos, practice tips and other critical resources."

Text Structure and Key Ideas

Understanding where writers place important information can help readers identify the significant ideas in a text. Many times, a writer will emphasize an idea by providing extensive details or by placing it toward the beginning or the end of a text.

Directions: Read the passage below. Then complete the activities.

1 A tremendous number of little toads, one or two months old, fell from a great thick cloud that appeared suddenly in a clear sky, in August 1804, near Toulouse, France, according to a letter from Prof. Pontus to M. Arago. (*Comptes Rendus*, 3-54.)

2 An issue of *Scientific American* magazine, dated July 12, 1873, reported that "A shower of frogs which darkened the air and covered the ground for a long distance is the reported result of a recent rainstorm at Kansas City, MO."

3 Some experts claim that small frogs and toads have never fallen from the sky, but in every purported case were "on the ground in the first place," or that there have been such falls "up from one place in a whirlwind, and down in another."

4 See, for instance, *Leisure Hours, 3-779* for accounts of small frogs, or toads, said to have been seen to fall from the sky. The writer says that all observers were mistaken and that the frogs or toads must have fallen from trees or other places overhead.

5 There are, it must be said, cases where the possibility of fallen frogs having "been there in the first place" is quite remote:

(continued)

6 Little frogs were found in **London**, after a heavy storm (July 30, 1838, *Notes and Queries, 8-7-437*).

7 Little toads were found **in a desert**, after a rainfall (*Notes and Queries, 8-8-493*).

8 At the same time, I do not completely dismiss the conventional explanation of whirlwinds as the [reason for] falling frogs. I think that there have likely been such occurrences. In the *London Times*, July 4, 1883, there is an account of a shower of twigs and leaves and tiny toads in a storm upon the slopes of the Apennines. This may have indeed been the work of a whirlwind.

9 That is one specific case, however. In others, while it is easy to say that small frogs that have fallen from the sky had been scooped up by a whirlwind, this gives no regard for mud, debris from the bottom of a pond, floating vegetation, or loose things from the shores. To accept a whirlwind as the cause, one would need to accept that a whirlwind somehow, very precisely, picked up frogs alone.

10 There is also the fact that, of all instances I have studied that attribute the fall of small frogs or toads to whirlwinds, only one actually identifies or places the whirlwind. Also, it seems to me that a pond going up would be quite as interesting as frogs coming down, and that anybody who had lost a pond would be heard from. Yet in *Symons' Meteorological Magazine*, a fall of small frogs, near Birmingham, England, June 30, 1892, is attributed to a specific whirlwind, without a word as to any special pond that had contributed. And something else that strikes my attention here is that these frogs are described as almost white.

11 I am afraid there is no escape for us: we shall have to accept that upon this earth exist some still-unknown locations: places with white frogs in them.

—Adapted from the writings and observations of Charles Fort

1. Why does the author begin the passage with the observations of frog and toad sightings?

   A. to reveal instances of frog and toad sightings before exploring what may have happened to cause the event

   B. to show the problem that frog and toad sightings posed in London and France

   C. to contrast the effects of frog and toad sightings in London with the effects of frog and toad sightings in the United States

   D. to present a solution for the problem of frogs and toads falling in France

2. Which paragraph from the passage begins with the author's own skepticism about a possible cause of frog and toad sightings?

   A. Paragraph 2

   B. Paragraph 3

   C. Paragraph 4

   D. Paragraph 10

3. Which of the following definitions best fits the meaning of the word **remote** as it is used in paragraph 5?

    A. unfriendly

    B. unlikely

    C. distant

    D. device

4. Read the list of excerpts from the passage below. Write a possible cause of frogs falling from the sky into the cause box. Then write the effects of this cause into the effects box.

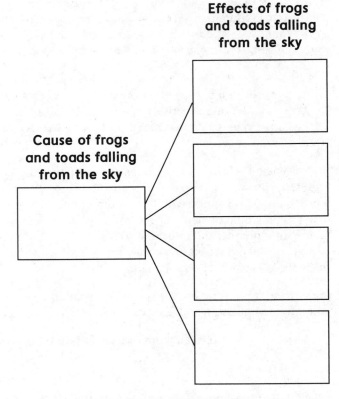

Effects of frogs and toads falling from the sky

Cause of frogs and toads falling from the sky

"Little frogs were found in London, after a heavy storm..."

"This may have indeed been the work of a whirlwind."

"Little toads were found in a desert, after a rainfall..."

"[A] shower of twigs and leaves and tiny toads . . . [fell] . . . upon the slopes of the Apennines."

 Test-Taking Tip

Drag-and-drop items are test questions that have you move words, phrases, numeric expressions, or images to a target location on the screen. You may be sequencing, classifying, or organizing information in this item type. As you drag and drop your answers into place, move and aim your answers accurately. Otherwise the computer may not place your answers where you want them to appear.

Writing Practice

All friends have some similarities, and that is what makes them friends. Even though they have similarities, they are not the same. All friends also have differences.

Directions: Write two paragraphs that compare and contrast two of your friends or acquaintances. You might decide to compare your friends in one paragraph and to contrast your friends in the other paragraph, or you might decide to compare and contrast them point by point. While writing, use descriptions along with comparisons and contrasts to make the similarities and differences clear to the reader.

_____

_____

_____

_____

_____

_____

_____

_____

_____

_____

_____

_____

_____

_____

_____

_____

_____

This lesson will help you practice analyzing the effects of transitional and signal words in nonfiction texts. Use it with core lesson 4.3 Analyze the Effects of Transitional and Signal Words to reinforce and apply your knowledge.

Key Concept

Writers use certain words and phrases to link ideas within sentences and between sentences.

Core Skills

- Determine the Relationships among Ideas
- Analyze Transitions between Paragraphs

Locating Transitions

Transitions are shifts in the text that show the writer has moved from one idea to the next. Transitions can happen between paragraphs or within paragraphs. The best way to locate transitions is to look for signal words or phrases. Signal words and phrases express the following relationships: addition, time order, relative location, relative importance, cause and effect, comparison, contrast, example, and conclusion.

Directions: Read the passage below. Then complete the activities.

How to Choose the Right Dog for You

1 Raising a puppy can be a great experience, but choosing a puppy is a big decision. You want to get the kind of dog that's right for you and your family. In addition, you want to pick a healthy puppy that will grow up to be a loyal pet for many years. How do you find the right puppy? Experts agree that you should follow several steps to ensure you choose the right pet.

2 First, before buying a dog, make sure you are getting the right kind of pet for your family. Think carefully about the breeds you are interested in, and decide which one will be best for your home. For instance, if you have young children who like to romp and play, you will probably want to get a breed that is large enough to play with your children. A Chihuahua, for instance, would not be a good choice, because it could be hurt easily while playing. On the other hand, the dog you choose should not be a large or aggressive breed if your children are very small. Seek advice from a dog breeder or veterinarian before making a choice.

3 After choosing the kind of dog you want, begin looking around. In general, large stores that sell puppies are not the best place to find a puppy because a dog from there might have health problems. Instead of heading for a large store, consider a reputable private breeder. If a private breeder is too expensive, you also might consider getting a dog from your city's animal shelter. When you get a dog from the animal shelter, you often only have to pay for the dog's license and required shots.

4 When you pick out a puppy from a litter, observe the puppies carefully from a distance and choose a puppy whose character you like.

5 After you have narrowed your choice to one puppy, examine it carefully. Inspect the dog to make sure its skin and fur look healthy. Make sure the puppy doesn't have ticks or fleas, and check its gums. Pink gums indicate good health, whereas white gums could indicate anemia caused by heartworm.

6 After you get your puppy home, continue to observe it to make sure it is the dog for you. If you need further advice, check with the breeder or your vet. If you follow the steps above, you will have a fine pet that will give you and your family years of loyalty and companionship.

1. Which phrase found in the first paragraph is a signal phrase?

   A. that's right

   B. in addition

   C. for many

   D. to ensure

2. What does the signal word *after* at the beginning of the sixth paragraph reveal about the shift in ideas between the fifth and sixth paragraphs?

   A. The signal word *after* shows that the sixth paragraph arrives at a conclusion from ideas in the fifth paragraph.

   B. The signal word *after* shows that the sixth paragraph contrasts the information that the fifth paragraph introduced.

   C. The signal word *after* shows that the sixth paragraph has shifted in time from the ideas in the fifth paragraph.

   D. The signal word *after* shows that the sixth paragraph presents an example of the ideas in the fifth paragraph.

3. What does the signal phrase *on the other hand* reveal about the shift in ideas in the second paragraph?

   A. It contrasts the small Chihuahua breed with a large or aggressive breed.

   B. It compares the small Chihuahua breed with a large or aggressive breed.

   C. It provides an example of large or aggressive breeds.

   D. It shows the effect of buying a small Chihuahua breed.

4. Write the steps of finding the best dog in the sequence suggested by the passage.

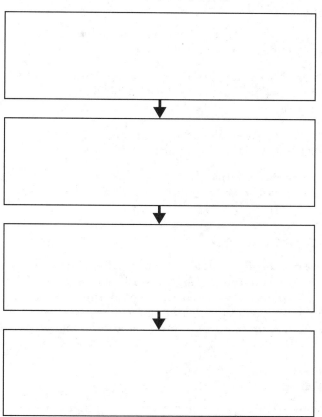

"Once you have narrowed your choice to one puppy, examine it carefully."

"After choosing the kind of dog you want, begin looking around."

"After you get your puppy home, continue to observe it to make sure it is the dog for you."

"First, before buying a dog, make sure you are getting the right kind of pet for your family."

5. The signal phrase *for instance* is used twice in the second paragraph. What transition does this signal phrase show?

A. It shows the effect of buying a Chihuahua on families with young children.

B. It provides examples of dogs that might or might not be appropriate for families with children.

C. It shows what happens in time order after bringing a Chihuahua home.

D. It reveals a relative location about the best places to find and buy different dogs.

 Test-Taking Tip

Signal words help you link ideas. When writing an extended response on a test, choose the appropriate signal words and phrases to transition between ideas within paragraphs and between paragraphs. For example, if you are placing your ideas in the order of importance, you should use signal words such as *first, more important, most important,* and *primarily.*

Analyzing Transitions

Transitions, whether they come within paragraphs or between paragraphs, tell the reader to slow down and focus on how the ideas have shifted. If signal words have not been used, you can infer transitions by paying attention to the relationship between ideas.

Directions: Read the passage below. Then complete the activities.

Why NASA Deserves Our Continued (If Not Increased) Support

1 The Space Age began in 1957, with the Soviet Union's successful launch of the unmanned Sputnik 1. The first manned space mission came a mere four years later, in 1961, when Soviet cosmonaut Yuri Gagarin became the first human being to orbit Earth. During the five decades since, human beings have explored outer space in the same way that Europeans explored the hitherto unfamiliar expanses of the Americas during the Age of Exploration—by physically going there. Impressive accomplishments—sending humans to the moon, manually placing the Hubble telescope in Earth's orbit—can be credited to the US National Aeronautics and Space Administration (NASA). Yet, despite NASA's extraordinary history, there has been continual discussion as to whether its continued existence is justified. Today we can state that the answer is "By all means, yes."

(continued)

2 Let's begin our analysis of this assertion by addressing the primary objection to it—that the United States cannot afford the expense. Space exploration costs a great deal of money. However, it is a mistake to think of NASA's budget as a waste of money that would be better spent on Earth. It *is* spent on Earth. When President Eisenhower created the agency in 1958, he said that one purpose for it was the development of new technologies adaptable for everyday use. NASA has excelled in this regard. To date, the organization has secured more than 6,000 patents, many of which have driven innovation in other fields. Thousands of inventions, such as cordless tools, water filters, smoke detectors, medical devices, cell phones, and home entertainment systems, can trace their technological lineage to one or more of NASA's patents.

3 Moreover, this pioneering of knowledge points to related advantages to space exploration—it answers questions about the material world and how it works, and it also leads to new questions that, when answered, uncover still further knowledge. Surely, this potential for learning is as expansive as space itself. Who knows what remains to be discovered about the universe and our place in it? Perhaps we'll stumble upon new supplies of needed natural resources, new clues about the origins of life, or even new forms of life itself—some of which, it isn't far-fetched to consider, might have much in common with us and perhaps a thing or two to teach us.

4 As we think about all of this, we should also look at our world's likely future. There is no guarantee that humankind must forever survive and develop. Some claim that there is an increasing amount of evidence that the opposite outcome is likely. The world's population is growing at an ever-faster rate, but we have limited natural resources. There are at present more than 7 billion human beings on Earth, many already living in poverty. The US Census Bureau estimates that there will be more than 9 billion humans by 2050. It seems unwise, therefore, not to put some effort toward finding new places for humans to live. This idea might seem like science fiction at present, but one decade's sci-fi is the next decade's science fact.

5 Finally, let's ponder a proposition that few people would dispute. Whatever the cause, a spirit of curiosity and adventure is part of what it means to be a human being. To state that this inquisitiveness must be limited to the world in which we find ourselves ignores the fact that we would know little about our world if not for that spirit of adventure. To squelch our natural urge to explore space is to deny our very humanity.

1. What is the shift in ideas between the first paragraph and the second paragraph?

   A. The first paragraph presents the problems of space exploration, and the second paragraph provides a solution to that problem.

   B. The first paragraph discusses the beginning of space exploration, and the second paragraph reveals a shift in time order.

   C. The first paragraph provides NASA's history, and the second paragraph provides examples of NASA's new technologies.

   D. The first paragraph presents some of NASA's accomplishments, and the second paragraph concludes that NASA should not be funded anymore.

2. Which of the following definitions best fits the meaning of the word **assertion** as it is used in paragraph 2?

   A. question

   B. declaration

   C. command

   D. request

3. What signal phrase could be placed at the beginning of this sentence from the second paragraph: "Thousands of inventions, such as cordless tools, water filters, smoke detectors, medical devices, cell phones, and home entertainment systems, can trace their technological lineage to one or more of NASA's patents"?

   A. In brief

   B. By contrast

   C. In conclusion

   D. For instance

 Test-Taking Tip

When responding to a writing prompt in a test, reread your sentences to make sure that your signal words and phrases make sense in context. Signal words or phrases that have similar meanings cannot necessarily be used interchangeably. Suppose you wanted to write a sentence that contrasted apples and oranges, for example: "Unlike oranges, apples have an edible, thin peel." You might remember that *in spite of* is another signal phrase that shows contrast. Even so, you would not be able to substitute "in spite of" for "unlike" in this sentence.

Writing Practice

Everyone has a variety of skills or talents. Some people are talented artists, but they might also be able to solve complex math problems. Other people are track stars who can also read music.

Directions: Write two paragraphs in which you describe two of your skills or talents. Think about the text structure that best fits the content of your paragraphs. Then use the correct signal words or phrases to transition between ideas within and between paragraphs. Each paragraph should focus on a different skill or talent.

_____

_____

_____

_____

_____

_____

_____

_____

_____

_____

_____

_____

_____

_____

_____

_____

_____

_____

_____

_____

This lesson will help you practice analyzing an author's purpose and point of view in two informational texts. Use it with core lesson 5.1 Determine Author's Purpose and Point of View to reinforce and apply your knowledge.

Key Concept

Authors have a reason for writing, and they often have an opinion about the topic of their writing.

Core Skills

- Determine Author's Purpose
- Establish Point of View

Identifying an Author's Purpose

Authors write texts for a specific purpose. A text may be written to inform you about a topic, to persuade you to think a certain way, or to entertain you.

Directions: Read the passage below. Then complete the activities.

The Nature of Waves

The Nature of Waves

A **wave** is a periodic or harmonic disturbance in space or through a medium (water, for instance) by which energy is transmitted. Water, sound, and light all travel in waves. The illumination a lamp provides comes from light waves, while the music emanating from a stereo comes from sound waves. The powers to preserve food and warm it come from electromagnetic waves, and the power that transmits signals to a television comes from radio waves. The energy that gives a waterbed its soothing motion comes from water waves.

Types of Properties of Waves

Waves transmit energy in different ways, and all phases of matter transmit waves. An example of a solid transmitting wave energy is an earthquake that takes place when rocks are under pressure and snap or slide into new positions. Waves that are felt and seen in water are examples of a liquid transmitting wave energy. Gases also transmit wave energy, as in an explosion, when heat, sound, and light waves are generated. Two basic types of waves exist: longitudinal waves and transverse waves.

Longitudinal Wave

Particles of the medium move back and forth in the same direction as the wave itself moves. An example of a longitudinal wave is a sound wave that occurs when a tuning fork is tapped. When a tuning fork is tapped, the prongs move from right to left in a rapid periodic motion. A sound wave is produced, and it moves parallel (right and left) to the moving prong.

Transverse Wave

Particles of the medium move at right angles to the direction of the wave's movement. An example of a transverse wave is one that occurs when a pebble is tossed into a still pond.

When a stone is dropped into a pond, the waves produced appear to move outward. These waves move at right angles to the dropped stone.

Waves have two components, a crest and a trough. A **crest** is the point of highest displacement in a wave, and a **trough** is the point of lowest displacement. Crests and troughs are easily visible in water waves.

(continued)

Two specific characteristics of a wave are length and frequency:

- **Wavelength** is defined as the distance between two successive wave crests or two successive wave troughs.

- **Wave frequency** is the number of wave crests that pass a given point per second.

Therefore, the shorter the wavelength is, the higher the wave frequency will be. In fact, a wave's speed equals the wavelength times the wave frequency.

When a source of a wave is in motion, a compression of the wavelength is detected. This can be demonstrated with sound waves. As a train passes while you are standing on the platform, you will notice a distinct drop in the pitch or sound quality. This drop in sound pitch is heard by the observers standing on the side during an automotive race such as the Indianapolis 500. Water waves demonstrate the same compression in the direction of motion. The water waves in the front of a boat are squeezed together, while those at the rear of the boat are far apart. This is referred to as the **Doppler Effect**. Scientists use the Doppler Effect to forecast tornadoes and to detect the motion of stars in our galaxy.

Sound Wave

Sound waves are longitudinal waves. A musical pitch, or tone, is heard when there is a definite frequency to a wave. The lower the frequency, the lower the tone. For example, the frequency of a bass speaker in a stereo system is lower than a tweeter, or high-frequency speaker, because the low-pitched sound of the bass results from a lower number of vibrations per second.

1. The author's purpose for writing this passage is to _____.

2. How does the following sentence support the author's purpose?

   "This drop in sound pitch is heard by the observers standing on the side during an automotive race such as the Indianapolis 500."

   A. It persuades the reader to attend a car race.

   B. It convinces the reader to be careful around noisy machinery.

   C. It gives an example to explain compression in sound waves.

   D. It helps the reader visualize the excitement of a car race.

3. How does the second sentence of the section on transverse waves support the author's purpose?

   A. It provides an example of transverse waves to inform the reader.

   B. It provides vivid sensory details to spark the reader's imagination.

   C. It uses figurative language to entertain the reader.

   D. It provides a reason to persuade the reader to agree with the viewpoint.

4. Which of the following definitions best fits the meaning of the word **frequency** used in this passage?

   A. what tunes you in to a radio station

   B. how often something happens

   C. the number of times an electric current changes direction

   D. the proportion of one type of item in a group

Recognizing an Author's Point of View

An author's point of view is the writer's attitude toward a topic. A point of view may be positive, negative, or neutral. It may be expressed directly or implied.

Directions: Read the passage below. Then complete the activities.

Excerpt from a speech made by George W. Bush

1 Both parties have been talking about education reform for quite a while. It's time to come together to get it done so that we can truthfully say in America, "No child will be left behind—not one single child."

2 We share a moment of exceptional promise—a new administration, a newly sworn-in Congress, and we have a chance to think anew and act anew.

3 All of us are impatient with the old lines of division. All of us want a different attitude here in the nation's capital. All in this room, as well as across the country, know things must change.

4 We must confront the scandal of illiteracy in America, seen most clearly in high-poverty schools, where nearly 70 percent of fourth graders are unable to read at a basic level. We must address the low standing of [American] test scores amongst industrialized nations in math and science, the very subjects most likely to affect our future competitiveness. We must focus the spending of federal tax dollars on things that work. Too often we have spent without regard for results, without judging success or failure from year to year.

5 We must face up to the plague of school violence, with an average of 3 million crimes committed against students and teachers inside public schools every year. That's unacceptable in our country. Change will not come by adding a few new federal programs to the old. If we work only at the edges, our influence will be confined to the margins. We need real reform.

6 Change will not come by disdaining or dismantling the federal role of education. I believe strongly in local control of schools. I trust local folks to chart the path to excellence. But educational excellence for all is a national issue, and at this moment is a presidential priority. I've seen how real education reform can lift up scores in schools and effectively change lives.

7 And real education reform reflects four basic commitments. First, children must be tested every year in reading and math. Every single year. Not just in the third grade or the eighth grade, but in the third, fourth, fifth, sixth and seventh and eighth grade. . . . Without yearly testing, we don't know who is falling behind and who needs help. Without yearly testing, too often we don't find failure until it is too late to fix. . . .

8 Secondly, the agents of reform must be schools and school districts, not bureaucracies. Teachers and principals, local and state leaders must have the responsibility to succeed and the flexibility to innovate. One size does not fit all when it comes to educating the children in America. School districts, school officials, educational entrepreneurs should not be hindered by excessive rules and red tape and regulation.

9 . . . If local schools do not have the freedom to change, they cannot be held accountable for failing to change. Authority and accountability must be aligned at the local level, or schools will have a convenient excuse for failure. "I would have done it this way, but some central office or Washington, D.C., caused me to do it another way."

10 . . . Third, many of our schools, particularly low-income schools, will need help in the transition to higher standards. When a state sets standards, we must help schools achieve those standards.

(continued)

11 We must measure, we must know; and if a school or school district falls short, we must understand that help should be applied. . . . Once failing schools are identified, we will help them improve. . . . We want success, and when schools are willing to accept the reality that the accountability system points out and are willing to change, we will help them.

12 Fourth, American children must not be left in persistently dangerous or failing schools. When schools do not teach and will not change, parents and students must have other meaningful options. And when children or teenagers go to school afraid of being threatened or attacked or worse, our society must make it clear it's the ultimate betrayal of adult responsibility.

13 Parents and children who have only bad options must eventually get good options, if we are to succeed all across the country. . . .

14 These four principles are the guides to our education reform package. Yet today I'm offering more than principles. I'm sending a series of specific proposals to the United States Congress; my own blueprint for reform. I want to begin our discussion in detail with the members of the House and the Senate, because I know we need to act by this summer so that the people at the local level can take our initiatives and plan for the school year beginning next fall.

15 . . . If somebody's got a better idea, I hope they bring it forward, because the secretary and I will listen.

16 We've got one thing in mind: an education system that's responsive to the children, an education system that educates every child, an education system that I'm confident can exist; one that's based upon sound fundamental curriculum, one that starts teaching children to read early in life, one that focuses on systems that do work, one that heralds our teachers and makes sure they've got the necessary tools to teach, but one that says every child can learn. And in this great land called America, no child will be left behind.

—From *Selected Speeches of George W. Bush* 2001–2008

1. Which of the following best expresses the author's point of view?

   A. High standards leave some children behind.

   B. Parents and children have too many choices in education.

   C. The education system is not working and needs to be changed.

   D. Education in the United States allows everyone to be successful.

2. Which of the following words best describes the author's point of view about the education system in the United States at the time of the speech?

   A. positive

   B. negative

   C. neutral

   D. optimistic

3. The author's point of view is expressed _____ because it is stated in paragraph 4.

4. According to the author's point of view, what is most needed in the US educational system?

A. reform

B. money

C. leaders

D. diversity

5. Write in the outer circles of the concept web the examples of proposed changes that the author uses to support his point of view.

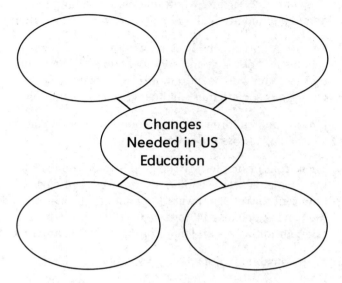

Test children every year in math and reading.

Create a uniform model for all children.

Help schools transition to higher standards.

Encourage schools and not bureaucracies to be agents of change.

Allow children to leave dangerous or failing schools.

Place more control at the federal level.

 Test-Taking Tip

During a test, as you are reading a question, circle or write key words that help you understand what the question is asking. For example, you might circle the words *point of view* or *author's purpose*.

Writing Practice

Many schools want to increase their students' access to technology, but they have limited funds to purchase these devices. One solution that has been proposed is to allow students to bring their own devices such as tablets and smart phones to school to use in class. Some people argue that allowing students to bring their own devices into school will create new problems.

Directions: Write a speech in which you give your opinion about this issue, clearly stating your point of view in your writing. Remember that your purpose is to persuade the listener to agree with your opinion. Use persuasive language, and provide reasons to support your opinion.

This lesson will help you practice analyzing how an author's purpose helps determine the text structure within two texts. Use it with core lesson 5.2 Analyze How Author's Purpose Determines Structure to reinforce and apply your knowledge.

Key Concept

Authors choose specific text structures to clarify what they want to say. The text structures engage the reader and help authors achieve a purpose.

Core Skills

- Analyze Text Structure
- Determine Author's Purpose

Text Structure in Informational Texts

All authors have a purpose for writing. The most common purposes are to inform, to persuade, and to entertain. An author of an informational text chooses an organization or structure that supports his or her purpose for writing. Some common text structures include sequence, compare and contrast, cause and effect, description, and problem and solution.

Directions: Read the passage below. Then complete the activities.

Earth and Space Science

Earth science is the study of planet Earth—its origin and the forces at work that are constantly changing the surface of the planet. Earth science differs from the life sciences in that Earth science focuses on nonliving rather than living things. It is a very broad field that covers the subjects of astronomy, geology, meteorology, paleontology, and oceanography.

Astronomy: The Study of Space

One of the oldest fields of study in science deals with how Earth was created and how this planet fits into the design of the universe. **Astronomy** is the study of the size, movements, and composition of the planets, stars, and other deep-space objects. By observing objects in space, astronomers hope to understand how our planet was created and how it evolved. A number of important theories have been advanced to explain the beginning of Earth and its universe.

The Beginning of the Universe

According to the leading theory, known as the *big bang theory,* a "cosmic egg" made up of dust and gas containing all the matter in the universe exploded. This explosion occurred 15 to 20 billion years ago, creating the basic atoms of our lightest gases from which the stars formed. The big bang theory accounts for the measured expansion of the universe and the background radiation found in all directions in outer space. According to the *open universe theory,* the universe will either continue the expansion indefinitely or begin a collapse. A different theory, called the *closed universe theory,* predicts that the total mass of the universe is large enough to gather up all matter into a concentrated central point and then gravitationally collapse at some point in the distant future. This collapse is referred to as the "big crunch."

(continued)

The most distant (but unknown) objects detected by science are known as **quasars** (quasi-stellar radio sources). The light and energy that has arrived from these objects is about 16 billion years old. It is likely that the energy that we receive now came from these objects during their formation. Every time scientists investigate deep-space objects, they must remember that information we receive now took time to get to Earth. Even the light from the Sun takes eight minutes to reach Earth. The nearest star to the Sun is Alpha Centauri, which is more than four light years away.

1. The author's main purpose for writing this piece is to _____.

2. Which best describes the overall structure of this passage?

    A. sequence

    B. compare and contrast

    C. cause and effect

    D. description

3. How does the overall structure help the author achieve his or her purpose for writing?

    A. It helps the reader understand what topics are included in astronomy.

    B. It helps the reader compare Earth and life sciences.

    C. It helps the reader understand the order in which major theories in astronomy were developed.

    D. It helps the reader understand how lack of funding causes limits on astronomy research.

4. Which best describes the structure of paragraph 3?

    A. sequence

    B. compare and contrast

    C. cause and effect

    D. description

 Test-Taking Tip

When faced with a multiple-choice test question, read the question and formulate an answer in your head. Then read the answer choices. Choose the answer that is most similar to your answer. Following these steps will help you eliminate any answer choices that you know are incorrect.

Text Structure in Literary Texts

Like authors of informational texts, literary writers also choose a text structure to convey their purpose. These structures, such as sequence, may be similar to those used by informational writers. Sometimes literary writers enhance the structure with special techniques such as alternating viewpoints, flashback, and parallel plots.

Directions: Read the passage below. Then complete the activities.

1 [T]hese other apartments were densely crowded, and in them beat feverishly the heart of life. And the revel went whirlingly on, until at length there commenced the sounding of midnight upon the clock. And then the music ceased, as I have told; and the evolutions of the waltzers were quieted; and there was an uneasy cessation of all things as before. But now there were twelve strokes to be sounded by the bell of the clock . . . . [B]efore the last echoes of the last chime had utterly sunk into silence, there were many individuals in the crowd who had found leisure to become aware of the presence of a masked figure which had arrested the attention of no single individual before. And the rumor of this new presence having spread itself whisperingly around, there arose at length from the whole company a buzz, or murmur, expressive of disapprobation and surprise—then, finally, of terror, of horror, and of disgust.

2 In an assembly of phantasms such as I have painted, it may well be supposed that no ordinary appearance could have excited such sensation. In truth the masquerade license of the night was nearly unlimited; but the figure in question had out-Heroded Herod, and gone beyond the bounds of even the prince's indefinite decorum. There are chords in the hearts of the most reckless which cannot be touched without emotion. Even with the utterly lost, to whom life and death are equally jests, there are matters of which no jest can be made. The whole company, indeed, seemed now deeply to feel that in the costume and bearing of the stranger neither wit nor propriety existed.

3 The figure was tall and gaunt, and shrouded from head to foot in the habiliments of the grave. The mask which concealed the visage was made so nearly to resemble the countenance of a stiffened corpse that the closest scrutiny must have had difficulty in detecting the cheat. And yet all this might have been endured, if not approved, by the mad revellers around. But the mummer had gone so far as to assume the type of the Red Death. His vesture was dabbled in blood—and his broad brow, with all the features of the face, was besprinkled with the scarlet horror.

4 When the eyes of Prince Prospero fell upon this spectral image (which with a slow and solemn movement, as if more fully to sustain its role, stalked to and fro among the waltzers) he was seen to be convulsed, in the first moment with a strong shudder either of terror or distaste; but, in the next, his brow reddened with rage.

—From "The Masque of the Red Death" by Edgar Allan Poe

1. The author's main purpose for writing this piece is to _____.

2. Which term best describes the overall structure?

    A. problem and solution

    B. parallel plots

    C. sequence

    D. flashback

3. How does the structure help achieve the author's purpose for writing?

    A. It helps the reader compare the feelings and actions of different characters at the masked ball.

    B. It helps the reader follow the events that occur during the masked ball.

    C. It helps the reader understand how earlier events influenced the masked character's current actions.

    D. It helps the reader see the events at the masked ball from different perspectives.

4. Which of the following techniques does the author use to help tell the story?

    A. alternating viewpoints

    B. parallel plots

    C. flashbacks

    D. time-order words

5. Which of the following definitions best fits the meaning of the word **sustain** as it is used in paragraph 4?

    A. nourish

    B. keep up

    C. undergo

    D. withstand

6. Read the sentences below the graphic organizer. Then write each of the sentences in a box of the graphic organizer to show the order in which the events occur.

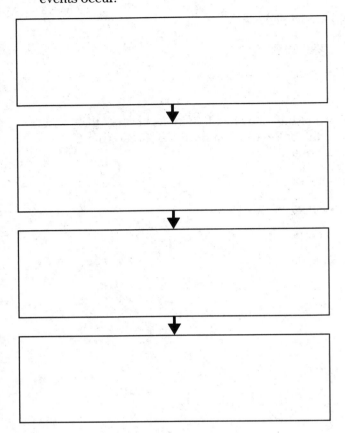

People were disturbed by the way the masked character was dressed.

The prince became angry.

People began to notice a masked character.

The music stopped around midnight, and the party got quieter.

 Test-Taking Tip

If possible, use your life experiences as the basis for your extended responses on a test. If you are writing something you know well, you will feel more confident and engaged. In addition, you will have a ready supply of real-life examples to use as evidence to support your ideas.

Writing Practice

News articles are structured in different ways, depending on the author's purpose. For example, an article written to inform citizens about a mayor's response to graffiti on public buildings might describe the problems along with several of the mayor's proposed solutions. However, a news article written to explain the history of a conflict between two nations might relate the events in the order in which they happened.

Directions: Write a one-paragraph newspaper article about a current event that interests you. Think about your purpose for writing. Then select an organizational structure such as sequence, problem and solution, cause and effect, or description to help you present your information.

This lesson will help you practice inferring an author's purpose in two informational texts. Use it with core lesson 5.3 Infer Author's Purpose to reinforce and apply your knowledge.

Key Concept

When an author does not explicitly state his or her purpose for writing a text, readers can use their prior knowledge and details from the text to infer the author's purpose.

Core Skills

- Use a Graphic Organizer
- Determine the Implicit Purpose in a Text

Inferring the Author's Purpose

Authors write with a specific purpose in mind. They might want to inform you about a topic, to persuade you to think a certain way, or to entertain you. They might even have more than one purpose. Whatever their reason for writing, authors do not always state the purpose explicitly. Sometimes you have to infer it by using context, details, and your own knowledge of the topic.

Directions: Read the passage below. Then complete the activities.

MEMO

Date: October 15
To: All Medical Staff
From: Wendy Lockwood, Human Resources Manager
Subject: Hand-washing guidelines

This memo is a follow-up to the recent training about workplace hygiene and safety. We would like to outline the key points addressed in the training about clean hands in the workplace. These guidelines are crucial for all medical staff to follow. However, they also serve as common-sense hygiene tips for everyone in a workplace setting.

To ensure that all germs and bacteria are released, be sure to follow these steps:

1. Place hands together under warm water. Using antibacterial soap, rub your hands together for at least 20 seconds.
2. Thoroughly wash both sides of the hands, the wrists, and under the fingernails.
3. Rinse well.
4. Completely dry your hands using a clean towel, which helps remove the germs. If using a disposable towel, be sure to throw it in the trash.

If water is not available, use an alcohol-based hand sanitizer. Place a small dollop of the product on the palm of one hand, and then rub it all over your hands and fingers until it dries.

Frequent hand-washing can help you and others avoid illness. You should wash your hands

- after using the bathroom.
- before and after eating or preparing food (especially raw meat).
- after sneezing, coughing, or blowing your nose.
- before and after tending to a wound.

(continued)

- after handling trash and/or hazardous materials.
- after touching objects contaminated by floodwater or sewage.
- after handling animals or their waste.
- when your hands are visibly dirty.

This information and a recording of last week's training presentation are available on our company's intranet. We strongly encourage all medical staff to review the information. Please help us adhere to the highest standards possible, ensuring the health and safety of our cohorts and patients.

Source: Centers for Disease Control and Prevention: www.cdc.gov/handwashing/

1. Wendy Lockwood's purposes for writing the memo are to persuade and to _____.

2. The main reason for including the bullet points is to convey that

   A. hands can become contaminated in many ways.

   B. animals should not be present in the workplace.

   C. people who are sick can spread disease.

   D. hands are susceptible to getting dirty.

3. Which of the following definitions best fits the meaning of the word **hazardous** as it is used in this passage?

   A. dirty

   B. slippery

   C. unpleasant

   D. dangerous

4. Which of the following is an implied purpose of the text?

   A. to highlight the work of researchers in the hospital

   B. to reduce training costs for the hospital

   C. to prevent the spread of disease in the hospital

   D. to address complaints from patients about the hospital

5. Choose the four terms from the memo that belong in the concept web.

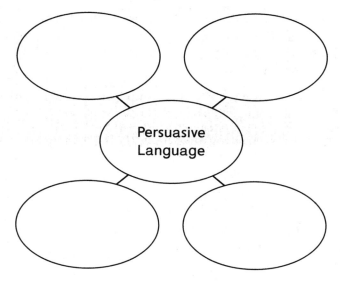

crucial   be sure to

key points   should

adhere   encourage

Using Context to Infer Implicit Purpose

If an author does not state why he or she is writing, you can use your knowledge and the details in the text to infer the purpose. It is also helpful to consider the author and the context.

Directions: Read the passage below. Then complete the activities.

President Gerald Ford gave this speech toward the end of the US involvement in the Vietnam War.

1 Instead of my addressing the image of America, I prefer to consider the reality of America. It is true that we have launched our bicentennial celebration without having achieved human perfection, but we have attained a very remarkable self-governed society that possesses the flexibility and the dynamism to grow and undertake an entirely new agenda, an agenda for America's third century.

2 So, I ask you to join me in helping to write that agenda. I am as determined as a president can be to seek national rediscovery of the belief in ourselves that characterized the most creative periods in our nation's history. The greatest challenge of creativity, as I see it, lies ahead.

3 We, of course, are saddened indeed by the events in Indochina. But these events, tragic as they are, portend neither the end of the world nor of America's leadership in the world.

4 Let me put it this way, if I might. Some tend to feel that if we do not succeed in everything everywhere, then we have succeeded in nothing anywhere. I reject categorically such polarized thinking. We can and we should help others to help themselves. But the fate of responsible men and women everywhere, in the final decision, rests in their own hands, not in ours.

5 America's future depends upon Americans—especially your generation, which is now equipping itself to assume the challenges of the future, to help write the agenda for America.

6 Earlier today, in this great community, I spoke about the need to maintain our defenses. Tonight, I would like to talk about another kind of strength, the true source of American power that transcends all of the deterrent powers for peace of our armed forces. I am speaking here of our belief in ourselves and our belief in our nation.

7 Abraham Lincoln asked, in his own words, and I quote, "What constitutes the bulwark of our own liberty and independence?" And he answered, "It is not our frowning battlements or bristling seacoasts, our army or our navy. Our defense is in the spirit which prized liberty as the heritage of all men, in all lands everywhere."

8 It is in this spirit that we must now move beyond the discords of the past decade. It is in this spirit that I ask you to join me in writing an agenda for the future.

—From "A War That Is Finished" by President Gerald R. Ford, April 23, 1975

1. The speaker was the president of the United States. Which of the following statements about the presidency is most relevant in determining the purpose of Ford's speech?

   A. The president is elected every four years.

   B. The president signs legislation.

   C. The president leads his or her political party.

   D. The president guides the nation and the military.

2. Which contextual information is most relevant in determining the purpose of Ford's speech?

   A. Many celebrations were held to celebrate the US bicentennial.

   B. Some Americans were discouraged by the outcome of the Vietnam War.

   C. The speech was made at Tulane University in Louisiana.

   D. President Ford served in the US Navy during World War II.

3. Which sentence from the speech best conveys Ford's overall purpose?

    A. "Instead of my addressing the image of America, I prefer to consider the reality of America."

    B. "I ask you to join me in writing an agenda for the future."

    C. "I am speaking here of our belief in ourselves and our belief in our nation."

    D. "We, of course, are saddened indeed by the events in Indochina."

4. President Ford's main purpose for writing and delivering this speech was to _____.

 Test-Taking Tip

If you are unsure of the answer to a question, you can click on "Flag for Review" in the upper right corner of the screen. A yellow flag will appear. Continuing with the remaining questions might help you figure out the answer to a difficult question. At the end of the test, you will come to a review screen, where your flagged questions will be marked. If time remains, you can return to those questions.

Writing Practice

Think about your favorite advertisement. It probably doesn't come right out and ask you to purchase the product. Instead, it tries to persuade you to want a product or service by listing features and using persuasive words to entice you.

Directions: Write a paragraph in which you convey your feelings about a product or service you enjoy without explicitly stating your purpose: to persuade the reader to agree with your opinion. Use persuasive language and provide details that will make your purpose clear without stating it explicitly.

This lesson will help you practice analyzing how authors differentiate and support their positions. Use it with core lesson 5.4 Analyze How Authors Differentiate Their Positions to reinforce and apply your knowledge.

Key Concept

Authors can strengthen their position by acknowledging viewpoints that differ from their own and by using evidence or reasoning to refute them.

Core Skills

- Identify an Author's Position
- Evaluate Arguments

Identifying an Author's Position

To support their positions, or opinions, on a topic, authors often introduce opposing, or conflicting, viewpoints. Then they strengthen their position by disproving, or refuting, conflicting viewpoints or by showing them to be unreasonable.

Directions: Read the passage below. Then complete the activities.

1 Women should have equal political rights with men as provided for in Senate Constitutional Amendment No. 8 because—

2 Women are equal to men intellectually. In fact, if we take the number of graduates from our schools and colleges, we must admit that they are farther advanced mentally.

3 Women should not be subject to taxation without representation any more than men. "Consent of the governed" means women as well as men, for they are subject to government as well as men.

4 Women are recognized in the family as a large part of the governing force. The state is only a large family composed of both sexes. Why should she not be considered in the government of the larger family?

5 Women have been given suffrage in numerous countries and in several states in this Union, and partial suffrage in nearly all civilized countries. We have no knowledge of such action having proved to be a failure or of such laws being repealed. Of course, [this] would be done were the experiment not a success.

6 Women are better morally, as evidenced by the criminals in the penitentiaries. For example, in the penitentiaries in California we have about three thousand men and about thirty women. The cases tried before the police courts probably average about the same. We must, therefore, admit that women would be a great factor in promoting honesty, equity and morality if given the ballot.

7 It is argued that all women do not wish to vote. The same argument applies to men. It has become common practice on election days to send [transportation] for a large percent of the male voters, and many who go voluntarily do so from a sense of duty. Women, being more faithful to duty, will exercise their right of franchise and do it cheerfully. Besides, their presence on such occasions will . . . guarantee that everything will be carried on respectably.

8 Women who are in touch with public affairs are none the less womanly. On the contrary, they are better and more companionable wives, more interesting mothers, because they have a common interest with their sons.

(continued)

9 The time was thought that to allow a girl a high school education would ruin her morals, destroy her religion, impair her health . . . and take away her desire to be a good wife and mother. Such theories are long since exploded. As we have progressed in these matters, let us progress in reference to suffrage; let us show the saloon element, the gambling element, the selfish element (for these are the opponents of women's suffrage) that this great state of California is really a progressive state in every way.

—From 1911 California voters' information manual by assemblyman H.G. Cattell

1. Which of the following statements best reflects the author's position?

   A. Women should be allowed to attend college.

   B. Women should be allowed to hold government office.

   C. Women should be allowed to vote in elections.

   D. Women should be allowed to hold peaceful protests.

2. An opposing viewpoint cited by the author is that

   A. all women do not want to vote.

   B. women do not have the morals to vote.

   C. women are not intelligent enough to vote.

   D. women cannot vote in other countries.

3. The author uses the following statement as _____ to support his assertion that women are morally superior to men: "In the penitentiaries in California we have about three thousand men and about thirty women."

4. Which of the following definitions best fits the meaning of the word **franchise** as it is used in paragraph 7?

   A. a business that sells a company's goods

   B. the right for an individual to vote

   C. a team that belongs to a sports league

   D. freedom from any type of restriction

 Test-Taking Tip

Before writing an extended response, take a few minutes to plan your response. You might want to use a graphic organizer to organize your thoughts. Consider using a flow chart to explain steps in a process or a Venn diagram to compare and contrast ideas. A diagram used to visually represent causes and effects can also work for problems and solutions. Finally, concept webs are helpful for showing relationships among ideas.

Analyzing Support for an Author's Position

To make their persuasive texts effective, authors provide evidence to support their positions. They also offer evidence to refute opposing viewpoints. Without evidence, readers are not likely to be convinced to agree with the author or to disagree with the opposing position.

Directions: Read the passage below. Then complete the activities.

1 Wednesday I will send to Congress a law designed to eliminate illegal barriers to the right to vote. . . . This bill will establish a simple, uniform standard which cannot be used, however ingenious the effort, to flout our Constitution.

2 It will provide for citizens to be registered by officials of the United States government if the state officials refuse to register them.

3 It will eliminate tedious, unnecessary lawsuits which delay the right to vote.

4 Finally, this legislation will ensure that properly registered individuals are not prohibited from voting.

5 I will welcome the suggestions from all the members of Congress—I have no doubt that I will get some—on ways and means to strengthen this law and to make it effective. But experience has plainly shown that this is the only path to carry out the command of the Constitution.

6 To those who seek to avoid action by their national government in their own communities, who want to and who seek to maintain purely local control over elections, the answer is simple:

7 Open your polling places to all your people. Allow men and women to register and vote whatever the color of their skin. Extend the rights of citizenship to every citizen of this land. . . .

8 There is no constitutional issue here. The command of the Constitution is plain.

9 There is no moral issue. It is wrong—deadly wrong—to deny any of your fellow Americans the right to vote in this country.

10 There is no issue of states' rights or national rights. There is only the struggle for human rights. . . .

11 The last time a president sent a civil rights bill to the Congress it contained a provision to protect voting rights in federal elections. That civil rights bill was passed after eight long months of debate. And when that bill came to my desk from the Congress for my signature, the heart of the voting provision had been eliminated.

(continued)

12 This time, on this issue, there must be no delay, no hesitation and no compromise with our purpose. We cannot, we must not, refuse to protect the right of every American to vote in every election that he may desire to participate in. And we ought not and we cannot and we must not wait another eight months before we get a bill. We have already waited a hundred years and more, and the time for waiting is gone.

13 So I ask you to join me in working long hours—nights and weekends, if necessary—to pass this bill. And I don't make that request lightly. For from the window where I sit with the problems of our country I recognize that outside this chamber is the outraged conscience of a nation, the grave concern of many nations, and the harsh judgment of history on our acts. . . .

14 But even if we pass this bill, the battle will not be over. What happened in Selma* is part of a far larger movement which reaches into every section and state of America. It is the effort of [African Americans] to secure for themselves the full blessings of American life.

15 Their cause must be our cause too. Because it is not just [African Americans], but really it is all of us, who must overcome the crippling legacy of bigotry and injustice.

16 And we shall overcome.

—From "We Shall Overcome" speech by Lyndon B. Johnson, March 15, 1965

* Police in Selma, Alabama, physically attacked hundreds of civil rights marchers.

1. What is Lyndon Johnson's position?

   A. Congress must work harder.

   B. Congress must draft a new bill.

   C. Congress must guarantee states' rights.

   D. Congress must pass the voting rights bill.

2. What is the opposing position that Johnson refutes in paragraph 10?

   A. The national government should determine election laws.

   B. States' rights take precedence over national rights.

   C. All people should have the right to vote in elections.

   D. The entire country agrees that change should be made.

3. Acknowledging and _____ opposing viewpoints help Johnson strengthen his position.

4. In which paragraph does Johnson provide evidence that discredits the opposition?

   A. 5

   B. 9

   C. 11

   D. 15

Writing Practice

Some schools have added service learning to their programs. In these programs, students are required to complete volunteer hours as a part of their coursework or even as a graduation requirement. Many times these volunteer programs are incorporated into the curriculum. For example, a history class studying World War II might volunteer at a local veterans' hospital.

Directions: Write an essay about whether service learning belongs in schools. Develop a logical argument in which you clearly state your opinion and introduce an opposing viewpoint. Indicate that you understand that position and explain how it is different from yours. Cite evidence to support your position and to refute the opposing position.

_____

_____

_____

_____

_____

_____

_____

_____

_____

_____

_____

_____

_____

_____

_____

_____

_____

This lesson will help you practice analyzing an author's intention and effect in two texts. Use it with core lesson 5.5 Analyze Author's Intention and Effect to reinforce and apply your knowledge.

Key Concept

Authors use several types of rhetorical devices to communicate their position and to achieve their goals for writing.

Core Skills

- Analyze Author's Purpose
- Determine Point of View

Identifying Rhetorical Devices

Authors write with goals, or intentions, in mind. Among the many techniques they use are rhetorical devices, which help authors create the desired effects on their audiences. Some common rhetorical devices are analogy, asking questions, enumeration, juxtaposition of opposites, qualification statements, repetition, and parallelism.

Directions: Read the passage below. Then choose the best answer to each question.

1 That winter had been a very severe one in Romania. The Danube froze solid a week before Christmas and remained tight for five months. It was as if the blue waters were suddenly turned into steel. From across the river, from the Dobrudja, on sleds pulled by long-horned oxen, the Tartars brought barrels of frozen honey, quarters of killed lambs, poultry and game, and returned heavily laden with bags of flour and rolls of sole leather. The whole day long the crack of whips and the curses of the drivers rent the icy atmosphere. Whatever their destination, the carters were in a hurry to reach human habitation before nightfall—before the dreaded time when packs of wolves came out to prey for food.

2 In cold, clear nights, when even the wind was frozen still, the lugubrious howling of the wolf permitted no sleep. The indoor people spent the night praying for the lives and souls of the travellers.

(continued)

3 All through the winter there was not one morning but some man or animal was found torn or eaten in our neighbourhood. The people of the village at first built fires on the shores to scare the beasts away, but they had to give it up because the thatched roofs of the huts in the village were set on fire in windy nights by flying sparks. The cold cowed the fiercest dogs. The wolves, crazed by hunger, grew more daring from day to day. They showed their heads even in daylight. When Baba Hana, the old . . . fortune-teller, ran into the school-house one morning and cried, "Wolf, wolf in the yard," the teacher was inclined to attribute her scare to a long drink the night before. But that very night, Stan, the horseshoer, who had returned late from the inn and had evidently not closed the door as he entered the smithy, was eaten up by the beasts. And the smithy stood in the centre of the village! A stone's throw from the inn, and the thatch-roofed school, and the red painted church!

—From "Ghitza" by Konrad Bercovici

1. What type of rhetorical device is the author using in the following sentence?

   "It was as if the blue waters were suddenly turned into steel."

   A. enumeration

   B. repetition

   C. parallelism

   D. analogy

2. The following sentence contains which type of rhetorical device?

   "Whatever their destination, the carters were in a hurry to reach human habitation before nightfall—before the dreaded time when packs of wolves came out to prey for food."

   A. qualifying statement

   B. analogy

   C. enumeration

   D. juxtaposition of opposites

3. Which of the following sentences is an example of enumeration?

   A. "The Danube froze solid a week before Christmas and remained tight for five months."

   B. "In cold, clear nights, when even the wind was frozen still, the lugubrious howling of the wolf permitted no sleep."

   C. "A stone's throw from the inn, and the thatch-roofed school, and the red painted church!"

   D. "The wolves, crazed by hunger, grew more daring from day to day."

4. Which of the following definitions best fits the meaning of the word **quarters** used in paragraph 1?

   A. coins worth twenty-five cents

   B. one-fourth portions of slaughtered animals

   C. lodgings for soldiers or crew members

   D. at close range or nearly in contact

Identifying an Author's Intention and Effect

Authors write for a purpose: to entertain, to inform, or to persuade. Authors also write with an intention, which combines purpose and point of view. The author's intention is what he or she hopes to accomplish with the written work. The author uses rhetorical devices to produce the desired effect.

Directions: Read the passage below. Then complete the activities.

1 There were no beds given the slaves, unless one coarse blanket be considered such, and none but the men and women had these. This, however, is not considered a very great privation. They find less difficulty from the want of beds, than from the want of time to sleep; for when their day's work in the field is done, the most of them having their washing, mending, and cooking to do, and having few or none of the ordinary facilities for doing either of these, very many of their sleeping hours are consumed in preparing for the field the coming day; and when this is done, old and young, male and female, married and single, drop down side by side, on one common bed,—the cold, damp floor,— each covering himself or herself with their miserable blankets; and here they sleep till they are summoned to the field by the driver's horn. At the sound of this, all must rise, and be off to the field.

2 There must be no halting; every one must be at his or her post; and woe betides them who hear not this morning summons to the field; for if they are not awakened by the sense of hearing, they are by the sense of feeling: no age nor sex finds any favor. Mr. Severe, the overseer, used to stand by the door of the quarter, armed with a large hickory stick and heavy cowskin, ready to whip any one who was so unfortunate as not to hear, or, from any other cause, was prevented from being ready to start for the field at the sound of the horn.

3 Mr. Severe was rightly named: he was a cruel man. I have seen him whip a woman, causing the blood to run half an hour at the time; and this, too, in the midst of her crying children, pleading for their mother's release. He seemed to take pleasure in manifesting his fiendish barbarity. Added to his cruelty, he was a profane swearer. It was enough to chill the blood and stiffen the hair of an ordinary man to hear him talk. Scarce a sentence escaped him but that was commenced or concluded by some horrid oath. The field was the place to witness his cruelty and profanity. His presence made it both the field of blood and of blasphemy. From the rising till the going down of the sun, he was cursing, raving, cutting, and slashing among the slaves of the field, in the most frightful manner. His career was short. He died very soon after I went to Colonel Lloyd's; and he died as he lived, uttering, with his dying groans, bitter curses and horrid oaths. His death was regarded by the slaves as the result of a merciful providence.

—From "Narrative of the Life of Frederick Douglass an American Slave" by Frederick Douglass

1. Judging from the rhetorical devices he uses, Frederick Douglass' intention was likely

   A. to convince readers that Mr. Severe's death was deserved.

   B. to convey how unfairly he and other slaves were treated.

   C. to clarify what it is like to work on a farm.

   D. to entertain readers with a tale from his childhood.

2. Which sentence best describes the effect of rhetoric in the narrative?

   A. It prompts people to be skeptical about the experiences of slaves.

   B. It stimulates a discussion about life in the rural south in the 1800s.

   C. It inspires people to make changes in their daily lives.

   D. It evokes an emotional response to the treatment of the slaves.

3. In the following excerpt from the text, the author uses the rhetorical device of _____.

   " . . . and when this is done, old and young, male and female, married and single, drop down side by side . . ."

4. Which of the following excerpts from the text does NOT convey the author's intention?

   A. "His career was short."

   B. "There were no beds given the slaves . . ."

   C. " . . . the cold, damp floor . . ."

   D. " . . . ready to whip any one . . ."

Language Practice

A participle is a verb that acts as an adjective. It modifies nouns and pronouns and comes in two forms: present, ending with *-ing*, and past, ending with *-ed*. Not all verbs with these endings are participles. When you use participles, make sure you use the correct form.

Directions: Circle the correct participial version of the verb.

1. The 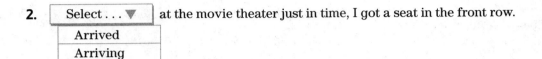 dog dashed after the mail truck.

   Select... ▼
   barked
   barking

2. 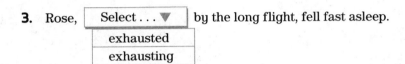 at the movie theater just in time, I got a seat in the front row.

   Select... ▼
   Arrived
   Arriving

3. Rose, 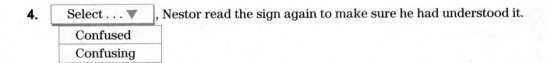 by the long flight, fell fast asleep.

   Select... ▼
   exhausted
   exhausting

4. 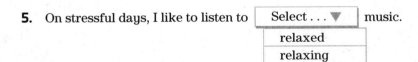, Nestor read the sign again to make sure he had understood it.

   Select... ▼
   Confused
   Confusing

5. On stressful days, I like to listen to 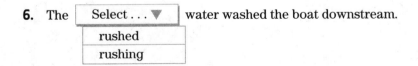 music.

   Select... ▼
   relaxed
   relaxing

6. The Select... ▼ water washed the boat downstream.

   rushed
   rushing

✔ Test-Taking Tip

To familiarize yourself with computerized tests, consider using an online test-taking tutorial. Tutorials provides information on how to navigate through the test, how to select an answer, and how to enter and edit text. You will also learn how to keep track of remaining time and how to monitor your progress.

Writing Practice

Have you ever read something that had a dramatic effect on you? Perhaps it helped you see an issue in a new way, or it included descriptions that evoked an emotional response. A writer's intention and use of rhetorical devices may create these effects. When you are reading, it is helpful to think critically about the devices the writer uses to achieve his or her goals.

Directions: Analyze one of the reading passages in this lesson. Summarize the excerpt, and explain the author's intention and effect. Describe at least two rhetorical devices the writer uses, and explain how those devices help the writer achieve his goals. Support your ideas with details and examples.

This lesson will help you practice identifying argument development in two texts. Use it with core lesson 6.1 Identify Argument Development to reinforce and apply your knowledge.

Key Concept

The purpose of an argument is to persuade the reader that a claim is reasonable. A well-developed argument includes reasons and evidence that support the writer's claim.

Core Skills

- Understand the Relationship among Ideas
- Analyze Text Structure to Evaluate an Argument

Developing an Argument

An argument starts with a claim, or a statement of the author's opinion or position on a topic. The author wants to persuade readers to believe or act on the claim. In a good argument, claims are supported by evidence such as reasons, facts, and examples. The conclusion of an argument may restate the author's claim, summarize the evidence, or call upon the reader to take action.

Directions: Read the passage below. Then complete the activities.

Thomas Paine, a British-American political activist and revolutionary, published the booklet "Common Sense" in 1776. In it, he spoke against the authority of the British government and the king, who he felt oppressed the people of America. He also believed that the Constitution of England encouraged oppression by the king, rather than freeing the people from tyranny. The king could still override elected officials and often did. "Common Sense" was the first publication to encourage colonists in America to declare independence. The peers referred to in the passage are nobility, who inherited their positions, while people in the commons were elected.

Common Sense

1 I offer a few remarks on the so much boasted constitution of England. That it was noble for the dark and slavish times in which it was erected, is granted. When the world was overrun with tyranny the least remove therefrom was a glorious rescue. But that it is imperfect, subject to convulsions, and incapable of producing what it seems to promise, is easily demonstrated. . . .

2 I know it is difficult to get over local or long standing prejudices, yet if we will suffer ourselves to examine the component parts of the English constitution, we shall find them to be the base remains of two ancient tyrannies, compounded with some new republican materials.

3 FIRST—The remains of monarchial tyranny in the person of the king.

SECONDLY—The remains of aristocratical tyranny in the persons of the peers.

THIRDLY—The new republican materials in the persons of the commons, on whose virtue depends the freedom of England.

4 The two first, by being hereditary, are independent of the people; wherefore in a CONSTITUTIONAL SENSE they contribute nothing towards the freedom of the state.

(continued)

5 To say that the constitution of England is a UNION of three powers reciprocally CHECKING each other, is farcical, either the words have no meaning, or they are flat contradictions.

6 To say that the commons is a check upon the king, presupposes two things:

7 FIRST—That the king is not to be trusted without being looked after, or in other words, that a thirst for absolute power is the natural disease of monarchy.

8 SECONDLY—That the commons, by being appointed for that purpose, are either wiser or more worthy of confidence than the crown.

9 But as the same constitution which gives the commons a power to check the king by withholding the supplies, gives afterwards the king a power to check the commons, by empowering him to reject their other bills; it again supposes that the king is wiser than those whom it has already supposed to be wiser than him. A mere absurdity!

—From "Common Sense" by Thomas Paine, 1776.

1. Write the statements below the chart in the appropriate columns.

Claim	Supports Claim	Does Not Support Claim

The king can reject bills that the commons passes.

Members of the peers are part of the old tyranny.

Members of the commons are elected by the people.

England's constitution does not encourage liberty.

2. Which of the following definitions best fits the meaning of the word **check** as it is used in paragraphs 6 and 9?

A. hold accountable

B. stop or slow down

C. detect the presence

D. determine the condition

3. In building his argument, Thomas Paine makes the _____ that the king and the peers do not contribute to freedom.

4. Which phrase best describes the evidence that Paine presents to support his argument?

A. contradictory to the claim

B. insufficient to support the claim

C. irrelevant to the claim

D. relevant to the claim

5. Which statement can be considered a fact that supports part of the claim that the constitution of England is absurd?

   A. The king has the power to reject the common's bills.

   B. The king is not to be trusted and should be looked after by the commons.

   C. The members of the commons are wiser and more reliable than the king.

   D. The members of the peers and the king are part of an ancient tyranny.

6. What type of conclusion does Paine reach in his argument?

   A. restatement of ideas

   B. call to action

   C. ideas that extend the argument

   D. combination of A, B, and C

Analyzing Argument Development

Whether an author's claim is unstated or clearly laid out in the text, you can gain a better understanding of the author's claim when you analyze the author's argument. When an argument is structured properly, the relationship among ideas is clear and readers can easily understand the author's point of view.

Directions: Read the passage below. Then complete the activities.

1 Female suffrage is a reform demanded by the social conditions of our times, by the high culture of woman, and by the aspiration of all classes of society to organize and work for the interests they have in common. . . .

2 It is an interesting phenomenon that whenever an attempt is made to introduce a social reform . . . there is never a lack of opposition . . . As was to be expected, the eternal calamity howlers and false prophets of evil raise their fatidical [prophetic] voices . . . in protest against female suffrage, invoking the sanctity of the home and the necessity of perpetuating customs that have been observed for many years.

3 Frankly speaking, I have no patience with people who voice such objections. . . . I remember very well that in the past, not so very long ago, the same apprehension and fears were felt with regard to higher education for our women. . . . We are now able to observe the results, and if these results are found to be detrimental to the social and political welfare of the country, it is our duty to undo what we have done and to return to where we were before.

4 Fortunately, nobody would think of such a thing. . . . Education has not atrophied or impaired any of the fundamental faculties of woman; on the contrary, it has enhanced and enriched them. . . . Thank God, people are no longer ready to cast ridicule upon what some used to consider the foolish presumption of women to know as much as the men, and this is doubtless due to the fact that the disastrous results predicted by the calamity howlers, the terrible prophets of failure, have not materialized.

(continued)

5 Very well; if you allow the instruction and education of woman in all the branches of science, you must allow woman to take on her place not only in domestic life, but also in social and public life. Instruction and education have a twofold purpose; individually, they redeem the human intellect from the perils of ignorance, and socially they prepare man and woman for the proper performance of their duties of citizenship. A person is not educated exclusively for his or her own good, but principally to be useful and of service to the others. Nothing is more dangerous to society than the educated man who thinks only of himself, because his education enables him to do more harm and to sacrifice everybody else to his convenience or personal ambition. The real object of education is public service, that is, to utilize the knowledge one has acquired for the benefit and improvement of the society in which one is living.

6 In societies, therefore, where woman is admitted to all the professions and where no source of knowledge is barred to her, woman must necessarily and logically be allowed to take a part in the public life, otherwise, her education would be incomplete or society would commit an injustice towards her, giving her the means to educate herself and then depriving her of the necessary power to use that education for the benefit of society and collective progress.

—From "The Woman and the Right to Vote" by Rafael Palma

1. What is the claim made in this passage?

A. Women are entitled to the right to vote.

B. Women participate in all aspects of education.

C. Women are admitted to all the professions.

D. Women participate in many aspects of public life.

2. How does the author feel about people who protest against women's right to vote?

A. He thinks they are correct.

B. He thinks they are doing their duty.

C. He thinks they have no reason to protest.

D. He thinks they should be better educated.

3. As a(n) _____ of another way in which allowing women into public life was beneficial, the author cites the successes of women in education.

4. Which statement best describes how Palma builds his argument?

A. He states his claim and supports it with facts, reasons, and examples.

B. He states his claim and supports it with his opinion on the topic.

C. He states his claim and supports it with expert opinions on the topic.

D. He states his claim and supports it with examples of ways to gain the vote.

5. Which sentence best describes the way the author connects his ideas in this passage?

   A. The author connects his ideas chronologically.

   B. The author connects his ideas logically.

   C. The author connects his ideas using the question-and-answer form.

   D. The author connects his ideas through comparison and contrast.

6. Which sentence best describes the author's conclusion?

   A. A woman has access to all sources of knowledge and all professions.

   B. A woman is not educated exclusively for her own good.

   C. It is not necessary to perpetuate customs that have been observed for many years.

   D. It is necessary and logical for women to participate in public life by voting.

 Test-Taking Tip

When you read a passage during a test, you need to eliminate information that is not necessary for answering questions. One way to do this is to read the passage, taking notes of important information, and then review the questions to see what information is covered and what is not.

Writing Practice

There are many reasons for developing an argument. Maybe you have strong feelings about a proposed law and want to write a letter to the editor. Maybe you are trying to convince your employer that you are the best candidate for an open position. When you develop an argument, you should make a clear claim that is supported by facts and evidence.

Directions: Write a paragraph making a claim that an action you support is the right action. It can be something that you advocate for in your personal life or an action that is more community based. Provide facts, reasons, and examples as evidence to support your claim. Finally, write a conclusion that summarizes your supporting evidence and reiterates your claim.

_____

_____

_____

_____

_____

_____

_____

_____

_____

_____

_____

_____

_____

_____

_____

_____

_____

_____

This lesson will help you practice identifying supporting evidence in two texts. Use it with core lesson 6.2 Identify Supporting Evidence to reinforce and apply your knowledge.

Key Concept

Authors use various types of reasoning in developing an argument. Some types of reasoning are useful, but others are ineffective.

Core Skills

- Evaluate Arguments
- Cite Specific Evidence

Supporting Evidence

Authors making a claim in an argument must support that claim with evidence such as facts, reasons, and examples. Authors use this supporting evidence to back up the claim and to persuade you, the reader, that the claim is reasonable. The evidence presented must be logical and connected to the claim. Emotional appeals and faulty logic do not qualify as supporting evidence.

Directions: Read the passage below. Then complete the activities.

Excerpt from "The One Man Power," *New York Times*, January 5, 1860

1 Mayor WOOD, in his eagerness to impress the public with the belief that he cannot justly be held responsible for defects or malfeasances in the City Government, overlooks or misrepresents one point of considerable importance. He states that there is no general supervision confided to the Mayor; —these are his words:

2 "While the Common Council, with the Mayor, can enact an ordinance, the administrative authority is not thus defined. This is diffused and uncertain. It is disseminated among several independent departments. There is no general head; there is no Chief Executive. Instead of one, there are eight coordinate Executives, separate and independent of each other, the Mayor having no supervisory control. These departments constitute the whole administrative municipal government of the corporation."

3 This is an entire mistake. The Charter makes the heads of nearly all the Departments directly responsible to the Mayor. The Comptroller and Corporation Counsel are, it is true, elected by the people, and are not accountable to the Executive; but the Croton Aqueduct Board, the Street Commissioner, the City Inspector, and the four Superintendents of Bureaux under him, are all appointed by the Mayor and Aldermen, and may at any time be removed by the Mayor and Board for cause. Any malfeasance or neglect of duty on the part of either of those officers, entitles the Mayor instantly to supersede them. What more does Mayor WOOD desire? What greater power is necessary to enable him to enforce proper vigilance and energy in the business of these Departments? In speaking of the Street Inspector the Mayor says:

4 "The Mayor, being without power, should not be held accountable by the public. If nuisances abound and the streets remain filthy, it will be unjust to lay the responsibility at his door. Until he has power to appoint and remove the subordinates upon whom it is incumbent to perform these duties, he should be relieved from any censure which attaches to the neglect. It is well for the public and myself to have an understanding upon the subject at the commencement of my administration."

(continued)

5 "The public and myself" should have an accurate understanding of the subject, if they have any at all: —yet the Mayor's words convey an impression in regard to the matter which is not correct. In the same paragraph the Mayor says: "The City Inspector and the Superintendents under him are appointed and removed in the same manner as the Street Commissioner;" and in regard to that officer, he says:

6 "Like the officers of the Croton Board, he derives his appointment, in the first instance, from the Mayor and Aldermen, but with a tenure of two years, unless sooner removed for cause, which removal requires the sanction of a majority of all the members elected to the Board of Aldermen."

7 His own admissions thus completely contradict his assertion that the Mayor is without power, and should therefore be without responsibility. He has power in every case of misconduct to remove the offender from office, and to demand the concurrence of the Board of Aldermen. Does he doubt the disposition of that Board to second promptly any effort he may make to remedy evils or punish mal-practices on the part of City officers? If so, he can very easily throw upon them the responsibility which he deprecates so much. Let him remove an officer for misconduct, and show clear cause for the proceeding, and he will be sustained by the public, whether the Board second his action or not. But the fact that he is not arbitrary and absolute, —that others share the power of punishment which is placed in his hands, cannot relieve him from the just responsibility which belongs to his office.

—from "The One Man Power," *New York Times*, January 5, 1860

1. The author's claim in this passage is that the Mayor

   A. is taking on too much responsibility.

   B. has no real power over city employees.

   C. is trying to shirk his responsibilities.

   D. was not responsible for removing officers.

2. What does the author say is the Mayor's claim?

   A. He has supervisory power over members of city government.

   B. He should be held responsible for removing officers for misconduct.

   C. He can get support from the Board for his actions to clean up government.

   D. He is not responsible for removing officers for misconduct in city government.

3. Which statement serves as evidence that is logically connected to the author's claim?

   A. The Mayor has no supervisory control over the Executives in the Common Council.

   B. The Mayor, being without power, is not held accountable by the public.

   C. The Mayor has the responsibility to provide the public with an accurate understanding of the distribution of power in the city.

   D. The Mayor has the power to remove an offender from office and to demand the concurrence of the Board of Aldermen.

4. The author provides evidence that
   _____ his claim by including the Mayor's statements that contradict his insistence that he has no power.

5. Which word best describes the Mayor's logic in explaining his lack of responsibility?

   A. faulty

   B. sound

   C. supporting

   D. connected

Connecting Claims and Evidence

When reading an argument, use reasoning to evaluate the author's argument and to determine whether it is valid. If the reasoning is logical and you can cite specific evidence that supports and connects directly to the author's claim, then you can safely say that the argument is valid and reasonable.

Directions: Read the following passage. Then complete the activities.

"Checkers" Speech, Richard M. Nixon

1 My Fellow Americans,

2 I come before you tonight as a candidate for the Vice-Presidency and as a man whose honesty and integrity has been questioned. . . .

3 I am sure that you have read the charges, and you have heard it, that I, Senator Nixon, took $18,000 from a group of my supporters.

4 [L]et me say this: Not a cent of the $18,000 or any other money of that type ever went to me for my personal use. Every penny of it was used to pay for political expenses that I did not think should be charged to the taxpayers of the United States.

5 It was not a secret fund. . . .

6 I just don't believe in that, and I can say that never, while I have been in the Senate of the United States, as far as the people that contributed to this fund are concerned, have I made a telephone call to an agency, nor have I gone down to an agency on their behalf.

7 And the records will show that, the records which are in the hands of the administration.

8 Let me tell you in just a word how a Senate office operates. First of all, the Senator gets $15,000 a year in salary. He gets enough money to pay for one trip a year, a round trip, that is, for himself, and his family between his home and Washington, D.C. and then he gets an allowance to handle the people that work in his office to handle his mail.

9 And the allowance for my State of California, is enough to hire 13 people. And let me say, incidentally, that this allowance is not paid to the Senator.

10 It is paid directly to the individuals, that the Senator puts on his pay roll, but all of these people and all of these allowances are for strictly official business; business, for example, when a constituent writes in and wants you to go down to the Veteran's Administration and get some information about his GI policy—items of that type for example. But there are other expenses that are not covered by the Government. And I think I can best discuss those expenses by asking you some questions.

11 Do you think that when I or any other senator makes a political speech, has it printed, should charge the printing of that speech and the mailing of that speech to the taxpayers?

12 Do you think, for example, when I or any other Senator makes a trip to his home State to make a purely political speech that the cost of that trip should be charged to the taxpayers?

13 Do you think when a Senator makes political broadcasts or political television broadcasts, radio or television that the expense of those broadcasts should be charged to the taxpayers?

14 . . . The answer is no. The taxpayers should not be required to finance items which are not official business but which are primarily political business.

(continued)

15 Well, then the question arises, you say, "Well, how do you pay for these and how can you do it legally?" And there are several ways, that it can be done, incidentally, and it is done legally in the United States Senate and in the Congress.

16 The first way is to be a rich man. So I couldn't use that.

17 Another way that is used is to put your wife on the pay roll. Let me say, incidentally, that my opponent, my opposite number for the Vice Presidency on the Democratic ticket, does have his wife on the pay roll and has had her on his pay roll for the past ten years. Now let me just say this: That is his business, and I am not critical of him for doing that. You will have to pass judgment on that particular point, but I have never done that for this reason:

18 I have found that there are so many deserving stenographers and secretaries in Washington that needed the work that I just didn't feel it was right to put my wife on the pay roll . . .

19 What are the other ways that these finances can be taken care of? Some who are lawyers, and I happen to be a lawyer, continue to practice law, but I haven't been able to do that. . . .

20 And so I felt that the best way to handle these necessary political expenses of getting my message to the American people and the speeches I made—the speeches I had printed for the most part concerned this one message of exposing this Administration, the Communism in it, the corruption in it—the only way I could do that was to accept the aid which people in my home State of California, who contributed to my campaign and who continued to make these contributions after I was elected, were glad to make.

21 And let me say that I am proud of the fact that not one of them has ever asked me for a special favor. I am proud of the fact that not one of them has ever asked me to vote on a bill other than my own conscience would dictate. And I am proud of the fact that the taxpayers by subterfuge or otherwise have never paid one dime for expenses which I thought were political and should not be charged [to] the taxpayers.

—from "Checkers" speech by Richard M. Nixon, September 23, 1952

1. What is Richard Nixon's claim in this speech?

   A. He did not receive money from supporters for political expenses.

   B. He did not use money from supporters for personal expenses.

   C. He hired his wife to manage his political expenses.

   D. He received money from the government for political expenses.

2. In this argument, what type of evidence is Nixon's statement that "the taxpayers should not be required to finance items which are not official business but which are primarily political business"?

   A. an example

   B. a verifiable fact

   C. an emotional appeal

   D. a supporting reason

3. Which of the following definitions best fits the meaning of the word **finance** as it is used in paragraph 14?

   A. manage large amounts of money

   B. provide funds for someone or for a venture

   C. raise the funds to contribute support for a project

   D. donate resources and monetary affairs of a government or organization

4. The author provides _____ as evidence that he used the money that was given to him for political expenses.

5. The fact that Nixon does not have proof that he has not given special favors for contributions makes his argument

   A. valid.

   B. faulty.

   C. reasonable.

   D. logical.

 Test-Taking Tip

When a test includes questions related to a text, it is often helpful to read the questions before reading the text. You can even jot down notes and key words to help you identify the information that you'll need to look for in the text. Then as you first read the text, keep the questions in mind and look for the information that you need to answer them correctly.

Writing Practice

Many people have done things that others have disagreed with. Look at Nixon's situation in his "Checkers" speech, for example. Then recall something that you have done or a decision that you have made that others disagreed with.

Directions: Build an argument defending something that you have done in your life or a decision that you made that others have disagreed with. Start with a claim, and then list supporting evidence that is connected to your claim. Scan your list, and decide whether any of your reasons are faulty or based on emotional appeals. If you find any, cross them off the list. Then write a paragraph using your evidence to support your claim.

_____

_____

_____

_____

_____

_____

_____

_____

_____

_____

_____

_____

_____

_____

_____

_____

_____

_____

_____

This lesson will help you practice evaluating relevance and sufficiency of supporting evidence in two texts. Use it with core lesson 6.3 Evaluate Relevance and Sufficiency to reinforce and apply your knowledge.

Key Concept	Core Skills
To create a reasonable argument, an author must provide relevant and sufficient evidence for his or her claim.	• Identify Relevant Information • Evaluate Arguments

Building a Case

To build an effective argument, writers must support their claim with evidence that is relevant not only to the claim, but also to the audience's interests and needs. Writers must also provide more than one piece of evidence to build a convincing argument. The validity of the argument depends on the relevancy and sufficiency of the evidence.

Directions: Read the passage below. Then choose the best answer to each question.

Corporate Memo on Sick-Leave Legislation

In response to the current influenza outbreak, the New York City Council is fast-tracking a piece of legislation. If passed, this would place statutory standards on the administration of corporate sick-leave policies. In a nutshell, it would require all New York City employers to provide the following:

- 10 paid sick days a year for full-time employees, and
- 5 paid sick days a year for employees working between 20 and 32 hours per week.

We strongly encourage employees to oppose this legislation. We have always acknowledged the importance of employee health. We also realize that our employees are more productive when their salary and position in the workforce are protected. Our current policy of granting sick leave on a documented, case-by-case basis is efficient and effective. It provides protection for our employees, their families, and society as a whole:

- It helps to maintain workplace health, in support of CDC guidelines. These guidelines suggest that people infected with influenza remain isolated for at least 24 hours after their fever breaks.
- It helps to maintain a healthy school environment for the children of our employees by allowing parents to remain home while their children are contagious.

Current law does not require employers to provide sick leave, paid or unpaid, under any circumstances. If, however, a company is held to a specific number of sick days, it is likewise obliged to compensate employees for their unused sick days. This amount must be paid yearly or when an employee leaves the company.

(continued)

Our current policy, then, is a vital tool for maintaining our bottom line. This, in turn, translates into benefits and job security for you, the employee.

- According to a March 2010 Department of Labor Statistics report, the cost of sick leave to a business or agency can average 81 cents per hour per employee. We are a mid-sized company. We employ approximately 1,200 full-time and part-time workers. Using the DLS report as a guide, let's consider some figures.

One full-time employee works 260 days a year. At 8 hours per workday, an individual works 2,080 hours per year. Multiply that by the number of employees (1,200), and there are 2,496,000 work hours per year in our company. Finally, multiply the number of work hours by the per-hour cost of sick leave ($.81), and you get $2,021,760 per year.

This is an unacceptable level of expense. It would force overall cost reduction. This cost reduction would most likely be administered through layoffs and reduced employee salaries. As an employee, voter, and citizen, this concerns you directly. Phone your city representative to protest this intrusion into the private sector—and remind him or her that you vote!

Source: Corporate Memo on Sick-Leave Legislation

---

1. Which statement is evidence that supports the claim that employees should oppose mandatory paid sick leave?

   A. Employees should support their company's position.

   B. The company can't afford mandatory paid sick-leave.

   C. The New York City council is trying to pass legislation for mandatory paid sick leave.

   D. The mandatory sick leave legislation is in response to the influenza outbreak.

2. Which statement is directly relevant to the audience?

   A. "We have always acknowledged the importance of employee health."

   B. "We employ approximately 1,200 full-time and part-time workers."

   C. "Our current policy, then, is a vital tool for maintaining our bottom line."

   D. "Our current policy translates into benefits and job security for you, the employee."

3. Which type of evidence does the author provide to support the claim that legislated sick leave would cost the company a lot of money?

   A. verifiable but faulty

   B. biased and repetitive

   C. relevant and sufficient

   D. valid but contradictory

4. The author links the evidence to the claim at the end of the passage by stating that

   A. the employees are directly affected by this legislation and should oppose it.

   B. the employees should oppose the legislation out of loyalty to the company.

   C. the company's management is going to oppose the legislation.

   D. the city leaders have doubts about the proposed legislation.

Evaluating Evidence in Various Texts

When you evaluate the evidence in a text, you look for appropriate evidence that supports the author's claim and is relevant to the topic and the audience's interests. You also check for sufficient evidence, in strength and amount, to support the claim.

Directions: Read the passage below. Then complete the activities.

Address Before a Joint Session of the Congress Reporting on the State of the Union

State of the Union, 1982

1 Today marks my first State of the Union address to you. . . .

2 When I visited this chamber last year as a newcomer to Washington, critical of past policies . . . , I proposed a new spirit of partnership between this Congress and this administration and between Washington and our state and local governments. In forging this new partnership for America, we could achieve the oldest hopes of our republic—prosperity for our nation, peace for the world, and the blessings of individual liberty for our children and, someday, for all of humanity.

3 It's my duty to report to you tonight on the progress that we have made. . . .

4 Seldom have the stakes been higher for America. . . . The situation at this time last year was truly ominous.

5 The last decade has seen a series of recessions. There was a recession in 1970, in 1974, and again in the spring of 1980. Each time, unemployment increased and inflation soon turned up again. . . .

6 Late in 1981 we sank into the present recession, largely because continued high interest rates hurt the auto industry and construction. And there was a drop in productivity, and the already high unemployment increased.

7 This time, however, things are different. We have an economic program in place, completely different from the artificial quick fixes of the past. It calls for a reduction of the rate of increase in government spending. . . . But reduced spending alone isn't enough. We've just implemented the first and smallest phase of a three-year tax-rate reduction designed to stimulate the economy and create jobs. . . .

8 I will seek no tax increases this year. . . . I promise to bring the American people—to bring their tax rates down and to keep them down, to provide them incentives to rebuild our economy, to save, to invest in America's future. . . . Seize these new opportunities to produce, to save, to invest, and together we'll make this economy a mighty engine of freedom, hope, and prosperity again.

(continued)

9   Now, the budget deficit this year will exceed our earlier expectations. The recession did that. It lowered revenues and increased costs. To some extent, we're also victims of our own success. We've brought inflation down faster than we thought we could. . . . [W]e've deprived government of those hidden revenues that occur when inflation pushes people into higher income tax brackets. . . .

10 We must cut out more nonessential government spending and rout out more waste . . .

11 The budget plan I submit to you on February 8th will realize major savings by dismantling the Departments of Energy and Education. . . . We'll continue to redirect our resources to our two highest budget priorities—a strong national defense to keep America free and at peace and a reliable safety net of social programs for those who have contributed and those who are in need. . . .

12 Our faith in the American people is reflected in another major endeavor. Our private sector initiatives task force is seeking out successful community models of school, church, business, union, foundation, and civic programs that help community needs. Such groups are almost invariably far more efficient than government in running social programs.

13 We're not asking them to replace discarded and often discredited government programs dollar for dollar, service for service. We just want to help them perform the good works they choose and help others to profit by their example. Three hundred and eighty-five thousand corporations and private organizations are already working on social programs ranging from drug rehabilitation to job training, and thousands more Americans have written us asking how they can help. The volunteer spirit is still alive and well in America. . . .

14 Our foreign policy is a policy of strength, fairness, and balance. By restoring America's military credibility, by pursuing peace at the negotiating table wherever both sides are willing to sit down in good faith, and by regaining the respect of America's allies and adversaries alike, we have strengthened our country's position as a force for peace and progress in the world. . . .

15 We have made pledges of a new frankness in our public statements and worldwide broadcasts. In the face of a climate of falsehood and misinformation, we've promised the world a season of truth—the truth of our great civilized ideas: individual liberty, representative government, the rule of law under God. We've never needed walls or minefields or barbed wire to keep our people in. Nor do we declare martial law to keep our people from voting for the kind of government they want. . . .

16 A hundred and twenty years ago, the greatest of all our presidents delivered his second State of the Union message in this chamber. "We cannot escape history," Abraham Lincoln warned. "We of this congress and this administration will be remembered in spite of ourselves." The "trial through which we pass will light us down, in honor or dishonor, to the latest [last] generation."

17 Well, that president and that congress did not fail the American people. Together they weathered the storm and preserved the Union. Let it be said of us that we, too, did not fail; that we, too, worked together to bring America through difficult times. Let us so conduct ourselves that two centuries from now, another congress and another president, meeting in this chamber as we are meeting, will speak of us with pride, saying that we met the test and preserved for them in their day the sacred flame of liberty—this last, best hope of man on Earth.

— From "Address Before a Joint Session of the Congress Reporting on the State of the Union" by Ronald Reagan

1. President Reagan uses Abraham Lincoln's words as _____ to support his claim that the country needs to work together to bring America through difficult times.

2. In which sentence does President Reagan present evidence to support his claim that government programs can be cut?

   A. "[W]e have strengthened our country's position as a force for peace and progress in the world.

   B. "We just want to help [private sector groups] perform the good works they choose and help others to profit by their example.

   C. "[Volunteer groups] are almost invariably far more efficient than government in running social programs.

   D. "[We do not] declare martial law to keep our people from voting for the kind of government they want.

3. Which of the following definitions best fits the meaning of the word **dismantling** as it is used in paragraph 11?

   A. rebuilding

   B. restructuring

   C. improving

   D. eliminating

4. Which statement is relevant evidence to support President Reagan's claim that the government will do its part to turn around the recession?

   A. He has promised the country a season of truth.

   B. He believes our foreign policy is fair, strong, and balanced.

   C. He will not raise taxes to pay for the new budget.

   D. He will not declare martial law to change how people vote.

5. President Reagan's argument is supported by several pieces of evidence related to his claim, but the lack of specific examples makes the evidence _____.

6. Which phrase best describes the evidence that the recession caused the budget deficit?

   A. interesting but biased

   B. connected but faulty

   C. relevant but not sufficient

   D. factual but not verifiable

✓ Test-Taking Tip

When you take a test that involves reading a text, scan the text for features such as headings and lists. As you scan, look in the text features and the text for words that you associate with the topic and words that are frequently repeated. These steps will help activate your prior knowledge about the topic and make it easier for you to answer questions about it.

Writing Practice

People write arguments for a number of reasons. They might be trying to convince others to invest in a project, or they could be writing a letter to the editor of a local newspaper to convince voters to support a certain political candidate.

Directions: Write a paragraph about a social program in your community that interests you, such as foster care or mental health services. In your paragraph, make a claim for the usefulness of this program and provide evidence to support your claim. Make sure that the evidence is relevant to your claim and that it is of interest to your audience. Be sure to provide more than one piece of evidence so your claim is sufficiently supported.

This lesson will help you practice evaluating the validity and reasoning used in arguments in two texts. Use it with core lesson 6.4 Evaluate Validity and Reasoning to reinforce and apply your knowledge.

Key Concept

Readers can use logical tests to determine whether the reasoning authors use in their arguments is valid.

Core Skills

- Cite Specific Evidence
- Evaluate Arguments

Understanding Validity and Reasoning

An argument's validity is the degree to which it is logically or factually reliable. A valid argument is supported with sound, or sensible, evidence. To create a valid argument, the writer must also connect ideas in a logical way to the claim and to each other, leading to a reasonable conclusion about the claim. An argument is invalid if the author exhibits bias or presents contradictory evidence.

Directions: Read the passage below. Then complete the activities.

Argument Against Women's Suffrage

1 Suffrage is not a right. It is a privilege that may or may not be granted. Politics is no place for a woman, consequently the privilege should not be granted to her. The mother's influence is needed in the home. She can do little good by gadding the street and neglecting her children. Let her teach her daughters that modesty, patience and gentleness are the charms of woman. Let her teach her sons that an honest conscience is every man's first political law; that no splendor can rob him nor no force justify the surrender of the simplest right of a free and independent citizen. The mothers of this country can shape the destinies of the nation by keeping in their places and attending to those duties that God Almighty intended for them. The kindly, gentle influence of the mother in the home and the dignified influence of the teacher in the school will far outweigh all the influence of all the mannish female politicians on earth.

(continued)

2 The courageous, chivalrous, and manly men and the womanly women, the real mothers and homebuilders of the country, are opposed to this innovation in American political life. There was a bill (the Sanford bill) before the last legislature which proposed to leave the equal suffrage question to women to decide first before the men should vote on it. This bill was defeated by the suffragettes because they knew that the women would vote down the amendment by a vote of ten to one. Do women have to vote in order to receive the protection of men? Why, men have gone to war, endured every privation, and death itself in defense of woman. To man, woman is the dearest creature on earth, and there is no extreme to which he would not go for his mother or sister. By keeping woman in her exalted position man can be induced to do more for her than he could by having the mix up in affairs that will cause him to lose respect and regard for her. Woman does not have to vote to secure her rights. Man will go to any extreme to protect and elevate her now. As long as woman is woman and keeps her place she will get more protection and more consideration than man gets. When she abdicates her throne she throws down the scepter of her power and loses her influence.

3 Woman suffrage has been proven a failure in states that have tried it. It is wrong. California should profit by the mistakes of other states. Not one reform has equal suffrage effected.

—From *An Argument Against Women's Suffrage*, J. B. Sanford,
Chairman of [California] Democratic Caucus, 1911

---

1. What is the author's claim in this passage?

A. Woman suffrage should not be allowed.

B. Woman suffrage has been a failure in other states.

C. Women belong in the home and in schools as teachers.

D. Women are gentle creatures and should be revered.

2. Which of the following definitions best fits the meaning of the word **suffrage** as it is used in paragraphs 1, 2, and 3?

A. the right to go to war

B. the right to vote

C. the securing of rights

D. the right to be a citizen

3. Which idea from this passage is a verifiable fact?

A. Women should keep their place in the home.

B. Women do not have to vote to secure their rights.

C. The Sanford bill was defeated by the suffragettes.

D. Men can protect women if women keep their exalted position.

4. The author of this passage presents a(n) _____ argument because the evidence he uses to support his claim is not _____ or logically sound.

5. Which statement best describes the author's argument?

A. biased and invalid

B. reasonable and valid

C. biased but logical

D. logical but unreasonable

Evaluating Validity and Reasoning in Texts

To evaluate the validity of an argument, check whether the evidence is accurate, is connected to the claim, and helps build a logical argument. To evaluate an argument's reasoning, make sure the evidence relates to and fully supports the claim. The argument's reasoning is not sound if the evidence does not support the claim.

Directions: Read the passage below. Then complete the activities.

Remarks by President Barack Obama at Campaign Event—Stamford, CT

1 We are here to build an economy where work pays off so that no matter what you look like or where you come from, you can make it here if you try. . . .

2 . . . We've got the best workers in the world. We've got the best entrepreneurs in the world. We have the best scientists and the best researchers in the world. We have the best universities and the best colleges in the world. We are a young nation, and we've got the greatest diversity of talent and ingenuity from every corner of the globe. . . . [N]o matter what the naysayers may say, no matter how dark the picture they try to paint, there's not another country on Earth that wouldn't gladly trade places with the United States of America. . . .

3 So what's standing in our way right now is not the lack of technical solutions to the deficit or to education or to energy. What's standing in our way is . . . the uncompromising view that says we should be going back to the old, top-down economics that got us into this mess in the first place. . . .

4 And I don't exaggerate when it comes to how my opponent and his allies in Congress view this economy. They believe . . . that if we give more tax breaks to some of the wealthiest Americans, and we get rid of regulations . . . , that somehow prosperity will rain down on everybody. . . .

5 So you're talking about each year, a tax cut that's equivalent of our defense budget for the next 10 years. . . . [T]his policy center . . . ran the numbers . . . And they determined that Governor Romney's plan would effectively raise taxes on middle-class families with children by an average of $2,000—to pay for this tax cut. . . . He'd ask the middle class to pay more in taxes so that he could give another $250,000 tax cut to people making more than $3 million a year. . . .

6 It's like Robin Hood in reverse. . . .

7 . . . They have tried to sell us this trickle-down, tax cut fairy dust before. . . . It didn't work then; it won't work now. It's not a plan to create jobs. It's not a plan to reduce our deficit. And it is not a plan to move our economy forward.

(continued)

8 . . . We need tax cuts for working Americans. We need tax cuts for families who are trying to raise kids, and keep them healthy, and send them to college, and keep a roof over their heads.

9 So that's the choice in this election. That's what this is about. That's why I'm running for a second term as President of the United States. . . .

10 . . . Four years ago, I promised to cut middle-class taxes—that's exactly what I've done, by a total of about $3,600 for the typical family. . . .

11 . . . [W]hen a construction worker has got some money in his pocket, he goes out and buys a new car. When a teacher is getting paid a decent wage, that means they can maybe take their family to a restaurant once in a while. And when the middle class is doing well, then business is doing well, and those at the top do well. Everybody does well. That's what we believe in—an economy that grows from the middle class out and the bottom up. That's the choice in this election. . . .

12 And over the course of the next three months, the other side is going to spend more money than we have ever seen on ads that basically say the same thing you've been hearing for months. They know their economics theory won't sell, so their ads are going to say the same thing over and over again, which is: The economy is not where it needs to be and it's Obama's fault. . . .

13 Their strategists admit it. They say . . . we're not going to put out any plans. We're just going to see if this works. . . .

14 They don't have that plan. I do. . . .

15 And if you still believe in me, and you're willing to stand with me, and knock on some doors for me, make some phone calls with me, work hard and organize and mobilize with me for the next three months, we will finish what we started in 2008, and we will show the world why the United States of America is the greatest nation on Earth.

—From "Remarks by the President at Campaign Event—Stamford, CT" by Barack Obama

1. What is the claim made in this speech?

   A. Top-down economics doesn't work.

   B. Americans are hard-working people.

   C. Romney's economic plan is to give rich people a tax cut.

   D. People should vote for Obama for a second term.

2. Which piece of evidence below is a verifiable fact?

   A. Obama cut taxes by about $3,600 for the middle-class family.

   B. The United States has the best workers in the world.

   C. Any country in the world would want to trade places with the United States.

   D. The United States is the best country on Earth.

3. The speaker gives Romney's tax plan as an example to _____ the idea that trickle-down economics doesn't work.

4. The evidence about middle-class families helping the economy when they have more disposable income is logically _____ to the idea that raising taxes on the middle class in order to give the rich a tax cut will not help the economy.

5. Which phrase best describes the evidence presented to support the speaker's claim?

   A. sound reasoning and valid evidence

   B. sound reasoning but invalid evidence

   C. faulty reasoning and invalid evidence

   D. faulty reasoning but valid evidence

6. Which of the following sentences most strongly supports the speaker's claim?

A. The opponent says that problems with the economy are Obama's fault.

B. The opponent spends money on ads that repeat the same message.

C. The opponent wants to cut taxes to stimulate the economy.

D. The opponent doesn't have a solid economic plan, but Obama does.

 Test-Taking Tip

When you take a test, go for the "low-hanging fruit" first; that is, answer all the questions that are easy for you to answer. Answering the easy questions first leaves you more time for the questions that you might find more challenging. This technique prevents you from getting stuck on a question that you might not immediately be able to answer, and it increases your chances of completing the greatest number of items.

Writing Practice

To get elected or appointed to a position, politicians and community leaders give campaign speeches. These carefully crafted speeches are designed to convince the audience that the speaker is the best person for the job.

Directions: Write a short campaign speech describing why you or someone else should be elected to a political position. This can be a position in your town, in a school community, or in a larger political body. Provide facts and reasons as evidence for your claim that you should be elected. Finally, write a few sentences evaluating the validity and reasoning of your claim, explaining how you connected your evidence to your claim logically and gave sound reasons for your claim.

_____

_____

_____

_____

_____

_____

_____

_____

_____

_____

_____

_____

_____

_____

_____

_____

_____

_____

_____

This lesson will help you practice evaluating logic and identifying hidden assumptions in two texts. Use it with core lesson 6.5 Evaluate Logic and Identify Hidden Assumptions to reinforce and apply your knowledge.

Key Concept	Core Skills
Authors may support their claims with arguments based on logical reasoning.	• Identify Stated Assumptions • Infer Hidden Assumptions

Evaluating Arguments Founded on Logical Reasoning

For some arguments, supporting evidence, such as facts, examples, and expert opinion, is not available or appropriate, so the writer needs to base the argument on logical reasoning instead. The writer starts by making an assumption and then builds the argument using the assumption as the basis for a series of deductions.

Directions: Read the passage below. Then complete the activities.

Overcoming Obesity

1 Doctors say that obesity causes or aggravates diseases such as diabetes, high blood pressure, and heart disease. In fact, about 90 percent of the type II diabetes cases worldwide are caused by excessive weight. The causes of obesity are too varied for doctors to be able to suggest a simple solution to the problem

2 According to the U.S. Centers for Disease Control and Prevention, "Overweight and obesity are both labels for ranges of weight that are greater than what is generally considered healthy for a given height." In medical terms, obesity means having a body-mass index (BMI) of 30 or higher. BMI is an estimate of total body fat. It is based on a calculation using a person's height and weight.

3 Despite the many negative effects of obesity, about 34 percent of adults and 17 percent of children 2–19 years old in the United States are obese. Obesity is also a problem in most other industrialized countries.

4 Some studies support an explanation of body weight called the "set-point theory." According to the set-point theory, a person's genes determine his or her preferred weight. The brain adjusts a person's metabolism and eating behavior to maintain weight at this genetically determined level. No one has proved the set-point theory. However, doctors have observed that most people's bodies resist a weight that is lower than the "normal" weight for that person.

(continued)

5 Some people believe that the set-point theory helps explain why people find it difficult to maintain weight loss. These people are fighting against their bodies' set points. To weigh less than their set points, they must constantly exercise and limit food intake.

6 There is evidence that environmental factors have a strong influence on weight gain and obesity. Researchers have found that obesity affects people in wealthier industrial countries more than people in poorer countries. Because there is a large food supply in industrial nations, the people there tend to eat more high-calorie, processed foods. Because they have access to transportation and do less manual labor, they have lower levels of physical activity.

7 Doctors believe that many weight-loss programs are mostly ineffective. As many as 95 percent of people who lose weight on a specific program will gain back the weight within five years. Because body weight is the result of genes, environment, metabolism, behavior, and socioeconomic status, there is no one solution for weight loss.

1. What is the claim in this passage?

   A. It is that 95 percent of people who lose weight on a diet will gain it back.

   B. It is that a person's BMI determines whether or not that person is obese.

   C. It is that people in wealthy countries have a higher risk for being obese.

   D. It is that the causes of obesity are too varied to suggest a simple solution.

2. Which statement is an assumption made in the passage?

   A. that a person's genes determine his or her preferred weight

   B. that obesity is a medical problem that needs to be solved

   C. that the BMI is based on a calculation using height and weight

   D. that people in industrialized countries have lower levels of physical activity

3. What purpose does the explanation of the set-point theory serve in this passage?

   A. It is a claim.

   B. It is a deduction.

   C. It is an assumption.

   D. It is a fact.

4. Which of the following definitions best fits the meaning of the word **intake** as it is used in paragraph 5?

   A. a quantity of something taken in

   B. an opening through which fluid flows

   C. a contraction or narrowing of fabric

   D. a shaft that serves to ventilate

5. The author of this passage builds an argument using a series of _____ from studies on obesity to support the claim.

Evaluating Arguments Based on Hidden Assumptions

Sometimes, the assumption on which a writer bases an argument is unstated, or "hidden." If the reasoning in the argument depends on the reader accepting an idea that is not explicitly stated, then this idea is the hidden assumption. The validity of this supposition affects the validity of the argument as a whole. It can be challenging to find this assumption.

Directions: Read the passage below. Then complete the activities.

[T]he works of the poet may be considered in a very different light from those of the painter and the statuary. Shak[e]speare, inimitable Shak[e]speare, will remain the subject of admiration as long as taste and literature shall exist. . . . [H]is writings will be handed down to posterity in their native beauty, although the present attempt to add to his fame should prove entirely abortive. Here, then, is the great difference. If the endeavor to improve the picture or the statue should be unsuccessful, the beauty of the original would be destroyed, and the injury be irreparable. In such a case, let the artist refrain from using the chisel or the pencil. [But] with the works of the poet no such danger occurs . . . [T]he critic need not be afraid of employing his pen, for the original will continue unimpaired. . . . That Shak[e]speare is the first of dramatic writers will be denied by few. I doubt whether it will be denied by any who have really studied his works, and compared the beauties which they contain with the very finest productions either of our own or of former ages. It must, however, be acknowledged, by his warmest admirers, that some defects are to be found in the writings of our immortal bard. The language is not always faultless. Many words and expressions occur which are of so indecent a nature as to render it highly desirable that they should be erased. Of these, the greater part are evidently introduced to gratify the bad taste of the age in which he lived. [T]he rest may perhaps be ascribed to his own unbridled fancy. But neither the vicious taste of the age, nor the brilliant effusions of wit, can afford an excuse for profaneness or obscenity. . . . [I]f these could be obliterated, the transcendent genius of the poet would undoubtedly shine with more unclouded lustre. To banish every thing of this nature from the writings of Shak[e]speare is the object of the present undertaking. My earnest wish is to render his plays unsullied by any scene, by any speech, or if possible, by any word that can give pain to the most chaste, or offence to the most religious of his readers.

—From *The Family Shakespeare* by Thomas Bowdler

1. What is the author's claim in this passage?

A. that families should read Shakespeare's plays

B. that Shakespeare is a widely admired dramatic writer

C. that Shakespeare wrote for the tastes and language of his age

D. that the language in Shakespeare's works should be cleaned up

2. What is the hidden assumption in this passage?

A. that Shakespeare compares favorably with modern productions of plays

B. that words that may offend readers lower the artistic quality of literature

C. that Shakespeare's works would be more beautiful without obscene words

D. that critics can change words in a passage and not damage the original work

3. Which assumption do you have to accept to evaluate the author's argument as valid?

    A. Changing a painting or a sculpture damages the work.

    B. Changing a painting or a sculpture does not damage the work.

    C. Changing the words in a work of literature damages the work.

    D. Changing the words in a work of literature does not damage the work.

4. When you evaluate this argument for validity, which statement would you decide is based on an invalid assumption?

    A. Shakespeare's works should be read by everyone who loves literature.

    B. Shakespeare's words fit with the language of his times and his culture.

    C. Shakespeare's genius would shine more if his works were censored.

    D. Shakespeare's plays are among the finest in dramatic literature.

5. The author of this passage _____ that Shakespeare's use of obscene language is a defect in his writing.

 Test-Taking Tip

When you are taking a computer-based test, remember that you will not be able to return to a question after you have submitted the answer. Before clicking the Submit button, reread the question and your answer. Make sure that you have correctly understood the question and answer choices and that you selected the answer you intended to select.

Language Practice

Verbs may be active or passive. If the subject of the sentence performs the action, the verb is active. If the subject receives the action, the verb is passive. A passive verb includes a form of the verb *be* and the past participle of the main verb.

Directions: Fill in the blank in each sentence with a passive form of the verb in parentheses.

1 Tests _____ (give) to determine whether students have mastered the material taught.

2 In England, tea _____ (drink) for many reasons: to warm you up, to cool you down, to wake you up, and to calm you down.

3 Last Sunday Jaime _____ (see) running a marathon in the city.

4 Tuxedos _____ (wear) only for formal occasions.

Writing Practice

Many arguments rest on hidden assumptions. This often happens when the writer or speaker believes that the audience understands and agrees with the assumption. Think about political campaign speeches. Candidates often talk about how their policies will not involve raising taxes. The underlying, unstated assumption is that no one wants to pay higher taxes.

Directions: Think of a way of behaving that most people believe is appropriate. Then write a short paragraph suggesting that people follow a rule at work based on this assumption, but do not state the assumption. Be sure to support your claim with logical reasoning. Then state your hidden assumption in a separate sentence.

_____

_____

_____

_____

_____

_____

_____

_____

_____

_____

_____

_____

_____

_____

_____

_____

_____

_____

This lesson will help you practice comparing the formats of two similar texts. Use it with core lesson 7.1 Compare Similar Topics in Different Formats to reinforce and apply your knowledge.

Key Concept

Different writers can present similar information in different formats. Each format fits the message the writer wants to convey.

Core Skills

- Compare Two Texts in Different Formats
- Compare Fiction and Nonfiction

Comparing Texts on Similar Topics

Two texts about the same topic can be presented in different ways. The texts might have differing formats; that is, they might be arranged differently. In addition, the writing could be influenced by the context, or the circumstances in which the author wrote. Format and context affect a reader's understanding of a text.

Directions: Read the passage below. Then complete the activities.

1 Some idea of the impression which Mammoth Cave makes upon the senses, irrespective even of sight, may be had from the fact that blind people go there to see it, and are greatly struck with it. . . . The blind seem as much impressed by it as those who have their sight. When the guide pauses at the more interesting point, or lights the scene up with a great torch . . . and points out the more striking features, the blind exclaim, "How wonderful! How beautiful!" They can feel it, if they cannot see it. They get some idea of the spaciousness when words are uttered. The voice goes forth in these colossal chambers like a bird. When no word is spoken, the silence is of a kind never experienced on the surface of the earth. . . . This, and the absolute darkness, to a person with eyes makes him feel as if he were face to face with the primordial nothingness. . . .

2 Here in the loose soil are ruts worn by cart-wheels in 1812, when, during the war with Great Britain, the earth was searched to make saltpetre. The guide kicks corn-cobs out of the dust where the oxen were fed at noon, and they look nearly as fresh as ever they did. In those frail corn-cobs and in those wheel-tracks, as if the carts had but just gone along, one seemed to come very near to the youth of the century, almost to overtake it.

3 Probably the prettiest thing they have to show you in Mammoth Cave is the "Star Chamber." . . . The guide takes your lantern from you and leaves you seated upon a bench by the wayside, in the profound cosmic darkness. He retreats down a side alley that seems to go down to a lower level, and at a certain point shades his lamp with his hat, so that the light falls upon the ceiling over your head. You look up, and the first thought is that there is an opening just there that permits you to look forth upon the midnight skies. You see the darker horizon line where the sky ends and the mountains begin. The sky is blue-black and is thickly studded with stars—rather small stars, but apparently genuine. At one point a long luminous streak simulates exactly the form and effect of a comet.

(continued)

4 As you gaze, the guide slowly moves his hat, and a black cloud gradually creeps over the sky, and all is blackness again. Then you hear footsteps retreating and dying away in the distance. Presently all is still, save the ringing in your own ears. Then after a few moments, during which you have sat in silence like that of the interstellar spaces, you hear over your left shoulder a distant flapping of wings, followed by the crowing of a cock. You turn your head in that direction and behold a faint dawn breaking on the horizon. It slowly increases till you hear footsteps approaching, and your dusky companion, playing the part of Apollo with lamp in hand, ushers in the light of day. It is rather theatrical, but a very pleasant diversion nevertheless.

—From "In Mammoth Cave" by John Burroughs

1 Mammoth Cave National Park was established in 1941. It preserves and protects the world's longest known cave system, along with a portion of the Green River valley and much of south central Kentucky. More than 400 miles of its caves have been explored to date.

2 Study has shown the park to be far more complex than first imagined, and not simply because of its labyrinthine underground. The area sustains a broad diversity of plant and animal life, in myriad specialized and interconnected ecosystems. More than 70 threatened, endangered, or state-listed species make their homes there. The Federal Endangered Species Act of 1973 gives park officials the means to ensure the survival of these species.

3 The cave system ecosystem ranks among the most diverse in the world, hosting more than 130 varieties of animal. These species are almost equally divided among the three classes of cave life: troglobites, which need a cave environment to survive; troglophiles, which can survive in or out of caves; and trogloxenes, which use caves primarily for refuge.

4 Even if one does not consider the abundance of life underground, the Mammoth Cave area merits its National Park status due solely to the extraordinary density and variety of its plant life. While . . . Great Smoky Mountains National Park, has approximately 1,500 flowering species in its more than 500,000 acres, Mammoth Cave National Park supports more than 1,300 species within only one-tenth of that acreage.

5 The park is open to visitors year-round. Most of its resources and facilities are available free of charge. The following fees are charged for cave tours, camping, and selected picnic shelters.

Cave Tour Fees			
Cave Tour	Adults	Youth*	Seniors
Mammoth Passage Tour	$5.00	$3.50	$2.50
Historic Tour	$12.00	$8.00	$6.00
Grand Avenue Tour	$24.00	$18.00	$12.00
Great Onyx Tour	$15.00	$11.00	$7.50
Violet City Lantern Tour	$15.00	$11.00	$7.50
River Styx Tour	$13.00	$9.00	$6.50
Star Chamber Tour	$12.00	$8.00	$6.00
Wild Cave Tour	$48.00	n/a	$24.00
Introduction to Caving	$23.00	$18.00	$11.50
Trog	n/a	$14.00	n/a
*Youth is 6–12 years of age.			

Campground and Picnic Shelter Fees	
Campsite/ Picnic Area	Fee *Senior discounts in ( )*
Mammoth Cave Campground	$17.00 *($8.50)*
Maple Springs Group Camp	$30.00
Houchins Ferry Campground	$12.00 *($6.00)*
Open-Air Picnic Shelter	$25.00/day; limited availability
Enclosed Picnic Shelter	$50.00/day; one shelter, available Sat/Sun March 1– Memorial Day; daily Memorial Day–Labor Day; Sat/Sun Labor Day–November 30

1. The _____ of both passages is Mammoth Cave.

2. Which contextual fact most affects your understanding of passage 1?

A. It is an excerpt from a longer work.

B. It was written in the late 19th century.

C. It is a work of nonfiction.

D. It was written by a nature essayist.

3. Who is the intended audience for passage 2?

A. park visitors

B. historians

C. families

D. conservationists

4. How do the main purposes of the two passages differ?

A. passage 1 was written to inform; passage 2 was written to entertain.

B. passage 1 was written to persuade; passage 2 was written to inform.

C. passage 1 was written to entertain; passage 2 was written to inform.

D. passage 1 was written to entertain; passage 2 was written to persuade.

Comparing Fiction and Nonfiction

It is not always easy to distinguish fiction from nonfiction, especially when the fictional tale is rooted in fact. By studying a text's characteristics, you can identify it as fiction or nonfiction. Pay particular attention to the text's context, purpose, and tone.

Directions: Read the passage below. Then complete the activities.

1 There were three sorts of persons distinguished by the Tribunal as suspected of heresy [belief disagreeing with a particular religion, in this case Catholicism]: those who were lightly suspected, those who were seriously suspected, and those who were violently suspected.

2 There were three methods of torture; the cord, fire, and water. In the first method, they tied the hands behind the back of the patient by means of a cord which passed through a pulley attached to the roof, and the executioners drew him up as high as possible. After suspending him for some time, the cord was loosened, and he fell within six inches of the ground. This terrible shock dislocated all the joints and cut the flesh even to the sinews. The process was renewed every hour and left the patient without strength or motion. It was not until after the physician had declared that the sufferer could no longer endure the torture without dying, that the Inquisitors sent him back to prison.

(continued)

3 The second was performed by means of water. The executioners stretched the victim over a wooden instrument like a spout . . . without any bottom but a stick passing across it. The body falling backwards, came to such a position that the feet were higher than the head. In this cruel position the executioners passed into the throat a piece of fine linen, wet, a part of which covered the nostrils. They then turned water into the mouth and nose and left it to filter so slowly that one hour at least was consumed before the sufferer had swallowed a drop, although it trickled without interruption. Thus the patient found no interval for respiration.

4 If by this second torment they could obtain no confession, the inquisitors resorted to fire. For this purpose the executioners tied the hands and feet in such a manner that the sufferer could not change his position. They then rubbed the feet with oil and lard, and other penetrating matter, and placed them before the fire, until the flesh was so roasted that the bones and sinews appeared in every part.

—From *Records of the Spanish Inquisition,* translated by Andrew Dickson White

1 Unreal!—Even while I breathed there came to my nostrils the breath of the vapour of heated iron! A suffocating odour pervaded the prison! A deeper glow settled each moment in the eyes that glared at my agonies! A richer tint of crimson diffused itself over the pictured horrors of blood. . . . I gasped for breath! There could be no doubt of the design of my tormentors—oh! . . . most demoniac of men! Yet, for a wild moment, did my spirit refuse to comprehend the meaning of what I saw. At length it forced—it wrestled its way into my soul—it burned itself in upon my shuddering reason.—Oh! for a voice to speak!—oh! horror!—oh! any horror but this! With a shriek, I rushed from the margin, and buried my face in my hands—weeping bitterly. . . .

2 "Death," I said, "any death but that of the pit!" Fool! Might I have not known that into the pit it was the object of the burning iron to urge me? Could I . . . withstand its pressure? And now, flatter and flatter grew the lozenge . . . . Its centre, and of course, its greatest width, came just over the yawning gulf. I shrank back—but the closing walls pressed me resistlessly onward. At length for my seared and writhing body there was no longer an inch of foothold on the firm floor of the prison. I struggled no more, but the agony of my soul found vent in one loud, long, and final scream of despair. I felt that I tottered upon the brink—I averted my eyes—

3 There was a discordant hum of human voices! There was a loud blast as of many trumpets! There was a harsh grating as of a thousand thunders! The fiery walls rushed back! An outstretched arm caught my own as I fell, fainting, into the abyss. It was that of General Lasalle. The French army had entered Toledo. The Inquisition was in the hands of its enemies.

—From "The Pit and the Pendulum" by Edgar Allan Poe

1. What is the topic of both of these passages?

   A. the key players in the creation of the Spanish Inquisition

   B. the purposes behind the formation of the Spanish Inquisition

   C. the methods of torture used during the Spanish Inquisition

   D. the events that led to the end of the Spanish Inquisition

2. What is the difference in the way the authors approach the subject?

   A. White criticizes the methods used by the inquisitors; Poe shows sympathy for the accused.

   B. White gives a factual account of torture methods; Poe focuses on the terror felt by the prisoner.

   C. White details the torture experienced by one man; Poe writes about the experiences of many.

   D. White writes from the point of view of the inquisitor; Poe writes from the point of view of the accused.

3. What is the main purpose of passage 1?

   A. to help

   B. to persuade

   C. to entertain

   D. to inform

4. Which of the following definitions best fits the meaning of the word **instrument** as it is used in paragraph 3 of passage 1?

   A. a device used to produce music

   B. a means of getting something done

   C. a measuring device

   D. a tool or an implement

5. The characteristics of "The Pit and the Pendulum" help me determine that its genre is _____.

 Test-Taking Tip

If you aren't happy with your score in one or more subject tests, consider retaking the test in those subjects. You can retake each subject up to three times a year. You will be at an advantage the second time around because you can focus your studying, and you'll be familiar with the test's format.

Writing Practice

One of the first decisions an author has to make is how he or she will address a topic. For example, will the writer tell a fictional story about the topic or write a nonfiction article? If nonfiction is chosen, will the writer shares facts, express opinions, or both? Writers must also select the format that will best convey their message to the audience.

Directions: Write two accounts of a significant event in your life, such as meeting a future spouse or partner, getting your first job, or learning how to drive a car. The first account should be informational. Provide facts and details about the event. Write the second account as if it were a fictional story or a persuasive essay. Use language that conveys your purpose.

_____

_____

_____

_____

_____

_____

_____

_____

_____

_____

_____

_____

_____

_____

_____

_____

_____

_____

This lesson will help you practice comparing two texts from similar genres. Use it with core lesson 7.2 Compare Similar Genres to reinforce and apply your knowledge.

Key Concept

Authors may use similar genres to address common themes or ideas.

Core Skills

- Determine Genre
- Compare Similar Genres

Identifying Genre

A genre is a category of writing that has specific characteristics. Identifying the differences in genres helps the reader understand the differences in the authors' purposes for writing.

Directions: Read the passages below. Then complete the activities.

1 Tea began as a medicine and grew into a beverage. In China, in the eighth century, it entered the realm of poetry as one of the polite amusements. The fifteenth century saw Japan ennoble it into a religion of aestheticism—Teaism. Teaism is a cult founded on the adoration of the beautiful among the sordid facts of everyday existence. It inculcates purity and harmony, the mystery of mutual charity, the romanticism of the social order. It is essentially a worship of the Imperfect, as it is a tender attempt to accomplish something possible in this impossible thing we know as life. . . .

2 The long isolation of Japan from the rest of the world, so conducive to introspection, has been highly favorable to the development of Teaism. Our home and habits, costume and cuisine, porcelain, lacquer, painting—our very literature—all have been subject to its influence. No student of Japanese culture could ever ignore its presence. It has permeated the elegance of noble boudoirs, and entered the abode of the humble. Our peasants have learned to arrange flowers, our meanest laborer to offer his salutation to the rocks and waters. In our common parlance we speak of the man "with no tea" in him, when he is insusceptible to the serio-comic interests of the personal drama. Again we stigmatize the untamed aesthete who, regardless of the mundane tragedy, runs riot in the springtide of emancipated emotions, as one "with too much tea" in him.

3 The outsider may indeed wonder at this seeming much ado about nothing. What a tempest in a tea-cup! he will say. But when we consider how small after all the cup of human enjoyment is, how soon overflowed with tears, how easily drained to the dregs in our quenchless thirst for infinity, we shall not blame ourselves for making so much of the tea-cup. Mankind has done worse. . . .

4 Those who cannot feel the littleness of great things in themselves are apt to overlook the greatness of little things in others. The average Westerner, in his sleek complacency, will see in the tea ceremony but another instance of the thousand and one oddities which constitute the quaintness and childishness of the East to him. He was wont to regard Japan as barbarous while she indulged in the gentle arts of peace: he calls her civilized since she began to commit wholesale slaughter on Manchurian battlefields. Much comment has been given lately to the Code of the Samurai—the Art of Death which makes our soldiers exult in self-sacrifice; but scarcely any attention has been drawn to Teaism, which represents so much of our Art of Life.

—From *The Book of Tea* by Kakuzo Okakura

A History of Japanese Americans in California: Immigration

1 One of the first groups of settlers that came from Japan to the United States, the Wakamatsu Tea and Silk Farm Colony under the leadership of John Schnell, arrived at Cold Hill, El Dorado County, in June 1869. Additional colonists arrived in the fall of 1869. These first immigrants brought mulberry trees, silk cocoons, tea plants, bamboo roots, and other agricultural products. The U.S. Census of 1870 showed 55 Japanese in the United States; 33 were in California, with 22 living at Gold Hill. Within a few years of the colony's founding, the colonists had dispersed, their agricultural venture a failure.

2 The 1880 Census showed 86 Japanese in California, with a total of 148 in the United States. Possibly these were students, or Japanese who had illegally left their country, since Japanese laborers were not allowed to leave their country until after 1884 when an agreement was signed between the Japanese government and Hawaiian sugar plantations to allow labor immigration. From Hawaii, many Japanese continued on to the United States mainland. . . .

3 Laborers for the Hawaiian sugar plantations were carefully chosen. . . . [A] systematic method of recruiting workers from specific regions in Japan was established. Natives from Hiroshima, Kumamoto, Yamaguchi, and Fukushima were sought for their supposed expertise in agriculture, for their hard work, and for their willingness to travel. . . .

4 Except for a temporary suspension of immigration to Hawaii in 1900, the flow of immigration from Japan remained relatively unaffected until 1907–08, when agitation from white supremacist organizations, labor unions, and politicians resulted in the "Gentlemen's Agreement," curtailing further immigration of laborers from Japan. A provision in the Gentlemen's Agreement, however, permitted wives and children of laborers, as well as laborers who had already been in the United States, to continue to enter the country. Until that time, Japanese immigrants had been primarily male. The 1900 Census indicates that only 410 of 24,326 Japanese were female. From 1908 to 1924, Japanese women continued to immigrate to the United States, some as "picture brides."

5 In Japan . . . go-betweens arranged marriages between compatible males and females. . . . [A]n exchange of photographs became a first step in this long process. Entering the bride's name in the groom's family registry legally constituted marriage. Those Japanese males who could afford the cost of traveling to Japan returned there to be married. Others resorted to long-distance . . . marriages. . . . [T]he bride would immigrate to the United States as the wife of a laborer. . . . For wives who entered after 1910, the first glimpse of the United States was the Detention Barracks at Angel Island in San Francisco Bay. New immigrants were processed there, and given medical exams. As a result, this was the place where most "picture brides" saw their new husbands for the first time.

—From "A History of Japanese Americans in California," National Park Service

1. Which genres are used in the two passages?

    A. The first passage is biography, and the second passage is historical fiction.

    B. The first passage is autobiography, and the second passage is biography.

    C. The first passage is an essay, and the second passage is a historical article.

    D. The first passage is a folktale, and the second passage is an essay.

2. The main purpose of both passages is to
_____ readers about Japanese culture.

3. What is the main difference in literary technique between the two passages?

    A. Passage 1 includes vivid descriptions and connotative language; passage 2 relies on facts and figures.

    B. Passage 1 begins in the 8th century; passage 2 begins in the 19th century, which affects the authors' perspectives.

    C. Passage 1 is about Teaism in Japan; passage 2 is about immigrants.

    D. Passage 1 contains a plot; passage contains only facts and figures.

4. How does the portrayal of the Japanese differ in these two passages?

    A. Passage 1 depicts the Japanese as hard working; passage 2 depicts the Japanese as lazy.

    B. Passage 1 shows the refinement of Japanese culture; passage 2 shows the plight of Japanese laborers in America.

    C. Passage 1 emphasizes the woman's place in Japan; passage 2 highlights the lack of Japanese women in America at the turn of the 20th century.

    D. Passage 1 depicts Japanese culture as more advanced than other cultures; passage 2 depicts Japanese culture as less advanced than American culture.

 Test-Taking Tip

When you are writing an extended response, pay attention to grammar, punctuation, and spelling. The computer-based scoring system will notice errors just as a human would. Study and practice the rules of grammar, punctuation, and spelling ahead of time so you can focus on the content of your essay. And don't forget to check for typographical errors before you submit your response.

Comparing Texts from Similar Genres

Some nonfiction texts, such as memoirs, biographies, or letters, are narratives. They tell the story of a person, event, time, or place. As you compare narrative texts of similar genres, pay attention to text features, literary techniques, tone, and the author's attitude toward his or her topic.

Directions: Read the passage below. Then complete the activities.

1 As we edged our way out to a better position, the sun rose and threw a series of three rainbows in the mist clouds as they floated up out of the shadowed depths. The lowest and clearest of these semicircles of irised spray seemed to spring from a patch of bright saffron sand, where it was laid bare by the melting snow. Now I know where the story of the gold at the end of the rainbow came from.

2 Carr and I tried to come through from the canyon by moonlight last night and had rather a bad time of it. First a fog obscured the moon. Then we tried to take a shortcut by following the telephone line, got lost in the dark, and stayed lost till the moon set and made it darker still. In cutting across the hills to get back into Hayden Valley, Carr fell over a snow bank and landed right in the middle of the road . . . .

3 After a while we were lost again, this time in a level space bounded on four sides by a winding creek. I know it was on four sides of the place, for we carefully walked off toward each point of the compass in rotation, and each time landed in the creek. We finally escaped by wading. How we got in without wading will always be a mystery. . . .

4 We passed the famous and only Mud Geyser an hour before daybreak. Things were in a bad way with him, judging from the noise. . . . Carr said it reminded him of something between a mad bull buffalo and a boatload of seasick tourists when the summer wind stirs up the lake. But Carr was too tired and disgusted to be elegant. Indeed, we were both pretty well played out. Personally, I felt just about like the Mud Geyser sounded.

—From *Down the Yellowstone* by Lewis R. Freeman, 1922

November 1st [1868]

1 I was extremely glad to receive yet one more of your ever welcome letters. . . . I am not surprised to hear of your leaving Madison and am anxious to know where your lot will be cast. . . . If you make your home in California, I know from experience how keenly you will feel the absence of the special flowers you love. . . . [However,] I think that you will find in California just what you desire in climate and scenery, for both are so varied.

2 March is the springtime of the plains, April the summer, and May the autumn. The other months are dry and wet winter. . . . I rode across the seasons in going to the Yosemite last spring. I started from the Joaquin in the last week of May. All the plain flowers, so lately fresh in the power of full beauty, were dead. Their parched leaves crisped and fell to powder. . . .

(continued)

3 After riding for two days in this autumn I found summer again in the higher foothills. Flower petals were spread confidingly open, the grasses waved their branches all bright and gay in the colors of healthy prime, and the winds and streams were cool. Forty or fifty miles further into the mountains, I came to spring. The leaves on the oak were small and drooping, and they still retained their first tintings of crimson and purple, and the wrinkles of their bud folds were distinct as if newly opened. . . .

4 A few miles farther "onward and upward" I found the edge of winter. Scarce a grass could be seen. . . . Soon my horse was plunging in snow ten feet in depth, the sky became darker and more terrible, many-voiced mountain winds swept the pines, speaking the dread language of the cold north. . . .

5 Descending these higher mountains towards the Yosemite, the snow gradually disappeared from the pines and the sky . . . and violets appeared again, and I once more found spring in the grand valley. Thus meet and blend the seasons of these mountains and plains, beautiful in their joinings as those of lake and land or of the bands of the rainbow. . . .

Ever yours most cordially,

J.M.

—From *Letters to a Friend* by John Muir

---

1. The genre of passage 1 is _____.
The genre of passage 2 is _____.

2. How do the authors' attitudes toward their topic differ?

A. Lewis: disgusted; Muir: fearful

B. Lewis: surprised; Muir: awestruck

C. Lewis: awestruck; Muir: amused

D. Lewis: amused; Muir: amazed

3. Which of the following definitions best fits the meaning of the word **keenly** as it is used in paragraph 1 of passage 2?

A. cleverly

B. intensely

C. sharply

D. sensitively

4. Compare the two passages by evaluating the topic, text features, and tone. Then write each passage's unique characteristics in the appropriate sections of the graphic organizer and the shared characteristics in the overlapping section.

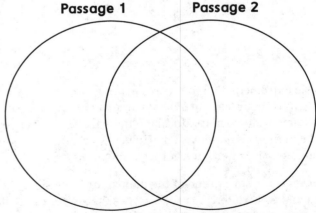

Passage 1   Passage 2

first person   humorous

nature   vivid description

date and signature   addresses reader

friendly but serious

Writing Practice

Biographies are about the life of a person written by someone other than that person. Autobiographies are about the life of the author. These genres are related, but each has its own distinct qualities, influenced by the author's purpose and point of view.

Directions: Write two paragraphs about yourself: the first as a biography and the second as an autobiography. The point of view of the biography should be objective and written in the third person. The autobiography should be subjective and written in the first person. Before you begin writing, choose your purpose for writing in each genre.

_____

_____

_____

_____

_____

_____

_____

_____

_____

_____

_____

_____

_____

_____

_____

_____

_____

_____

_____

This lesson will help you practice analyzing opposing arguments expressed in two texts. Use it with core lesson 7.3 Analyze Two Arguments to reinforce and apply your knowledge.

Key Concept

In order to choose which side of an argument to support, a reader must evaluate the evidence and logic used by each side.

Core Skills

- Compare Arguments
- Evaluate Evidence in Opposing Arguments

Comparing and Contrasting Two Arguments

For every argument in favor of an opinion, there is likely to be an argument that disputes, or argues against it. When reading an argument, begin by identifying the claim. Then analyze the evidence to determine whether the claim is valid and supported.

Directions: Read the passages below. Then complete the activities.

1 Not very long before birth the human embryo is strikingly similar to the embryo of the ape; still earlier, it presents an appearance very like that of the embryos of other mammals lower in the scale, like the cat and the rabbit . . . Indeed, as we trace back the still earlier history, more and more characters are found which are the common properties of wider and wider arrays of organisms. [A]t one time the embryo exhibits gill-slits in the sides of its throat which in all essential respects are just like those of the embryos of birds and reptiles and amphibian . . . Can we reasonably regard these resemblances as indications of anything else but a community of ancestry of the forms that exhibit them?

2 Yet a still more wonderful fact is revealed by the study of the very earliest stages of individual development. The human embryo begins its very existence as a single cell,—nothing more and nothing less . . . I do not think we could ask nature for more complete proof that human beings have evolved from one-cell ancestors as simple as modern protozoa . . . They at least are real and not the logical deductions of reason. . . .

3 And now . . . we may look to nature for fossil evidence regarding the ancestry of our species. Much is known about the remains of many kinds of men who lived in prehistoric times, but we need consider here only one form which lived long before the glacial period in the so-called Tertiary times. In 1894 a scientist named Dubois discovered in Java some of the remains of an animal which was partly ape and partly man. So well did these remains exhibit the characters of Haeckel's hypothetical ape-man, *Pithecanthropus*, that the name fitted the creature like a glove. Specifically, the cranium presents an arch which is intermediate between that of the average ape and of the lowest human beings. It possessed protruding brows like those of the gorilla. The estimated brain capacity was about one thousand cubic centimeters, four hundred more than that of any known ape, and much less than the [human average]. Even without other characters, these would indicate that the animal was actually a "missing link" in the scientific sense,—that is, a form which is near the common progenitors of the modern species of apes and of man. . . . So *Pithecanthropus* is a part of the chain leading to man, not far from the place where the human line sprang from a lower primate ancestor. . . .

4 The foregoing facts illustrate the conclusive evidence brought forward by science that human evolution in physical respects is true. Even if we wished to do so, we cannot do away with the facts of structure and development and fossil history, nor is there any other explanation more reasonable than evolution for these facts.

—From *The Doctrine of Evolution: Its Basis and Its Scope* by Henry Edward Crampton, 1911

1 [I]t would be indeed strange, if no honest man could be found to tell . . . the truth regarding Darwinism. This has occurred sooner than I dared to hope. This chapter can announce the glad tidings that even in "social-democratic science" Darwinism is doomed to decay. Much printer's ink will, of course, be yet wasted before it will be so entirely dead as to be no longer available as a weapon against Christianity; but a beginning at least has been made.

2 In the December [issue] of the ninth year of the *Sozialistische Monatshefte*, a social-democratic writer, Curt Grottewitz, undertakes to bring out an article on "Darwinian Myths." It is stated there that Darwin had a few eminent followers, but that the educated world took no notice of their work; that now, however, they seemed to be attracting more attention. "There is no doubt that a number of Darwinian views, which are still prevalent to-day, have sunk to the level of untenable myths. . . ."

3 Grottewitz very frankly continues: "The difficulty with the Darwinian doctrines consists in the fact that they are incapable of being strictly and irrefutably demonstrated. The origin of one species from another, the conservation of useful forms, the existence of countless intermediary links, are all assumptions, which could never be supported by concrete cases found in actual experience." Some are said to be well established indirectly by proofs drawn from probabilities, while others are proved to be absolutely untenable. Among the latter Grottewitz includes "[natural] selection," which is indeed a monstrous figment of the imagination. There was moreover really no reason for adhering to it so long. It is eminently untrue, that the biological research of the last few years proved for the *first* time the untenableness of this doctrine, as Grottewitz seems to think. Clear thinkers recognized its untenableness long ago . . .

4 It is certainly a very peculiar phenomenon; for decades we behold a doctrine reverently re-echoed; thoughtful investigators expose its folly, but still the worship continues.

—From *At the Deathbed of Darwinism* by Eberhard Dennert, 1904

---

1. What is the claim of Crampton's argument?

A. Human embryos are similar to ape embryos.

B. Humans are physically similar to other types of primates.

C. Fossils provide a record of the evolution of humans over time.

D. Humans have evolved from other species over the centuries.

2. Crampton's argument about evolution is credible because the evidence is based on _____.

3. Which of the following definitions best fits the meaning of the word **scale** as it is used in paragraph 1 of Crampton's argument?

A. a device used to measure weight

B. a thin plate covering the skin, as on a fish

C. a series of tests used to rate performance

D. a graduated series of order

4. What is the claim of the Dennert's argument?

    A. Evolution cannot be proved.

    B. Darwinism damages Christianity.

    C. Darwinism is not widely accepted.

    D. Natural selection is impossible.

5. Dennert _____ Darwin's theory of evolution.

6. Which of these additional claims are most likely to be made by Crampton? Which would be made by Dennert? Write each claim in the correct side of the chart.

Crampton	Dennert

Humans were created in God's image.

Unused traits disappear as a species evolves.

Humankind began with a single cell.

There is no relation between human and monkey.

Analyzing Evidence in Two Arguments

When comparing opposing arguments, readers must carefully evaluate the evidence provided by each author and decide whether it is relevant, accurate, sufficient, credible, and logical, and supports the claim.

Directions: Reread the passages in the previous section. Then choose the best answer to each question.

1. How does the information about Pithecanthropus support Crampton's argument?

    A. It shows that other well-regarded scientists supported Darwin's theory of evolution.

    B. It proves that humans are more highly evolved than other primates.

    C. It supports the claim of the physiological relationship between humans and apes.

    D. It indicates that the *Pithecanthropus* is not the "missing link."

2. Which types of evidence does Crampton use to support his argument?

    A. logic and scientific research/analysis

    B. expert opinion and scientific research/analysis

    C. logic and witness statements

    D. witness statements and expert opinion

3. What type of evidence does Dennert's argument provide?

A. scientific research

B. opinion

C. logic

D. records of events

4. What evidence in Crampton's argument contradicts the claim of Dennert's argument?

A. Cats and rabbits are on the lower end of the evolutionary scale.

B. Humans and apes are primates with similar structures.

C. A "missing link" between ape and human once existed.

D. Amphibians, reptiles, and birds have similar embryonic structures.

✔ Test-Taking Tip

How much should you write for an extended response? The answer is as much as you feel is necessary to clearly answer the question and to provide supporting evidence. If you do not have much to say about the topic, do not try to stretch your material. Adding extraneous or irrelevant information just to add more length can harm your overall score.

Writing Practice

You need to compare and contrast opposing arguments to determine which argument you agree with. To make an informed decision, compare the arguments and evaluate the evidence for accuracy, relevance, and sufficiency. Once you have analyzed the two arguments, you can decide which argument to support.

Directions: Briefly compare and contrast two sides of an argument that you've recently read or heard, such as a debate between two politicians or a disagreement between friends about what movie to go see. Which argument was stronger? Why? Did you agree with either of their arguments? Explain why or why not. Support your viewpoint with examples.

_____

_____

_____

_____

_____

_____

_____

_____

_____

This lesson will help you practice evaluating the impact of genre and format. Use it with core lesson 7.4 Evaluate the Impact of Genre and Format to reinforce and apply your knowledge.

Key Concept

By comparing genres that present similar ideas, readers can identify differences in scope, impact, purpose, and intended audience.

Core Skills

- Compare Text and Image
- Compare Textual Genres

Comparing Textual and Visual Genres

The genre and format that writers choose depends in part on their purpose. Writers, as well as visual artists, consider the impact, or effect, that they want to have on their audience. The same topic presented strictly as text or in a visual format can affect readers in different ways.

Directions: Read the passages, and look at the time line below. Then complete the activities.

Niagara, June 10, 1843

1 The whirlpool I like very much. It is seen to advantage after the great falls; it is so sternly solemn. The river cannot look more imperturbable, almost sullen in its marble green, than it does just below the great fall. But the slight circles that mark the hidden vortex seem to whisper mysteries the thundering voice above could not proclaim—a meaning as untold as ever. . . .

2 It is fearful, too, to know . . . that whatever has been swallowed by the cataract is like to rise suddenly to light here, whether uprooted tree, or body of man or bird.

3 The rapids enchanted me far beyond what I expected. They are so swift that they cease to seem so; you can think only of their beauty. The fountain beyond the Moss Islands I discovered for myself. [I] thought it for some time an accidental beauty which it would not do to leave, lest I might never see it again. After I found it permanent, I returned many times to watch the play of its crest. In the little waterfall beyond, Nature seems, as she often does, to have made a study for some larger design. She delights in this—a sketch within a sketch, a dream within a dream. Wherever we see it, the lines of the great buttress in the fragment of stone, the hues of the waterfall copied in the flowers that star its bordering mosses, we are delighted; for all the lineaments become fluent, and we mold the scene in congenial thought with its genius.

4 People complain of the buildings at Niagara, and fear to see it further deformed. I cannot sympathize with such an apprehension. The spectacle is capable of swallowing up all such objects; they are not seen in the great whole, more than an earthworm in a wide field.

5 And now farewell, Niagara. . . . I will be here again beneath some flooding July moon and sun. Owing to the absence of light, I have seen the rainbow only two or three times by day, the lunar bow not at all. However, the imperial presence needs not its crown, though illustrated by it.

—From *At Home and Abroad; or, Things and Thoughts in America and Europe* by Margaret Fuller Ossoli

Niagara Falls Geology Facts & Figures

- The Niagara River is about 36 miles in length and is the natural outlet from Lake Erie to Lake Ontario. . . .

- More than 6 million cubic feet of water go over the crestline of the Falls every minute during peak daytime tourist hours. . . .

- The rapids above the Falls reach a maximum speed of 25 mph, with the fastest speeds occurring at the Falls themselves (recorded up to 68 mph). The water through the Whirlpool Rapids below the Falls reaches 30 mph, and at Devil's Hole Rapids, 22 mph.

- . . . The huge volume of water rushing from the Falls is crushed into the narrow Great Gorge, creating the Whirlpool Rapids that stretch for 1 mile. The water surface here drops 50 feet and the rushing waters can reach speeds as high as 30 feet per second.

- The whirlpool is a basin 1,700 feet long by 1,200 feet wide, with depths up to 125 feet. This is the elbow, where the river makes a sharp right-angled turn. . . .

- When the Niagara River is at full flow, the waters travel over the rapids and enter the pool, then travel counter-clockwise around the pool past the natural outlet. Pressure builds up . . . and this pressure forces the water under the incoming stream. The swirling waters create a vortex, or whirlpool. . . .

- The [green] color [of the water] comes from . . . dissolved salts and "rock flour," very finely ground rock. [These are] picked up primarily from the limestone bed. [They]probably also [come] from the shales and sandstones under the limestone cap at the falls.

—From "Niagara Falls Geology Facts & Figures" by Niagara Parks

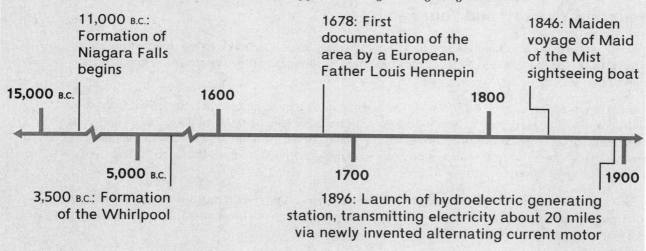

11,000 B.C.: Formation of Niagara Falls begins

1678: First documentation of the area by a European, Father Louis Hennepin

1846: Maiden voyage of Maid of the Mist sightseeing boat

15,000 B.C.   1600   1800

5,000 B.C.   1700   1900

3,500 B.C.: Formation of the Whirlpool

1896: Launch of hydroelectric generating station, transmitting electricity about 20 miles via newly invented alternating current motor

1. "Niagara, June 10, 1843," "Niagara Falls Geology Facts & Figures," and the time line are about the same topic, but their _____ are different.

2. Which of the following definitions best fits the meaning of the word **apprehension** used in paragraph 4 of "Niagara, June 10, 1843"?

   A. capture

   B. comprehension

   C. understanding

   D. concern

3. Which statement best describes the impact of "Niagara, June 10, 1843" on readers?

   A. Readers learn statistics about the features of Niagara Falls.

   B. Readers understand the author's feelings about Niagara Falls.

   C. Readers agree that buildings should be built at Niagara Falls.

   D. Readers learn about of the history of Niagara Falls.

4. Which statement best describes how the time line compares to "Niagara Falls Geology Facts & Figures"?

   A. The time line visually organizes information about the history of Niagara Falls, whereas the passage describes a person's visit to the falls.

   B. The time line gives interesting facts about the water at Niagara Falls, whereas the passage explains the best sites to visit there.

   C. The time line organizes the events of a person's visit to Niagara in a visual way, whereas the passage describes the events on the trip.

   D. The time line visually organizes information about the history of Niagara Falls, whereas the passage lists significant facts about the falls.

Evaluating Differences between Genres

Readers can evaluate the differences between genres by recognizing each genre's unique characteristics. It is helpful to reflect on the intended audience of a piece of writing and to compare the impact of different genres. Also consider the scope, or breadth, of the information presented.

Directions: Read the passage below. Then complete the activity.

Evacuating Yourself and Your Family

1 Evacuations are more common than many people realize. Fires and floods cause evacuations most frequently across the U.S. and almost every year, people along coastlines evacuate as hurricanes approach. . . .

2 In some circumstances, local officials . . . require mandatory evacuations. In others, evacuations are advised or households decide to evacuate to avoid situations they believe are potentially dangerous. When community evacuations become necessary local officials provide information to the public through the media. In some circumstances, other warning methods, such as sirens, text alerts, emails or telephone calls are used. . . .

3 If the event is a weather condition, such as a hurricane, you might have a day or two to get ready. However, many disasters allow no time for people to gather even the most basic necessities, which is why planning ahead is essential.

4 Plan how you will assemble your family and supplies and anticipate where you will go for different situations. Choose several destinations in different directions so you have options in an emergency and know the evacuation routes to get to those destinations. Follow these guidelines for evacuation:

- Plan places where your family will meet, both within and outside of your immediate neighborhood. . . .

- If you have a car, keep a full tank of gas in it if an evacuation seems likely. . . . Gas stations may be closed during emergencies and unable to pump gas during power outages. Plan to take one car per family to reduce congestion and delay.

(continued)

- Become familiar with alternate routes . . . out of your area. . . .

- Leave early enough to avoid being trapped by severe weather.

- Follow recommended evacuation routes. Do not take shortcuts; they may be blocked.

- Be alert for road hazards such as washed-out roads . . . and downed power lines. . . .

- Take your emergency supply kit unless . . . it has been contaminated.

- Listen to a battery-powered radio and follow local evacuation instructions.

- Take your pets with you, but understand that only service animals may be permitted in public shelters. Plan how you will care for your pets in an emergency.

—From "Evacuating Yourself and Your Family" by the Federal Emergency Management Agency

Story of an Eye-Witness

1 The earthquake in San Francisco shook down hundreds of thousands of dollars' worth of walls and chimneys. But the conflagration that followed burned up hundreds of millions of dollars' worth of property. There is no estimating within hundreds of millions the actual damage wrought.

2 Not in history has a modern imperial city been so completely destroyed. San Francisco is gone. Nothing remains of it but memories and a fringe of dwelling houses on its outskirts. Its industrial section is wiped out. Its business section is wiped out. Its social and residential section is wiped out. The factories and warehouses, the great stores and newspaper buildings, the hotels and the palaces . . . are all gone. . . . Within an hour after the earthquake shock, the smoke of San Francisco's burning was a lurid tower visible a hundred miles away. And for three days and nights this lurid tower swayed in the sky, reddening the sun, darkening the day, and filling the land with smoke.

3 On Wednesday morning at a quarter past five came the earthquake. A minute later the flames were leaping upward. In a dozen different quarters south of Market Street, in the working-class ghetto, and in the factories, fires started. There was no opposing the flames. There was no organization, no communication. All the cunning adjustments of a twentieth-century city had been smashed by the earthquake. The streets were humped into ridges and depressions and piled with the debris of fallen walls. The steel rails were twisted into perpendicular and horizontal angles. The telephone and telegraph systems were disrupted. And the great water mains had burst.

4 By Wednesday afternoon . . . half the heart of the city was gone. . . . East, west, north, and south, strong winds were blowing upon the doomed city. The heated air rising made an enormous suck. Thus did the fire of itself build its own colossal chimney through the atmosphere. . . .

(continued)

> **5** San Francisco . . . is like the crater of a volcano, around which are camped tens of thousands of refugees. . . . All the surrounding cities and towns are jammed with the homeless ones, where they are being cared for by the relief committees. The refugees were carried free by the railroads to any point they wished to go, and it is estimated that over one hundred thousand people have left . . . . The government has the situation in hand, and, thanks to the immediate relief given by the whole United States, there is not the slightest possibility of a famine. The bankers and business men have already set about making preparations to rebuild San Francisco.
>
> —From *The Story of an Eye-Witness* by Jack London

1. Evaluate the characteristics that appear below the Venn diagram. Then write each passage's unique characteristics in the outer sections of the circles and the shared characteristics in the overlapping section.

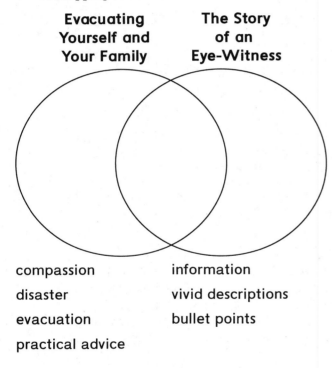

Evacuating Yourself and Your Family   **The Story of an Eye-Witness**

compassion

disaster

evacuation

practical advice

information

vivid descriptions

bullet points

2. Which conclusion could the reader draw about the intended audience of passage 1?

A. They are people who want to prepare for a natural disaster.

B. They are people who have experienced a natural disaster.

C. They are people who want to learn about the weather.

D. They are people who work for the Federal Emergency Management Agency.

3. How does the format support the author's purpose in writing "The Story of an Eye-Witness"?

A. The use of bullets helps explain key concepts about earthquakes.

B. The visual format allows the reader to keep track of the sequence of events.

C. This format allows for rich details that appeal to the reader's emotions.

D. This format allows the writer to be persuasive about earthquake preparedness.

4. In a comparison of how the two passages cover the topic of evacuation, the scope of passage 1 is _____ the scope of passage 2.

A. narrower than

B. broader than

C. equal to

D. superior to

 **Test-Taking Tip**

As you plan to write an extended response, ask yourself, "What is my purpose for writing?" and "Who is my intended audience?" The audience and purpose will influence your choice in genre and format.

Writing Practice

Many people enjoy playing sports or participating in a performing art such as singing or dancing. Knowing the rules or understanding the skills not only helps you play or perform, but it can also enhance your viewing of games or performances.

Directions: Write two paragraphs, each in a different format. In the first paragraph, use bullet points or numbered lists to provide information about the rules of a sport or skills needed to perform a certain song, dance, and so on. In the second paragraph, use descriptive details to write a narrative account of a game or a performance.

_____

_____

_____

_____

_____

_____

_____

_____

_____

_____

_____

_____

_____

_____

_____

_____

Lesson 1.1

Main Idea in Informational Text, p. 1

1. **B** The heading above each section explains what the section is about, which helps you identify the main idea. The title provides information about what the entire passage is about, but does not focus on specific sections. The first and last sentences provide a detail, not the main idea of the sections.

2. **A** Answer A is the only detail that is about the start of work.

3. **C** Answer C tells the main idea of the section. The other sentences are not related to rates.

4. **D** The Change Order section explains how change orders need to be used when the scope of work changes, which includes additional work. The other sections are about different aspects of the PT system.

5. The _____main idea_____ of the passage is that employees must follow the guidelines for using the PT system.

6. **A** The topic sentence is presented at the start of the passage so employees know what the remaining text is about. The topic sentence is not the least important information and it is not required for readers to understand the remainder of the passage or the reverse.

Main Idea in Literary Text, p. 3

1. **A** Answer A explains the main idea of the excerpt. The other sentences do not reflect the details in the passage.

2. **C** The lack of imagination makes the man ill-equipped for the harsh environment. The other details are not about his shortcomings.

3. **D** Answer D explains the main idea of the paragraph. The other sentences are details or untrue.

4. **A** The excerpt is about how instinct is more important than knowledge in severe cold.

5. **B**

6. **D** There is no topic sentence in this passage. It does not have a topic sentence because the author uses details to imply the main idea.

Language Practice, p. 4

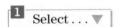
Select . . . ▼

    B. In fact, reality shows

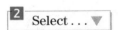
Select . . . ▼

    C. their everyday life, and when the

Select . . . ▼

    B. entertaining to viewers, but they

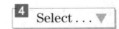
Select . . . ▼

    D. larger profit margin, so hit reality

Writing Practice, p. 5

Make sure your paragraph has a main idea that is expressed by a topic sentence or implied by the supporting details. All of your supporting details should support the main idea.

Answers will vary. Sample answer: Bruce Springsteen was called "The Boss" long before he was a famous singer. He earned the name from the musicians he paid to back him up in his early days. After they performed at a club, the club manager or owner would pay Bruce because he was the person they hired. Bruce would then give the musicians their share of the earnings. The musicians would tease him by calling him "The Boss."

Lesson 1.2

Identifying Supporting Details, p. 7

1. Information about mythology and the calendar are _____supporting_____ details that develop the main idea.

2. **D**   Answer D best supports the main idea that Greeks and Romans contributed to the culture of surrounding areas. It provides examples—traditions and technology—of contributions they made to other cultures. Answers A, B, and C give information about Greeks and Romans, but they do not link this information to the surrounding cultures.

3. **C**   The main idea of paragraph 4 is that mythology had an important role in Greek and Roman culture. Answer C is the only detail that supports this main idea. Answers A, B, and D give details about the Romans and culture, but they do not mention mythology or the Greek or Roman gods.

4. You would expect to find a supporting detail about the Greek government in paragraph _____2_____.

5. **B**   Answer choice B is a supporting detail that gives a description of the organizational structure and an example of one group. Answers A, C, and D do not relate to the structure of Roman society. Answer A is a detail about myths; Answer C is a detail about athletics, and Answer D is a detail about the Roman calendar.

Using Details to Make Generalizations, p. 9

1. **D**   Answer D is supported by the detail: "There are many different kinds of marshes, ranging from prairie potholes to the Everglades, coastal to inland, freshwater to saltwater." Answer A is incorrect because marshes have an abundance of plant life. The paragraph does not mention anything about marshes being fragile, so Answer B is incorrect. Answer C is both unrelated to the paragraph and factually inaccurate.

2. **B**   Answer B describes one way that marshes help decontaminate water. Answer A describes the types of marshes, Answer C describes the location of marshes, and Answer D describes threats to marshes, but none of these are related to water quality.

3. **A**   Answer A lists different kinds of plants and animals found in a marsh. Answers B, C, and D describe the make-up of marshes and threats to marshes, but they do not support a generalization about the ecosystem.

4. **C**

Language Practice, p. 10

 Select . . . ▼

    C. is the distinctive octopus.

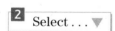 Select . . . ▼

    B. makes the octopus different from many animals.

 Select . . . ▼

    D. it can blend in with almost any environment.

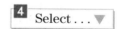 Select . . . ▼

    A. the octopus can release a puff of black ink.

Writing Practice, p. 11

Make sure your paragraph has at least three types of supporting details. Your supporting details may include descriptions, examples, reasons, and facts.

> Answers will vary. Sample answer: As Hurricane Ida prepares to hit the island of Galveston, people are preparing for the worst. Hurricanes are often disastrous for people who do not fully prepare. The mayor ordered an emergency evacuation of all residents Thursday morning. Before leaving, many people boarded up windows and secured valuable items, causing the city to look like a ghost town. People in the surrounding area are encouraged to prepare for the storm by assembling emergency kits that include water, dry food, flashlights, a battery-operated radio, blankets, and a first-aid kit. As the storm approaches, people can expect heavy winds, increased rainfall, and a possible storm surge. People are warned to seek shelter indoors, away from windows and possible flying debris.

Lesson 1.3

Direct and Implied Main Ideas, p. 13

1. The overall main idea of this passage is expressed _____indirectly_____.
2. **B** Answer choices A, C, and D are all supporting details. Only answer B describes what the entire passage is about.
3. **A** The main idea of the first paragraph is stated explicitly in the first sentence. The other choices are supporting details.
4. **D** Paragraph 7 contains the implied main idea that the United States expanded through territorial wars with other countries.

Implied Main Ideas and Supporting Details, p. 15

1. To identify the _____main idea_____ of "The Golden Windows," look for details in the boy's dialogue and actions at the top of both hills that tell what the passage is about.
2. **D** The main idea is not directly stated. Instead, readers must identify the implied main idea by looking at how the supporting ideas are related.
3. **A** The main idea of the passage is that "things are not always as they seem." This is suggested when the boy realizes that his own house looks to have golden windows from a distance.
4. **B** When the girl tells him that he has mistaken the house, it supports the main idea that "Things aren't always what they seem."
5. **C**

Writing Practice, p. 17

Remember that your passage should have a main idea supported by your details. The main idea can be stated directly or indirectly. Support your main idea with facts, examples, descriptions, or other details.

> Answers will vary. Sample answer: What do a box of cereal, a fluffy red sweater, and a power drill all have in common? It is likely that their packaging all contained a bar code. Bar codes are an amazing invention. To many people they just look like a line of black and white bars with some numbers underneath. However, there is more to a bar code than meets the eye. These black and white stripes are read by computers. They contain a variety of information from a product description to the price. Stores use these bar codes to make sure that sales clerks ring up the proper price of merchandise. It can also help track what products have been sold so there is a record of inventory, making it easier for managers to order new merchandise. For these reasons, bar codes are an important modern invention.

Lesson 1.4

Summarizing Key Information, p. 19

1. One major _____theme_____ of the passage is the pain and discomfort of clothing made for slaves.

2. **B** As the passage gives descriptions of the uncomfortable clothing worn by slaves, Answer B is the best summary of the main idea. The clothing was described as uncomfortable and painful, not luxurious or practical. There was no explanation of a relationship between clothes and a slave's life.

3. **D** The main idea of the passage is that the clothing was uncomfortable. Answer D described how uncomfortable the shoes were. The other answers were part of the passage, but are not closely related to the main idea, and so would not be included in the summary.

4. **D** Answer choice D describes how painful the new flax shirts were to wear. This detail supports the main idea that the clothing was uncomfortable. None of the other choices support the main idea that the clothing was uncomfortable.

5. **A**

Summarizing a Text, p. 21

1. The statement above is a __**paraphrase**__ of paragraph 1.

2. **C** The text describes precautions that travelers should take when traveling during hurricane season. Answer C is the best summary of the main idea. The other answers are details that were included in the paragraph, but do not express the main idea.

3. **D** The main idea is to be prepared when traveling. Answer D is an important detail about how to be prepared. The other answer options do not relate specifically to being prepared while traveling during the upcoming hurricane season.

4. **A** Answer choice A best summarizes all the details in the paragraph. The other choices paraphrase only one detail each or contain inaccurate information.

5. **A** This passage includes boldfaced headings, "Travel Alert" and "Hurricane Season." These headings tell you what the most important information to include in a summary would be. The text does not include italicized text or section headings. The paragraph breaks do not indicate the most important information that would be included in a summary.

6.

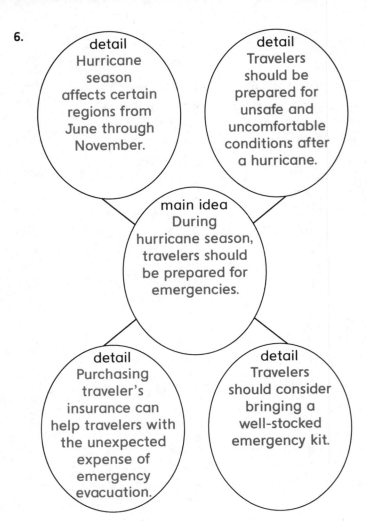

- detail
Hurricane season affects certain regions from June through November.

- detail
Travelers should be prepared for unsafe and uncomfortable conditions after a hurricane.

- main idea
During hurricane season, travelers should be prepared for emergencies.

- detail
Purchasing traveler's insurance can help travelers with the unexpected expense of emergency evacuation.

- detail
Travelers should consider bringing a well-stocked emergency kit.

Writing Practice, p. 23

Make sure your paragraph states the main idea and supporting details in concise statements. When you describe a book or movie, important details to include are the characters, settings, main events, a conflict, and how the conflict was resolved.

> Answers will vary. Sample answer: "The Kane Prophecy" is a book written by Oliver Scott. This book is set many years in the future after the collapse of current civilizations due to an outbreak of a deadly virus. A group of people led by a boy named Hunter begin to suspect they are not alone in the world, and they follow signs of another group of survivors. At first they are hesitant to join the group, because they are worried they may be infected. As the story progresses, the two groups join forces and discover that the world was not what they once believed. Together, the two groups build a new colony and fight off an army that seeks to keep them out of a fortified city of survivors. In the end, they realize that they have become immune to the virus and that immunity holds the promise of a healthy future for all society.

Lesson 1.5

Using Fictional Elements to Determine Theme, p. 25

1. The actions of the Measuring-Worm express the story's _____theme_____, or central message.

2. C   In the story, the inchworm slowly creeps up the cliff over the course of a year and is the only one who is successful in rescuing the boys. The passage is about persistence, not about working together, judging appearances, or being strong.

3. A   The perseverance of the inchworm is an important detail in identifying the theme. The other sentences describe different things that happen in the story, but they do not directly relate to the central theme.

4. D

Synthesizing Multiple Main Ideas to Determine Theme, p. 26

1. D   The story is told from the narrator's point of view, allowing the reader to understand the lessons both characters learned. When these lessons are synthesized, they reveal the theme. The story is not told from the perspective of the king, patriot, or Great Head Factotum.

2. B   The story is a satire, which uses humor to help us understand culture. The use of the term *patriot* highlights the man's dishonesty and disloyalty. The other sentences provide details about the main character but do not help to identify the theme.

3. C   In the short story, both the king and the patriot are dishonest in their words and actions. These actions reveal the theme. The other statements do not describe the theme.

4.   The theme can be determined by ___synthesizing___ information from the characterization of the king and the patriot, the language used in the dialog, and the outcome of the interaction between the characters.

Writing Practice, p. 27

Make sure your short story has a theme that is either stated or implied. Your story can reveal the theme through characterization, point of view, setting, plot, language, and conflict.

> Answers will vary. Sample answer: Many, many years ago there was a spider called Anansi who lived outside a village of hardworking animals. One day Anansi was hungry but too lazy to fix his own dinner. He could smell the wonderful things his neighbors were making and decided to explore. He came across Rabbit making a fine yam stew. "Mmmm…that smells wonderful," Anansi flattered Rabbit. "Can I have a bowl?" Rabbit replied yes but informed Anansi that it wasn't ready yet. Anansi wanted to look for other food, but he did not want to miss out on the yam stew. Then, he had an idea. "Rabbit, I will tie this yarn to my leg," Anansi said, smiling. "When the stew is ready, give it a little tug, and I'll come back." Anansi continued on his way until he met Monkey. Monkey was making a lovely bean soup. Once again, Anansi was in too much of a hurry to wait, so he tied some yarn to another leg and bid Monkey to give it a pull when the bean soup was ready. Anansi continued his explorations around the village. Before long, he had a piece of yarn tied to each leg. 'How clever I am," Anansi thought to himself. "Soon I will have eight yummy suppers, without doing any work!" Just then, Anansi felt a tug on the yarn from Rabbit. "Time for supper!" he smiled. But before he could go, he felt another and another and another tug. Each piece of yarn pulled Anansi in a different direction, and with each pull his legs got longer and thinner. Finally, Anansi was able to roll into the water, which washed away the yarn. However, to this day, Anansi the Spider has very thin, long legs.

Lesson 2.1

Sequence of Time, p. 29

1. D   The phrases "When" and "But today" tell you that picking out a comfortable pairs of athletic shoes was easier before there were so many brands and styles.

2. C   The word "Finally" is used to tell you that style and special features are the last things to consider when you are looking for shoes to purchase.

3. A   "When" means "at the same time" or "while."

4. B

5.

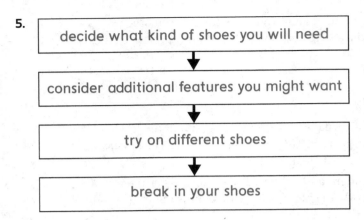

decide what kind of shoes you will need

↓

consider additional features you might want

↓

try on different shoes

↓

break in your shoes

Sequence in a Process, p. 31

1. In the section "How Was Natural Gas Formed?", the sequence of events describes a ____process____.

2. **A** Each section of the text explains a process, and in both cases they are explained in chronological order. The sections themselves are also arranged in chronological order.

3. **C** Bolded headings is the only feature used in this passage to show the organization of the text.

4. **B** The passage explains that scientists use seismic surveys to find the right places to drill wells. Then they study rock samples and take measurements. Since the process described in the section is in chronological order, this means that studying samples and taking measurements takes place after seismic surveys.

Writing Practice, p. 31

Make sure your paragraph uses past tense and includes at least four steps in a process. Also make sure that it includes an out-of-sequence event that uses transition words to tell when the event occurred.

> Answers will vary. Sample answer: I taught Sara how to write an e-mail last week. I began by showing her how to get to her e-mail login page. But even before doing that, I had to show her how to open the Web browser! I showed her how to log in with her user name and password, then I explained that "Compose" meant "Write a New Message." We typed my e-mail address in the "To" field and then typed "My First E-mail" in the subject line. I told her to write me a special message in the main box. Lastly, she hit the "Send" button and away it went. She was excited to hear my smartphone beep when I received her incoming message.

Lesson 2.2

Inferring a Writer's Meaning, p. 33

1. **B** The author's description of Dick Baker's character and way of dress indicate that he is not rich, nor is he particularly educated. The references to gold are a metaphor telling us that he has a good heart. The other statements do not describe Dick Baker.

2. However, the narrator ____implies____ that he, himself, has doubts about the cat's near-human intelligence.

3. **C** The actions of the cat, such as laying low, observing the miners, sleeping on their coats, is normal for cats. That the owner sees the cat's napping and watching as "superintending" is interpreting his behavior as being like a human. The owner does not imply that the cat has supernatural powers, is notably impressive, or is like a circus animal.

4. **D** Dick Baker says the cat "never *could* altogether understand that eternal sinkin' of a shaft an' never pannin' out anything." The reader can infer that the cat does not think mining underground is worthwhile.

5. **B** The language used by the character to describe the event indicates that he found it amusing. He does not express sadness, satisfaction, or fear.

Citing Evidence, p. 36

1. **D** The impenetrable darkness and the mist covering the hills are *examples* to support the author's idea that it was the type of night when one ought to be indoors, not opinions, readers' inferences, or facts.

2. The narrator's descriptions of what he sees and his opinions about what he sees are two types of _____evidence_____.

3. **A**

4. **C** The narrator's description of his own feelings is the best evidence to support an inference about him feeling uneasy in the house. The other excerpts do not express unease.

Writing Practice, p. 37

Make sure your paragraph includes at least two explicit facts, two explicit opinions, and one implied detail about the person you are writing about.

> Answers will vary. Sample answer: My cousin Reynaldo is the most impressive person I know. He is raising three kids and he runs his own business. And now he is starting a Master's program in business administration. Amazingly, he always seems so calm and cool when I see him; he never seems tired. I aspire to be as successful as my cousin when I reach that stage in my life. (*Note: Implied detail is that the writer is younger than his or her cousin.*)

Lesson 2.3

Identifying Literary Elements, p. 39

1. Scrooge, his clerk, and his nephew are the three _____characters_____ in this passage.

2. **C** The phrases describe the story's setting, specifically the weather of the place where the story takes place.

3.

Setting	Character
3 PM on Christmas Eve	Scrooge's control over the coal-box
description of the fog	nephew's response to Scrooge
Scrooge's counting-house	Scrooge's reaction to his nephew

4. **C** The nephew calls Scrooge dismal and morose, so Scrooge is in a bad mood. A and B describe the nephew, not Scrooge. The clerk, the nephew, and the people outside are cold, but Scrooge is not described this way.

Analyzing Relationships in Text, p. 41

1. **A** The room can be considered the setting, and the observations made about the room relate directly to the plot.

2. **D** In the story, the tavern owner shows the rooms to Coroner Golden and the deputy sheriff, who are investigating an incident involving a young woman.

3. **B** The text explains that the tavern is old and that the owner does not want to change the tavern and will not update it for his clientele.

4. A key detail that ties the story's plot to its setting is the color of the ____wallpaper____.

5. **C**

6. **A** The deputy sheriff has some suspicions, but he also makes important observations before coming to any conclusions.

Writing Practice, p. 43

Make sure your paragraph describes an important event and includes details about the place where the event occurred, including why this place was important.

> Answers will vary. Sample answer: My sister's wedding was all the more memorable because of where she held it, with all of the pluses and minuses of that place. She held it on the beach at sunset, so it was beautiful and romantic. The wedding vows related the couple's love to the size of the ocean, which you could see behind them. The only problem for the guests was the sand: people either had to go barefoot or try to walk to their seats in their dress shoes. The only problem for my sister was the wind: that ocean breeze was so strong it almost blew her veil right off her head. In most of the photos, she's trying to keep it from flying away.

Lesson 2.4

Interpreting Implied Relationships between Ideas, p. 45

1. **B** The similar sentence structure in paragraphs 2 and 3 and using the word "unstable" and then "stable" is a clue that the author is contrasting cold and warm air masses. Comparing would show what is the same about the two types of air masses, but the author is showing differences. The author does not explain how one air mass becomes another.

2. **B** The fact that the weather in Canada is cold and dry is implied, and must be inferred by the reader based on explicit details. The other answer options are explicit in the text and are not inferred.

3. In paragraph 3, language patterns and the ____proximity____ of ideas help readers infer that the author is comparing the different movements of cold air masses and the resulting fronts.

4. **C** The text does not say explicitly that cold air masses produce more rain, but because they can produce heavy loads of precipitation while warm air masses produce drizzle, this is a reasonable inference. Drizzle is a form of rain that occurs with some warm air masses. Gusty winds are not steady, so they would not occur with warm air masses. Choice B is explicitly stated in the passage and need not be inferred.

Citing Evidence of Implied Relationships, p. 48

1. **B** This statement helps the reader predict that Court will overturn DOMA. The writer uses the many laws and regulations that do not apply to same-sex spouses to show that the law doesn't treat people equally, so the writer is not implying that DOMA will be upheld. The Court of Appeals was not considering a case about Government-integrity rules, so those answers are not reasonable inferences.

2. **B** The idea that DOMA is in violation of the Fifth Amendment is the strongest evidence that the Court's decision is based on existing legislation. None of the other answers mention existing laws or regulations.

3. **B** The logical inference reader can make based on these two sentences is that DOMA denies rights and responsibilities to some couples, therefore diminishing their dignity and integrity. Couples of opposite sex are not deprived of anything under the law, so all couples do not have diminished dignity and integrity.

4. **D** The information throughout the text emphasizes that DOMA asks the federal government to deny rights already recognized by the state. This idea could be applied to other decisions made by the court. The other answer choices are not related to rights granted by the state or federal government.

5. **C**

Writing Practice, p. 49

Make sure your paragraph describes two different cities with two similarities and two differences. Also make sure it includes a detail about one city that implies a favorable comparison with the other.

> Answers may vary. Sample answer: New York and San Francisco are two of the most interesting cities in the United States, although both are very expensive to live in. New York has live music, shows, and art exhibits every day of the week. San Francisco has amazing attractions of architecture and nature inside the city and around it. New Yorkers can dine on cheap and delicious food from anywhere in the world. San Franciscans can dine in restaurants serving food straight from a nearby organic farm. But for me, the most important difference is the weather: New York's winters are too cold and its summers are just too hot. Along the Pacific Ocean is where I'd rather be.

Lesson 2.5

Examining Complex Literary Texts, p. 51

1. **B** The title and the first sentences of the last paragraphs indicate that the narrator is talking about a cat. He uses first person and mentions his childhood and his marriage, so the reader also knows he is talking about his life.

2. **C** The following phrases support this answer: "perhaps, some intellect . . . will reduce my phantasm [fantasy/nightmare] to the commonplace [ordinary]"; "nothing more than an ordinary succession of very natural causes and effects." Because the narrator states that he is telling the story "without comment," it is unlikely he is trying to persuade readers. He also says that readers might find the events less terrifying than he does. Finally, he is not concerned with readers understanding why he has written his account—rather, he wonders if readers will understand the events themselves.

3. **C** The main idea is that the narrator married someone who also loved animals, and together they adopted many different types of pets. The narrator does not say that his wife had pets before their marriage. Nor does he say that she was agreeable; he says the pets are agreeable. In addition, he states that his wife procured (got) pets for him, not that she allowed him to do so.

4. **D**

Understanding Complex Informational Texts, p. 53

1. **D** From the title and the end of the second paragraph, we see that the speaker is concerned with the affordability, or cost, of higher education.

2. **C** The difference between the rise in tuition costs and the rise in income is the strongest evidence that tuition is not affordable.

3. By imagining a college graduate sending a check for $1000 to a bank each month, you are ___visualizing___ the details of the text.

4. **C** Paragraphs 7 through 9 lay out the different steps taken by the government both to protect students from being exploited by lenders and to help them to obtain and repay loans.

5. **A** The first sentences of paragraphs 9 and 10 tell us that the speaker is glad changes have been made, but is not satisfied that the problem of tuition affordability has been resolved.

Language Practice, p. 54

1 Select . . . ▼

    C. one

2 Select . . . ▼

    A. they

3 Select . . . ▼

    A. him or her

4 Select . . . ▼

    D. it

Writing Practice, p. 55

Make sure your paragraph explains a rule or procedure and that it uses vocabulary that is specific to that activity.

> Answers will vary. Sample answer: In boxing, the classic one-two combo consists of a jab followed by a cross. Because the jab is the thrown from the more forward side of the body, it is used to establish the appropriate distance between the striker and his or her opponent. It is immediately followed by a cross, which comes from the rear hand and requires the rotation of the torso and hips to cover the same distance. This movement of the whole body adds force to the cross, which is why it is considered a power punch. The striker can follow the jab-cross combination with a hook, an uppercut, or both.

Lesson 3.1

Identify Connotative and Figurative Meanings, p. 57

1. **B** The young men of the Pony Express didn't actually gallop across the country into history. "Galloping into history" is used as a metaphor to evoke a specific image in the reader's mind.

2. **D** The author creates a sense of excitement by using phrases like "breakneck speed" and "glorious history."

3. **B** The author's attitude about the subject is complimentary. Only the positive parts of the Pony Express are described in this passage.

4. The sentence "Then the Pony Express and its riders ended their exciting chapter in American history." is an example of a _____metaphor_____.

5. **A** **Breakneck** evokes the image of someone moving so quickly as to actually break his or her neck. A Pony Express rider moving that fast is going at a dangerous speed.

6. **D**

Understanding Connotative and Figurative Meaning in Literary Text, p. 59

1. **D** The author gains the readers' sympathy for Rip Van Winkle by describing Dame Van Winkle as constantly nagging him and possessing the ability to terrify even the most composed of men.

2. The _____tone_____ in the third paragraph is one of amusement.

3. **B** "Adherent" is used when talking about Wolf, so it could mean "pet," but then it is used again when talking about a group of men. It is always used in a positive sense, so it cannot mean "enemy." Neither Rip Van Winkle nor Nicholas Vedder served as teachers.

4. **A**   In the fourth paragraph, the author paints a picture of the men idly chatting, Nicholas Vedder tranquilly smoking his pipe. In the fifth paragraph however, Dame Van Winkle "suddenly [broke] in upon the tranquility," "call[ed] all the members to task," and then attacked Vedder for encouraging her husband's habits of idleness.

5.

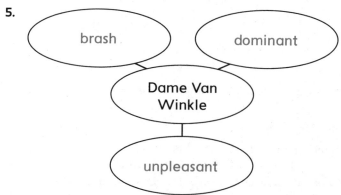

6. **B**   The first paragraph of the text talks about Dame Van Winkle's constant nagging of her husband. He is so "henpecked" that he is forced to go outside. The meaning of *henpecked* can be inferred from the previous descriptions of Dame Van Winkle's actions and how Rip Van Winkle reacted.

Language Practice, p. 60

1. Select . . . ▼
    A. knew

2. Select . . . ▼
    C. their

3. Select . . . ▼
    B. pair

4. Select . . . ▼
    B. whether

Writing Practice, p. 61

Your paragraph should use connotative and figurative language to accurately convey how you felt during the experience. Your word choices should also contribute to the overall mood of your text, indicating the type of reaction you would like the reader to have after reading.

> Answers will vary. Sample answer: I could see them from the wings, hundreds of people packed into the tiny theater like sardines in a tin. There were so many of them and they just stared at the stage, dourly waiting for someone to entertain them. A burst of anxiety bubbled through my stomach and up my sternum, threatening to spill out of my mouth as an ear-piercing scream. I knew my lines. I knew my cues. But I didn't know if I could do this.

Lesson 3.2

Identifying Author's Tone in an Informational Letter, p. 63

1. **B**   The topic of the letter is a complaint, so the tone will be negative. Anger and frustration are both appropriate tones for letters of complaint.

2. **D**   "Imagine my surprise" is the author's way of saying, "Can you believe this?" The other sentences in the paragraph detail what happened with little or no extra editorializing.

3.   In paragraph 1, the word ___headaches___ is a metaphor that conveys the tone by showing the author's frustration with the staff.

4. C   The writer of the letter is frustrated but ends the letter respectfully. He does not use aggressive language and maintains polite formalities in his greetings.

5. In paragraph 3, replacing "As the cherry on top," with "Thankfully," would change the _____tone_____ of the sentence to gratitude.

Analyzing Tone in a Literary Text, p. 66

1. C   The genre of the story is mystery, and mysteries are commonly suspenseful.

2. B

3. D   Short, terse phrases and sentences build tension in the story, which pushes the reader forward to find out what happens next.

4. A   The mystery itself and the short sentences contribute to the intense tone.

5. A   Mr. Sedgwick's lengthy inner monologue reveals his thinking and suspicions. This knowledge works to continue building tension about what has become of the coin and who is responsible. The paragraph slows the pace of the action but does not focus on Robert's search, name Darrow as the definite culprit, or focus solely on Mr. Blake.

6.

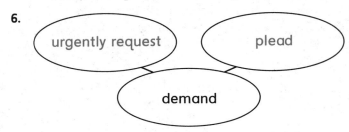

urgently request

plead

demand

Writing Practice, p. 67

Your paragraph should include connotative words, figurative language, and sentence structures that express your tone and match your purpose for writing.

> Answers will vary. Sample answer: I have so many responsibilities now that I am an adult. I have to decide when to go to bed, and if I stay up late, too bad! I still have to get up early and get to work on time. I make my own breakfast and get myself lunch. I buy the groceries and cook the food. And don't get me started on laundry! I have to do it. No one is going to nag me about it or do it for me. I deposit my paychecks and pay the bills. It's all so much responsibility.

Lesson 3.3

Choosing the Right Word, p. 70

1. C   The author uses words like "nightmare" and "murdered" to describe the atrocities happening. These details are meant to persuade the American public that the war is necessary. The other choices offer words that describe the strengths of the United States' military and the organization of Saddam Hussein's regime, but these are not used to to persuade Americans that Operation Liberty Shield is necessary.

2. C   In paragraph 4, the author calls the people working with Saddam Hussein thugs because he believes their actions described in the paragraph are criminal. Bush does not imply that his soldiers were in prison or come from any other countries. Paragraph 4 does not mention attempts at diplomacy.

3. B   Calling Hussein's rule a "dictator's regime" shows the author's dislike of his leadership. The other options refer to details from the paragraph not related to the author's direct feelings.

4.

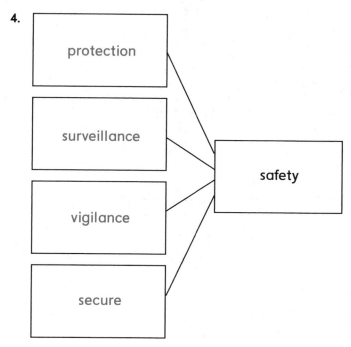

5. **B** *Attacked* has a negative connotation. It brings to mind acts of violence that deserve revenge. None of the other choices describe the negative connotation that *attacked* elicits.

Analyzing and Evaluating Word Choice in Various Texts, p. 72

1. Susan B. Anthony gave this speech and chose her words to _____persuade_____ people that women have the right to vote.

2. **D** Anthony begins her speech by addressing "friends and fellow citizens." She wants all the American public to rally behind the idea of votes for women. None of the other choices describe all of the people she was trying to reach with her speech.

3. **B**

4. The phrase *throw to the winds* in paragraph 2 is an example of _____figurative_____ language.

5. **A** *Mockery* has a negative connotation and conveys that talk of liberty has no meaning for people who cannot vote. *Silly* trivializes the women's plight. *Difficult* does not express Anthony's scorn. *Encouraging* ignores the frustration women might feel when their "liberty" is discussed.

6. **B** Anthony wants other people to become angry and take up the cause of suffrage for women. She is not describing a hopeful situation for women who want to vote. She does not want people to become depressed. And although her speech may excite some people, Anthony's intention was clearly to get people angry enough to change the law.

Writing Practice, p. 73

Make sure that your paragraph uses descriptive language, such as metaphors, similes, and connotative word choices. Also ensure that you clearly state your perspective on the topic and use words that align with your feelings.

> Answers will vary. Sample answer: I think the closing of six schools in the Kansas City school district is a despicable use of the school board's power. Education isn't just an issue for families with school-aged children. It's the backbone of our community; without it we are stuck in a slump. The schools that are closing are of course the schools that are needed the most—the schools where kids get their sole hot meal, the schools where teachers often play the role of parents, the schools where they're safe for a few hours each day.

Lesson 4.1

Identifying Text Structure, p. 75

1. C   The passage uses sequence to narrate the events of the *Titanic's* first trip.
2. D   The size of the *Titanic* is contrasted with the ships that the *Titanic* dwarfs.
3. B   The word "next" is specific to the sequence text structure. It shows what happens in time order.
4. One _____cause_____ of the large crowds at the departure of the *Titanic* was that many friends and family of the ship's passengers wanted to say good-bye.

Variations in Organization, p. 78

1. A   The events in the paragraph are told from start to finish. This is known as chronological order, or time order.
2. B
3. A   This passage relates a story with the events told in the order in which they happened. The story moves from the beginning to the end.

4.

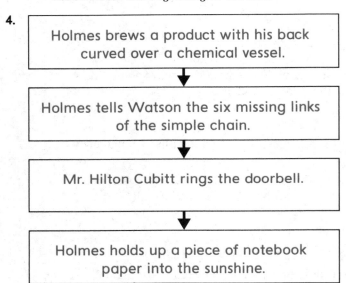

Holmes brews a product with his back curved over a chemical vessel.

↓

Holmes tells Watson the six missing links of the simple chain.

↓

Mr. Hilton Cubitt rings the doorbell.

↓

Holmes holds up a piece of notebook paper into the sunshine.

Writing Practice, p. 79

Make sure your paragraph uses the compare-and-contrast text structure and highlights two family traditions. Also make sure that it includes words such as *although, both,* and *in contrast* to show the comparisons and contrasts.

Answers will vary. Sample answer: My family loves to celebrate holidays with great food and lots of family time. Our biggest holiday celebration each year is our Thanksgiving feast, which is always at my Aunt Gloria's house. She cooks a turkey big enough to feed 25 hungry guests, including all 14 of my cousins and even some close family friends. Everyone brings a dish to share and we have a contest each year for the best pie. It's loud and boisterous. In contrast, just my immediate family gathers to celebrate New Year's Day. Although it's also a family gathering that involves food, it's different because it's just the five of us. My dad makes his famous pancakes and my mom makes omelets with our favorite ingredients. We drink hot chocolate and share our resolutions for the new year. My brother builds a fire and we play card games and enjoy a peaceful afternoon together.

Lesson 4.2

Distinguishing between Text Structures, p. 81

1. **D** Paragraph 3 establishes the order of steps that GDL systems require teenagers to complete. These steps must be completed in order, so sequence is the way this text structure is organized.

2. **D** One solution to the problem of teen drivers' high crash risk is giving teen drivers more driving experience. Research proves that this solution makes teens safer drivers.

3. Paragraph _____5_____ presents causes for why teens have a hard time managing risky behavior behind the wheel.

4.

Effects of the GDL

"States with stronger, comprehensive GDL systems see a higher reduction in teen crashes."

"GDL reduces teen driver exposure to high crash risk situations, such as nighttime driving and teen passengers."

Text Structure and Key Ideas, p. 83

1. **A** The writer begins the passage with frog and toad sightings (effects) and introduces the causes for these events later.

2. **D** The first sentence of paragraph 10 emphasizes the author's skepticism that whirlwinds are the cause of frog and toad sightings. In the other paragraphs, the author cites the opinions of other authors or experts.

3. **B**

4.

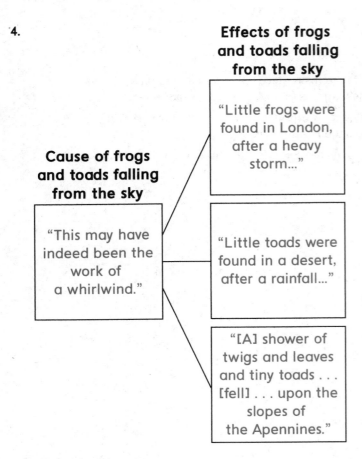

Effects of frogs and toads falling from the sky

Cause of frogs and toads falling from the sky

"This may have indeed been the work of a whirlwind."

"Little frogs were found in London, after a heavy storm…"

"Little toads were found in a desert, after a rainfall…"

"[A] shower of twigs and leaves and tiny toads . . . [fell] . . . upon the slopes of the Apennines."

Writing Practice, p. 85

Make sure your paragraphs show a clear compare-and-contrast structure. You should have included descriptions of your friends to support the points you are comparing and contrasting.

Answers will vary. Sample answer: When you meet my best friend Tanisha, the first thing that you will notice is the bright smile that is always painted on her dimpled face. When she smiles, her eyes curl at the corners and even sparkle a bit. I first met Tanisha in second grade, and she was laughing about something that I don't remember anymore. In fact, Tanisha thinks that everything is funny. Once, we were eating lunch and she laughed so hard that she couldn't catch her breath for a couple of minutes. My other friend, Amanda, is much quieter and more serious. Like Tanisha, Amanda likes to laugh, but she doesn't laugh as much as Tanisha does.

When Amanda gets stressed, she likes to find a quiet space and listen to music. Unlike Amanda, Tanisha deals with stress by being around her friends. To relax, both Tanisha and Amanda like to go to the movies or to the mall. But even though they love the mall, they like to buy different things. Amanda always shops for accessories like earrings and scarves while Tanisha loves shoes. In fact, Tanisha has so many shoes that she once gave away a garbage bag full of shoes to a clothing drive, and she still had a mountain of shoes left in her closet. Despite their differences, Tanisha and Amanda are great friends to me, and I hope we stay friends forever.

Lesson 4.3

Locating Transitions, p. 87

1. **B** *In addition* is a signal phrase. The transition indicates that the writer is providing more information about something. The other answer choices are not considered signal phrases.

2. **C** The signal word *after* explains what to do when you get the puppy home. This transition reveals a shift in time from the ideas in the fifth paragraph. The transition word *after* is not used in this paragraph to reveal a conclusion or to contrast information.

3. **A** The signal phrase *on the other hand* indicates a contrast between the small Chihuahua breed and larger or aggressive breeds. This phrase indicates a difference between the two breeds of dogs. It is not used to compare these dogs, provide examples, or show the effects of purchasing a small dog.

4.

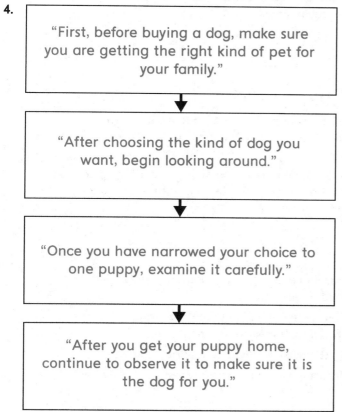

5. **B** The signal phrase *for instance* points to examples of dogs that may or may not be appropriate for families with small children. The paragraph suggests that families with playful children may like a larger dog and that a Chihuahua may not be appropriate. This phrase does not indicate other transitions such as cause and effect, time order, or relative location.

Analyzing Transitions, p. 90

1. **C** The first paragraph provides important information about NASA's history. The list at the end of the second paragraph provides examples of NASA's technological inventions.

2. **B**

3. **D** This sentence provides examples of NASA's impact on technological inventions. The signal phrase *for instance* best reveals this relationship shift. The term "In brief" is not appropriate here because the sentence does not provide a summary. "By contrast" indicates something will be contrasted, which does not happen in these sentences. "In conclusion" would indicate that the paragraph or passage is coming to a conclusion, which is not correct.

Writing Practice, p. 91

Make sure each paragraph clearly focuses on one particular skill or talent and uses signal words or phrases to transition between the ideas.

> Answers will vary. Sample answer: I am a talented musician. I have been playing the trumpet since I was nine. When I was in middle school, I won a Young Musician's Award. In addition, I have entered many local competitions, and I have competed in several other states, including Michigan, Indiana, and Illinois. At family gatherings, my brothers sing and I play the trumpet to accompany them.
>
> I am also really good at board games. My family and I play Scrabble every Saturday night, and I usually win by at least 50 points. There are other board games that I play well, including Monopoly, checkers, and chess. I am trying to learn a lot of new games; for example, I am trying to learn certain card games. I started playing hearts and bridge a couple months ago, and I am getting better every day. I think the combination of these two talents make me unique.

Lesson 5.1

Identifying an Author's Purpose, p. 93

1. The author's purpose for writing this passage is to _____inform_____.
2. **C** The purpose of this text is to inform the reader about different waves. The sentence gives an explanation of how compression can be heard in sound waves. Answer C is the only answer that supports the author's purpose of informing.
3. **A** This sentence provides an example of transverse waves. In an informative text, the author's goal is to explain a concept. In order to do this, informative texts often contain facts, definitions, and examples.
4. **B**

Recognizing an Author's Point of View, p. 95

1. **C** This passage outlines George W. Bush's plans for reforming education. His point of view is that there are problems with the education system that need to be changed.
2. **B** The writer lists a series of problems with the education system including poor performing schools and lack of accountability. His point of view about the education system is negative.
3. The author's point of view is expressed _____explicitly_____ because it is stated in paragraph 4.
4. **A** The author lists changes that need to occur in the education system. Therefore, his point of view is that the education system needs reform.

5.

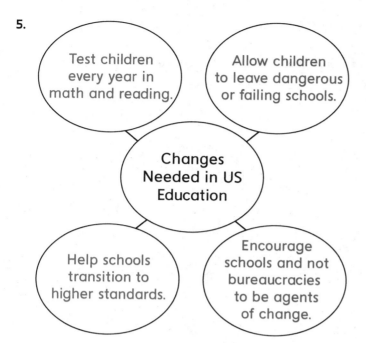

Writing Practice, p. 97

Make sure your text has a clearly stated topic sentence that expresses your point of view. You should give reasons to support your answers.

> Answers will vary. Sample answer: Students should be allowed to bring their own devices to school. It is very expensive for schools to provide the latest technology. Allowing students to bring their own devices will increase the number of units available. Schools will save money by having fewer machines to take care of and not needing to keep the machinery updated and current. There are advantages to students as well. They will be able to take e-books and textbooks with them wherever they go, as well as share information with others. Having their own devices gives students more control over their own learning. They can do research on topics the teacher is discussing. Finally, bring-your-own-device programs are helpful to teachers. When students submit assignments online it is more efficient—some programs even grade papers automatically for the teacher. Teachers will notice that their students are more engaged and involved in the lessons. Since these programs benefit schools, students, and teachers, I believe we should encourage bring-your-own-device programs in schools.

Lesson 5.2

Text Structure in Informational Texts, p. 99

1. The author's main purpose for writing this piece is to _____inform_____.

2. **D** The author defines and then describes various concepts important to astronomy, so the organizational structure is description.

3. **A** Using the descriptive structure, the author informs readers about Earth and space science by defining and explaining the topics included in these fields.

4. **C** In paragraph 3, the author explains the effect of the events described in the big bang theory and in the closed universe theory, so the structure that best describes the paragraph is cause and effect.

Text Structure in Literary Texts, p. 101

1. The author's main purpose for writing this piece is to _____entertain_____.

2. **C** The events are told in the order in which they occur, so the story has a sequence structure.

3. B Presenting the events in sequence allows readers to follow the storyline and to focus on the details and language.

4. D The author's use of time-order words such as *then* and *when* helps support the organizational structure by showing the sequence of key events.

5. B

6.

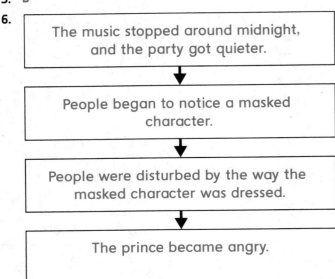

The music stopped around midnight, and the party got quieter.

↓

People began to notice a masked character.

↓

People were disturbed by the way the masked character was dressed.

↓

The prince became angry.

Writing Practice, p. 103

Make sure the text structure you choose helps you present information in a way that conveys the purpose of your article.

Answers will vary. Sample answer: On October 23, the Environmental Committee of the city council recommended that the city expand the new recycling bin program. The committee met the previous evening to discuss the recent replacement of the 19-gallon recycling bins with 34-gallon bins in precinct A. Miguel Rostro, the committee chairman, reported that because the bins are larger, the city has been able to reduce pickup of recycled materials from two days a week to one. He explained that this reduction would help compensate for the cost of the new bins. Committee member Marie Beaufort noted that the public has provided mostly positive feedback. She added that many people have commented that the new bins are easier to use, because they can be rolled to the street rather than carried. Ms. Beaufort said that most complaints have been about the difficulty of storing the larger containers in garages. Given the mostly favorable comments, the committee voted to recommend the expansion of the new program.

Lesson 5.3

Inferring the Author's Purpose, p. 105

1. Wendy Lockwood's purposes for writing the memo are to persuade and to ____inform____.

2. A The bullet points indicate many times when it is appropriate to wash one's hands, implying that hands can become contaminated in many ways. Although animals are mentioned, their presence in the workplace is not. It is true that people who are sick can spread disease and that hands are susceptible to getting dirty, but these are just two of the many reasons for washing one's hands.

3. D

4. C The memo does not mention the work of researchers, training costs, or patient complaints.

5.

Using Context to Infer Implicit Purpose, p. 106

1. D Knowing it is the president's responsibility to guide the nation and the military—and thus plan for the future—is the most relevant detail. The presidential election cycle, the responsibility for signing legislation, and the leadership of political parties are not relevant to the speech.

2. B The fact that the speech was written toward the end of the Vietnam War helps you understand that Ford wanted the American people to set aside their feelings about the war and focus instead on the future of the United States. The upcoming bicentennial was not directly related to Ford's main purpose. The fact that Ford gave the speech on a college campus explains why he refers to "your generation," but it does not hint at his main purpose. Ford's service in the US Navy is not related to the purpose of his speech.

3. B The knowledge that the president's responsibility is to set the agenda helps you understand that Ford's implied purpose was to focus people on moving forward after the Vietnam War. Choices A and C are details that support Ford's purpose, but they do not convey the purpose itself. With choice D, Ford acknowledges the events in Vietnam, but feelings about Vietnam are not his focus.

4. President Ford's main purpose for writing and delivering this speech was to _____persuade_____.

Writing Practice, p. 107

Your paragraph should convey your positive feelings about a product or service through the use of persuasive vocabulary and examples rather than by explicitly stating your opinion.

> Answers will vary. Sample answer: Do you enjoy going to the ballpark, watching the game while you munch on a warm, delicious hot dog? Now you can have that experience at home with the Hot-Diggety. This device cooks hot dogs to perfection. Simply place two hot dogs and two buns into the convenient slots. In seconds, out pops a fresh, toasty hot dog that you can place inside the softly grilled bun. Simply add your favorite toppings, and you can have the total ballpark experience right in your own living room. This inexpensive and efficient machine is easy to store and clean and will be a hit the next time you have your friends over to enjoy the game.

Lesson 5.4

Identifying an Author's Position, p. 109

1. C While college and the government are mentioned, the author is arguing that women should be granted the right to vote. Peaceful protests are not mentioned in the passage.

2. **A** The author begins paragraph 7 with the statement "It is argued that all women do not wish to vote" and goes on to refute the validity of this statement. The author does not claim that opponents doubt women's intelligence and morals, nor that women cannot vote in other countries. In fact, he uses the fact that women *can* vote in other countries to support his own position.

3. The author uses the following statement as _____evidence_____ to support his assertion that women are morally superior to men: "In the penitentiaries in California we have about three thousand men and about thirty women."

4. **B**

Analyzing Support for an Author's Position, p. 112

1. **D** Lyndon Johnson's position is that Congress should pass the voting rights bill. He does ask Congress to work hard to do so, but that is not his position. Johnson wants Congress to pass the current bill, not draft a new one. And although he refers to states' rights, he does not ask Congress to guarantee those rights.

2. **B** In paragraph 10, Johnson introduces and refutes the opposing argument that election issues are under the authority of individual states.

3. Acknowledging and _____refuting_____ opposing viewpoints help Johnson to strengthen his own position.

4. **C** In paragraph 11, Johnson describes what happened when Congress considered a similar bill. This previous experience explains why Johnson is insisting that Congress pass the new bill with the provisions intact. Paragraph 5 hints at this incident but does not provide details. Johnson refutes the opposition's argument in paragraph 9 and refers to bigotry in paragraph 15, but he does not provide evidence.

Writing Practice, p. 113

Your essay should clearly state your position and support it with evidence. To strengthen your argument, your essay should acknowledge an opposing position and explain, through the use of evidence, why it is not valid.

Answers will vary. Sample answer: Service learning is the active involvement of students in performing community service. Students may volunteer at school or in the community. Some service-learning activities are a part of the curriculum, while others are independently conceived. Both approaches offer many benefits to students, schools, and the community and should be a part of the school experience.

Some might argue that a school's main priority should be to focus on learning. However, there is a reason that "learning" is half of the term "service learning." These projects enhance and extend students' learning to a degree that traditional classroom work cannot. For example, consider a literature class that reads novels about immigrant experiences. Students then visit a community farm where recent refugees are provided with jobs and given the opportunity to use their farming experience to start a new future. As students work at the farm alongside the refugees, they gain a deeper understanding of the obstacles refugees face than they could get from reading a book. Consider the example of another student who, for her service learning project, organizes a blanket and towel drive for an animal shelter. She creates posters, writes letters, and speaks to a variety of groups to solicit donations. Not only does the shelter benefit, but the student gains organizational and communication skills. These examples and many others show that service learning not only benefits the community, but it also enriches students' learning by providing authentic experiences they could not receive in the classroom.

Lesson 5.5

Identifying Rhetorical Devices, p. 115

1. **D**   Using an analogy, the author compares the water to steel. By comparing the water to something readers can picture, the author helps to create a strong visual of the setting. Because the sentence does not list items or repeat phrases or ideas, the author has not used the rhetorical devices of enumeration, repetition, or parallelism.

2. **A**   The second part of the sentence provides more information to convey why nightfall was so dangerous. Because the author does not make a comparison, list items, or present two opposing ideas or situations, he has not used the rhetorical devices of analogy, enumeration, or juxtaposition of opposites.

3. **C**   This sentence lists various buildings that were close to where the mauled body was found. Therefore, the reader can understand how serious the wolf attack was to the community. None of the other sentences lists a series of examples or details.

4. **B**

Identifying an Author's Intention and Effect, p. 117

1. **B**   The author uses rhetorical devices such as enumeration and juxtaposition of opposites, as well as vivid descriptions of the life of a slave, to convey how unfairly slaves were treated. The author conveys that the slaves were glad that Mr. Severe died but does not indicate that the death was deserved. Although the slaves work on a farm, the passage does not include any details about what the work was like. The passage is not a tale about his childhood but a description of what life was like for slaves.

2. **D**   The author's use of rhetorical devices helps to create an emotional response in the reader. Skepticism is not a likely response. Readers might discuss life in the rural south, but the topic is more specific than that. And the passage is not a cautionary tale that would prompt readers to make changes in their lives.

3.   In the following excerpt from the text, the author uses the rhetorical device of __enumeration__ .

4. **A**   This excerpt, unlike the others, does not convey the inhumane circumstances in which the slaves lived.

Language Practice, p. 118

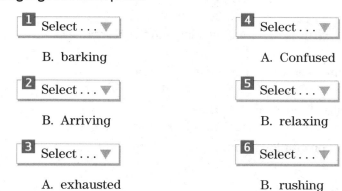

1. Select . . . ▼
   - B. barking

2. Select . . . ▼
   - B. Arriving

3. Select . . . ▼
   - A. exhausted

4. Select . . . ▼
   - A. Confused

5. Select . . . ▼
   - B. relaxing

6. Select . . . ▼
   - B. rushing

Writing Practice, p. 119

Make sure your paragraph discusses the author's intent and effect and mentions the use of rhetorical devices.

> Answers will vary. Sample answer: In the excerpt from Konrad Bercovici's story "Ghitza," a Romanian village suffers from attacks by hungry wolves during a harsh winter. The author's intention is to entertain readers by transporting them to another place and time. He communicates this intention in two main ways. First, he creates vivid descriptions, such as "the crack of whips and the curses of the drivers rent the icy atmosphere" and "cold, clear nights, when even the wind was frozen still." The author also employs rhetorical devices. For example, he uses an analogy to compare a frozen river to steel. This analogy conveys just how cold and hard the river is. Other rhetorical devices in "Ghitza" include a qualifying statement to explain why the carters needed to get to safety by nightfall, as well as enumeration to emphasize how close to home the wolf attacks are: "A stone's throw from the inn, and the thatch-roofed school, and the red painted church!" These rhetorical devices and the many rich details have the desired effect of helping readers feel the desperation of the villagers.

Lesson 6.1

Developing an Argument, p. 121

1.

Claim	Supports Claim	Does Not Support Claim
England's constitution does not encourage liberty.	The king can reject bills that the commons passes. Members of the peers are part of the old tyranny.	Members of the commons are elected by the people.

2. **A**

3. In building his argument, Thomas Paine makes the _____ claim _____ that the king and the peers do not contribute to freedom.

4. **D** The evidence that Paine presents to support his claim is relevant to the claim. The other descriptions do not describe the evidence.

5. **A** The king, according to the constitution, can reject bills of the commons. The other statements are all opinions which may be based on facts, but cannot be considered facts themselves in this argument.

6. **A** Paine's conclusion is a restatement of ideas, that the constitution is faulty. The other types of conclusions do not apply to his argument.

Analyzing Argument Development, p. 123

1. **A** Answer A explains the claim made by the passage. The other sentences express reasons and facts provided as evidence.

2. **C** The author says he has no patience for people who protest this right. The other sentences are not exact expressions of his opinion or are untrue.

3. As an _____ example _____ of another way in which allowing women into public life was beneficial, the author cites the successes of women in education.

4. **A** The author states his claim and supports it with facts, reasons, and examples. Options B and C describe ways to support an argument that the author does not use, and D describes a faulty way to support an argument.

5. **B** The author connects his ideas logically. The other options describe other ways of connecting or presenting ideas.

6. **D** The author concludes that it is only logical for women, who are allowed to participate in every other aspect of life, to be allowed to participate fully in public life, which includes voting. The other statements are summarizations of evidence.

Writing Practice, p. 125

Make sure your paragraph clearly states your claim. Provide facts, reasons, and examples as evidence to back up your claim. Conclude by reiterating your opinion and summarizing the evidence that backs up your claim.

> Answers will vary. Sample answer: Shopping for your food at farmers' markets and local farms boosts your local economy and improves your diet. The food at farmers' markets is as fresh as it can possibly be because it does not have to be shipped from far away. Also, if your local farms grow organic food, the food is free of pesticides, hormones, and other chemicals that can harm your health. Communities who support their local farms benefit from the healthier food these farms produce, while the farmers benefit financially from the community support: a win-win situation for everyone.

Lesson 6.2

Supporting Evidence, p. 127

1. **C** The author is claiming that the Mayor is avoiding his responsibilities. The other statements are all claims by the Mayor himself.

2. **D** The Mayor is claiming that he cannot remove people from government positions for misconduct. The other statements are all claims by the author about the Mayor's powers.

3. **D** The Mayor can remove offenders with the approval of the Board. The other statements are arguments the Mayor gives for not being held responsible for misconduct.

4. The author provides evidence that _____supports_____ his claim by including the Mayor's statements that contradict his insistence that he has no power.

5. **A** The Mayor's logic is faulty, as he contradicts himself. The other words describe ways in which the evidence would work to back up his argument.

Connecting Claims and Evidence, p. 130

1. **B** Nixon admitted that he received $18,000, but claimed that he did not use it for personal expenses. The other answer options are false.

2. **D** Nixon offered this rationale as a reason politicians need contributions to finance political business.

3. **B**

4. The author provides _____records_____ as evidence that he used the money that was given to him for political expenses.

5. **B** Nixon does not have any proof that he did not give special favors to supporters for that money, but he uses that absence as evidence to support his argument. The missing proof makes his argument faulty. The other options would only be true if he had proof.

Writing Practice, p. 131

Make sure that your argument does not include any emotional appeals or faulty reasoning.

> Answers will vary. Sample answer: To gain experience as an apprentice chef, I decided to take a year off before returning to school. I wanted to go to culinary school after high school, but I had no experience at all in cooking. I needed to learn the basics. I knew that I would not have time to learn all of the techniques I needed to know in addition to studying for exams. I gained the experience I needed, and then went back to school to finish my education.

Lesson 6.3

Building a Case, p. 133

1. **B** The fact that the company can't afford mandatory sick leave is evidence given to support the claim that employees should vote against the legislation. The other answer choices are information about the legislation, but these statements do not provide reasons to support the claim.

2. **D** The effect on employee benefits and job security is directly relevant to the audience. The other answer options are general information about the company.

3. **C** The author provides several pieces of evidence directly related to the company's cost for sick leave.

4. **A** The author provides relevant evidence and links the employees to the results of this legislation. This makes the claim persuasive. The other options are false or misleading.

Evaluating Evidence in Various Texts, p. 136

1. President Reagan uses Abraham Lincoln's words as ___evidence___ to support his claim that the country needs to work together to bring America through difficult times.

2. **C** Reagan states that the private sector is more successful at running social programs in order to justify his claim that the Department of Education and other social programs can be cut from the budget. The other statements are not directly related to the claim.

3. **D**

4. **C** The promise to not raise taxes is relevant to the claim. Reagan believes that not increasing taxes will help people and businesses recover from the recession. The other statements are not relevant.

5. President Reagan's argument is supported by several pieces of evidence related to his claim, but the lack of specific examples makes the evidence ___insufficient___.

6. **C** The president briefly provides relevant evidence that the recession caused the budget deficit (it lowered revenues and increased costs), but those two details are not sufficient evidence to support his claim.

Writing Practice, p. 138

Make sure your argument has sufficient and relevant supporting evidence for your claim.

> Answers will vary. Sample answer: Food stamps are an important social service program that should continue to be fully funded by the government. People who are in the terrible position of choosing between paying for their rent and buying groceries have no opportunity to get ahead in life or to help themselves. They have to either go without shelter or go without food. This problem is not only reserved for the unemployed. People who have jobs that do not pay enough to cover living expenses can also end up needing food stamps to make sure they and their families are well fed. If the government wants people to help themselves, they first need to make sure that these people do not go hungry and that their most basic needs are met. Only people whose basic needs are provided for can take advantage of opportunities to better their lives.

Lesson 6.4

Understanding Validity and Reasoning, p. 139

1. **A** The author claims that suffrage for women should not be allowed. The other statements are all evidence he presents to support his claim.

2. **B**

3. **C** The defeat of the Sanford bill can be verified. The other statements are the author's opinion.

4. The author of this passage presents an _____invalid_____ argument because the evidence he uses to support his claim is not _____reasonable_____ or logically sound.

5. **A** The writer's argument is biased because it is based solely on his unsupported opinion, and therefore it is invalid. Even his factual evidence about the reasons for the suffrage bill's defeat cannot be fully verified: there may have been other aspects of the bill that were not acceptable and led to its being voted down. The other descriptions of the author's argument are inaccurate.

Evaluating Validity and Reasoning in Texts, p. 141

1. **D** The passage claims that people should vote for President Obama for a second term. The other sentences express reasons and facts provided as evidence for this claim or a minor detail from the passage.

2. **A** Obama's tax cut is a verifiable fact. The other sentences are opinions.

3. The speaker gives Romney's tax plan as an example to _____support_____ the idea that trickle-down economics doesn't work.

4. The evidence about middle-class families helping the economy when they have more disposable income is logically _____related_____ to the idea that raising taxes on the middle class in order to give the rich a tax cut will not help the economy.

5. **A** The author connects his ideas logically and produces verifiable facts, providing sound reasoning and valid evidence for his claim that he should be re-elected to continue the progress he started.

6. **D** The last sentence states that Obama has a plan, which supports his claim that he should be re-elected. The other sentences describe the opponent's actions but do not directly support Obama's claim that he will be the best person to move the economy in a positive direction.

Writing Practice, p. 143

Make sure you provide facts, reasons, and examples as evidence to back up your claim. When you evaluate your claim, state why your claim is valid and your reasoning is sound.

> Answers will vary. Sample answer: Our schools need a representative on the school board who knows about the issues that current students face. I have two children in the school system, one who utilizes special education services, so I have direct experience with the issues and needs of a variety of students. I have also spent much of my free time volunteering in my children's classes, speaking with teachers about problems they encounter and possible solutions to those problems. As a parent and a volunteer, I am an ideal candidate for the position of representative on the school board.

> My argument is valid because I have given examples of my experience that are directly related to the position I seek. My reasoning is sound because I logically relate my evidence to the claim that I am an ideal candidate for school board representative because I know about current school issues.

Lesson 6.5

Evaluating Arguments Founded on Logical Reasoning, p. 145

1. **D** The author claims there are too many causes of obesity for doctors to be able to suggest just one solution to solve the problem. The other answer options are evidence and reasoning that builds to support the claim at the start of the argument.

2. **B** The author makes the assumption that obesity is a medical problem that needs to be solved. The other answer options define terms and explain causes of obesity.

3. **B** The explanation of the set-point theory serves as a deduction in a series of deductions that support the claim that obesity is a complex problem to solve. The other answer options are other parts of an argument.

4. **A**

5. The author of this passage builds an argument using a series of ____deductions____ from studies on obesity to support the claim.

Evaluating Arguments Based on Hidden Assumptions, p. 146

1. **D** The author claims that Shakespeare's work should have obscene words taken out to clean it up and make it more beautiful. The other choices are statements he makes to build his argument.

2. **B** The author bases his argument on the unstated assumption that offensive words lower the artistic quality of literature. The other answer options are stated ideas.

3. **D** The author's argument depends upon the reader accepting that changing literature does not damage the original work or change it in an unacceptable way.

4. **C** The author bases his idea that Shakespeare would be more beautiful if censored on the invalid assumption that literature can be censored and not damaged in the process.

5. The author of this passage ____assumes____ that Shakespeare's use of obscene language is a defect in his writing.

Language Practice, p. 148

1. are given/may be given
2. is drunk
3. was seen
4. are worn

Writing Practice, p. 149

Make sure you provide logical reasoning based on your hidden assumption.

Answers will vary. Sample answer: Please be sure to clean and put away dishes that you use in the company kitchen. Clean countertops, start the dishwasher if it is full, and check the floor for any stray garbage that needs to be put into the wastebasket. Place any leftover food in the refrigerator, but remember that it will be removed each Friday in order to make sure that food is not left too long. Check that the table is clear before you leave the room. If we all chip in and help, the kitchen will remain clean.

My hidden assumption is that people want to have a clean kitchen in their workplace.

Lesson 7.1

Comparing Texts on Similar Topics, p. 152

1. The _____topic_____ of both passages is Mammoth Cave.

2. **B** Knowing that passage 1 was written in the late 19th century helps readers understand why certain vocabulary was used and why certain references were made, such as the "great torch" in paragraph 1, the "youth of the [19th] century" in paragraph 2, and lanterns in paragraph 3. The facts described in the other answer choices might enlighten readers, but they do not necessarily affect readers' understanding.

3. **A** Passage 2 provides information about the park and fees associated with visiting. The information is probably more general than historians or conservationists would need. The text doesn't speak directly to families, but instead to park visitors in general.

4. **C** Passage 1 uses connotative language and vivid descriptions to talk about Mammoth Cave. Its main purpose is to entertain. Passage 2 provides facts and pricing information about the park. Its main purpose is to inform. Passage 1 may have also been written to inform and to persuade readers of the cave's wonder and beauty, but passage 2 is strictly informational, rather than entertaining or persuasive.

Comparing Fiction and Nonfiction, p. 154

1. **C** Passage 1 is a factual account of the torture methods used during the Spanish Inquisition. Passage 2 details the thoughts and feelings of one of the accused during his torture. Neither passage mentions the key players in the creation of the Spanish Inquisition, the purposes behind its formation, or the events that led to its ending.

2. **B** Passage 1 is entirely fact-based; passage 2 details the narrator's emotions and thoughts during his experience. Passage 1 does not reveal the author's opinion about the methods of torture, does not detail the torture experienced by one man, and is not written from the point of view of the inquisitor. In Passage 2, Poe expresses the terror felt by the prisoner.

3. **D** Passage 1 is an informational text written mainly to inform people about what happened during the Spanish Inquisition. While the passage may also be entertaining, that is not its main purpose. It was not written to help or persuade readers.

4. **D**

5. The characteristics of "The Pit and the Pendulum" help me determine that its genre is _____fiction_____.

Writing Practice, p. 155

Make sure that the first account focuses on facts and details about the event. The second account should use language (vivid descriptions or connotative, persuasive terms) to indicate your chosen genre.

> Answers will vary. Sample answer: Account 1: Kelly met her husband on April 26, on the 5:25 bus from Beele Street. Although the driver of this route was usually late, he was punctual that afternoon. Kelly, wet from the unexpected rain, ran to make it to the bus in time. She touched her pass to the electronic reader and stepped carefully down the aisle, water dripping from her drenched clothing. A lurch caused her to bump into a fellow passenger. Kelly apologized, and he smiled. After that day, they rode together daily without more than a "hello" until the afternoon of June 1, when she asked the man about himself. Many more conversations followed.

> Account 2: The 5:25 was actually on time that afternoon, so I dashed—and splashed—through puddles for the last block. My favorite weatherman hadn't predicted rain, so I was soaked to the bone, but sweating at the same time. As I shuffled my way down the slick aisle toward the back, the driver pulled sharply away from the curb and sent me staggering into the arms of a tall, broad man wearing a neat overcoat. After uttering an involuntary expletive, I stuttered an apology. Then I gazed up at his face, trying not to stare too hard at his bright blue eyes and sun-kissed skin. He gave me a wide smile, and somewhere up in heaven a choir of angels broke into song.

Lesson 7.2

Identifying Genre, p. 158

1. **C** The first passage is an essay, which is characterized by an author's viewpoint and logic or facts that back up this viewpoint. The second passage is a historical article. A historical article contains facts and figures, rather than opinion and logic, about a historical topic.

2. The main purpose of both passages is to _____inform_____ readers about Japanese culture.

3. **A** Passage 1, an essay, includes some of the same literary techniques as fiction, while passage 2, a historical article, includes literary techniques that are typical of informational text. Although passage 1 does begin in the 8th century and passage 2 in the 19th, these are details of content and not literary technique. Teaism and immigrants are the topics, not literary techniques, of the passages. Passage 1 does not contain a plot.

4. **B** Answer choice B highlights the differences in focus in the portrayal of the Japanese in the two passages. The other answer choices are either incorrect or only half right.

Compare Texts from Similar Genres, p. 160

1. The genre of passage 1 is __memoir or autobiography__. The genre of passage 2 is _____letter_____.

2. **D** Lewis writes about his experience in nature with amusement, and Muir seems amazed by the variations in California's climate and scenery.

3. **B**

4.

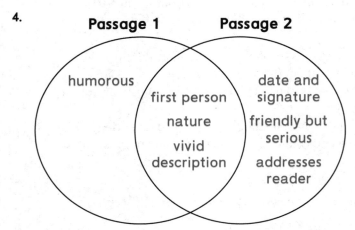

Writing Practice, p. 161

Both of your paragraphs should be about the same topic—you—but have different styles of narration. The biography should be in the third person; the autobiography should be in the first person. Both should contain factual information, but your viewpoint should be clearly presented in the autobiography.

Answers will vary. Sample answer: Marilyn Jordan spent her early life in St. Louis, leaving the only home she'd ever known for a brand new life in Iowa with an overworked husband, a beat-up Chevy, and not nearly enough winter clothes. Iowa in January was cold, and Marilyn wasn't sure she'd ever get the chance to leave their tiny apartment on the edge of town. She needed friends, she needed a job, she needed something to do. Petersen's Department Store seemed like the perfect fit.

We subscribed to the newspaper from the very first year of marriage, and in those early days nothing made me happier than to hear the *thwack* of newsprint against our thin front door at 6:30 every morning. Chuck would bring in the paper and then head to work. Nestled in bed, I would scan what was considered news in the little town and then search for a reason to get up and do something with my day. Eventually, I started paging through the want ads. One morning I noticed that Petersen's was hiring in the men's department. I could do a job like that.

Lesson 7.3

Comparing and Contrasting Two Arguments p. 163

1. **D** The author implicitly conveys the claim in the first paragraph, by explaining how a human embryo is much like embryos of other species. In the second paragraph, he says, "I do not think we could ask nature for more complete proof that human beings have evolved from one-cell ancestors as simple as modern protozoa…" In the fourth paragraph, he concludes with, "…we cannot do away with the facts of structure and development and fossil history, nor is there any other explanation more reasonable than evolution for these facts." Answers A, B, C are details that support the claim.

2. Crampton's argument about evolution is credible because the evidence is based on ____**facts**____.

3. **D**

4. **A** Dennert begins by saying that "Darwinism is doomed to decay," then goes on to cite an article that shows that Darwinism can't be defended because it can't be proven. Dennert uses the points in answers C and D to support his claim. He also states that Darwinism goes against Christianity, but this tells more about his reason for opposing Darwinism and is not the claim of the overall argument.

5. Dennert ____**disputes**____ Darwin's theory of evolution.

6.

Crampton	Dennert
Unused traits disappear as a species evolves.	Humans were created in God's image.
Humankind began with a single cell.	There is no relation between human and monkey.

Analyzing Evidence in Two Arguments, p. 164

1. **C** Crampton uses the *Pithecanthropus* to show that apes evolved, their skulls changed shape, and eventually that ape-man evolved to become a human. Crampton does not mention whether the scientist who discovered *Pithecanthropus* supported Darwin's theory. Crampton does not use the example to show how highly evolved humans are, but rather how closely related they are to apes. He believes that *Pithecanthropus* is the missing link.

2. **A** Crampton uses scientific research and analysis for the basis of his evidence. He also makes logical inferences based on facts. Crampton does not use expert opinion or witness statements.

3. **B** Dennert only uses opinion to defend his claim. It is not logic, because it is not rational and does not take into account evidence that supports the theory of evolution. His argument merely explains the opinion of another writer that Darwinism cannot be proven. He does not cite research or records of events.

4. **C** The evidence of a "missing link" is used as proof that Darwinism has basis in fact. While Crampton mentions the other points, these statements do not contradict Dennert's claim.

Writing Practice, p. 165

Make sure that your essay addresses the entire question, including a comparison of the two arguments and your opinion about the topic. Your writing should explain how you came to your conclusion.

> Answers will vary. Sample answer: My neighbor, a teacher, is in favor of using tablet computers instead of textbooks in her classroom. She explained that tablets actually cost less than textbooks. They prepare students to use technology productively, just as they will when they get a job. Tablets can make use of technological tools that make them more engaging than textbooks. She also pointed out that one tablet is much lighter than many books, so the risk of injuries to students is greatly reduced because students will no longer be forced to carry extremely heavy backpacks full of books. My father argued that tablets were just gizmos that will distract students from learning. He explained that he thinks students will spend their time surfing the Internet, so they won't learn the material as they would reading from a textbook.
>
> I find my neighbor's argument to be the most persuasive. It is hard to dispute evidence, even when it contradicts personal beliefs.

Lesson 7.4

Comparing Textual and Visual Genres, p. 167

1. "Niagara, June 10, 1843," "Niagara Falls Geology Facts & Figures," and the time line are about the same topic, but their ____formats____ are different.

2. **D**

3. **B** "Niagara, June 10, 1843" is a personal narrative. The author's purpose in writing the text was to entertain readers about a trip to Niagara Falls with vivid descriptions, figurative language, and sensory details. The author was not writing to persuade, inform, or explain.

4. **D** The time line visually communicates the history of the falls while the passage provides facts about the falls. The time line does not contain interesting facts about the waters or tell of a person's trip. The passage does not describe the history, nor does it discuss the best places to visit.

Evaluating Differences between Genres, p. 170

1.

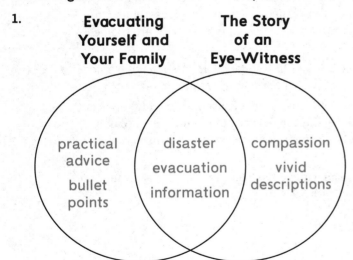

Evacuating Yourself and Your Family: practical advice, bullet points

disaster evacuation information

The Story of an Eye-Witness: compassion, vivid descriptions

2. **A** Although readers might have experienced a natural disaster, want to learn about the weather, or work for the Federal Emergency Management Agency, the intended audience is people who would like to prepare for a future natural disaster. It contains many facts and gives directions to help these people plan for evacuation. It does not talk in detail about past natural disasters, weather in general, or working for FEMA.

3. **C** The purpose of this text is to entertain and inform. The use of a narrative allows the writer to use rich descriptive details that appeal to the reader's emotions. The passage does not contain bullets or any special visual formatting. It is also not written to be persuasive.

4. **B** In a comparison of how the two passages cover the topic of evacuation, the scope of passage 1 is <u>broader than</u> the scope of passage 2.

Writing Practice, p. 171

You should have written in two different genres. The purpose of the first paragraph is to explain how to play a sport or do a performance. The purpose of the second text is to entertain the reader with a narrative about a game or performance.

> Answers will vary. Sample answer: Basketball is a game played between two teams of five players on a court. Players on each team try to capture the ball and shoot the ball through a hoop to score points for their team. The opposing team tries to keep the other team from scoring. The game is divided into four periods. At the end of the four periods, the team that scored the most points is declared the winner. Many rules govern play. For example:
>
> - Players may not carry the ball as they run; this is called traveling. Instead, players must bounce, or dribble, the ball or pass it to a teammate.
> - The ball must be kept inside the boundaries of the court.
> - When trying to steal the ball from an opposing team member, players must not make physical contact.

It was the fourth period, with only 10 seconds left, and the Tigers were one basket behind. With the Tigers on offense, the orange-uniformed players expertly passed the ball from player to player, but the quick-footed visiting Sharks tenaciously blocked every attempt to advance to the basket. Finally, the Tigers' center planted himself at the three-point line and shot the ball. My fellow fans and I shot up from our seats and screamed as we watched the ball soar in a perfect arc and bounce off the rim of the basket. The ball bounced on the floor as the final buzzer honked. A collective wail arose from the stands as the Sharks hugged one another in victory and the Tigers hung their heads, once again shut out of the championships.